FORECASTING THE UNITED KINGDOM ECONOMY

Forecasting the United Kingdom Economy

J. C. K. ASH
University of Reading

D. J. SMYTH
Claremont Graduate School
California

SAXON HOUSE / LEXINGTON BOOKS

Published by

SAXON HOUSE, D. C. Heath Ltd.
Westmead, Farnborough, Hants, England

Jointly with

LEXINGTON BOOKS, D. C. Heath & Co.
Lexington, Mass. U.S.A.

ISBN 0 347 01020 2
LC No. 73-10907

Printed in Great Britain by Robert MacLehose and Co. Ltd., Glasgow

Contents

List of figures

List of tables

Preface

This book undertakes an analysis of the accuracy of the short-run forecasts of the British economy made by the Treasury, the National Institute of Economic and Social Research, the Organisation for Economic Co-operation and Development, the London Business School (published in *The Sunday Times*) and a group of practising business economists (published in *The Sunday Telegraph*).

Forecasts of the major aggregates of the United Kingdom economy are important both to the Government and to the private sector. Forecasting plays a key role in the formulation of official policies aimed at regulating aggregate demand and controlling the balance of payments. At the private level, industry, institutions and individuals can frame coherent strategies for purchases, sales, investment and finance only by explicitly recognising at the outset the complex interdependence between their own operations and future developments in the macroeconomic environment. As a result there has been increasing interest, in recent years, in forecasting the British economy.

If forecasts are substantially in error then the policy measures applied by the Government may be inappropriate, and the return on personal and corporate decisions is likely to be inferior to that which would have resulted had actions been based on somewhat more accurate predictions. It is thus of some importance to have some idea of the accuracy of the forecasts, and the assessment provided in this book should be of use not merely to students of the British economy but to anyone who makes decisions using predictions of the short-run behaviour of the economy.

Annual, half-yearly and quarterly forecasts are considered. We primarily examine the accuracy of forecasts of gross domestic product and its major components (consumption expenditure, public authorities' current expenditure, gross fixed investment, stockbuilding and exports and imports of goods and services) although some more disaggregated analysis is also undertaken. We assess forecasts of individual variables over time and examine the accuracy of predictions for individual time periods. The forecasts are compared with predictions generated by naïve models and with forecasting performance in other countries.

Chapter 1 provides an introduction to macroeconomic forecasting in the United Kingdom and describes how the various forecasting teams arrive at their predictions. Chapter 2 explains the procedures we use to assess forecasting accuracy. Annual forecasts by the Treasury over the period 1951 to 1971 and by the National Institute from 1963 to 1971 are studied in Chapter 3. Chapter 4 deals with fourth quarter forecasts by the National Institute. Chapters 5 and 6 are mainly concerned with quarterly forecasts by the National Institute; Chapter 5 examining forecasts of gross domestic product and its major components, and Chapter 6 undertaking a disaggregated investigation of the forecasts of components of personal income and expenditure, gross fixed investment and the balance of payments on current account. Half-yearly forecasts by the Treasury, National Institute, OECD, London Business School and *The Sunday Telegraph* are evaluated and compared in Chapter 7. How well United Kingdom forecasts compare with those made for other countries is the subject of Chapter 8. Chapter 9 presents the book's conclusions.

Acknowledgements

We wish to express our thanks to all those who have directly contributed to the preparation of this book. Throughout the project, invaluable research assistance was generously given by Sally Ash. She also read and checked the complete text and tables. Mary Handslip performed a mass of computations with commendable patience, speed and accuracy. Three of our students, David Anderson, Bill Boyes and Tony Broome, helped us with data collection and processing. The final manuscript was expertly typed by Mary Gammons. We are equally grateful to our university colleagues and other economists, including some of the forecasters, for their encouraging and critical comments on preliminary reports of our research.

An earlier version of Chapters 3 and 4 was presented to the Second World Congress of the Econometric Society held at Cambridge, September 1970.

1 Macroeconomic Forecasting in the United Kingdom

1. Introduction

This book analyses the accuracy of short-run forecasts of the major economic aggregates of the United Kingdom economy. These forecasts have been made by the Treasury, the National Institute of Economic and Social Research, the Organisation for Economic Co-operation and Development, the London Business School and *The Sunday Telegraph*. Most of the forecasts evaluated are for the latter part of the 'sixties and the early 'seventies but one series of Treasury forecasts examined goes back to 1951. In all, we examine the accuracy of some three thousand forecasts.

If forecasts are quantitative, in the sense that some numerical level or change is predicted, then it is inevitable that most of them will be incorrect. So to ask the question 'Are the forecasters right or wrong?' is trivial. Rather one should ask 'How accurate are the forecasts?' which immediately leads one to a set of further questions: 'Are the forecasts more accurate than predictions generated by crude "non-economic" processes such as extrapolation or simple assumptions such as "no--change"?'; 'Are there systematic errors in the forecasts?'; 'Have the forecasts improved or deteriorated over time?'; 'Are some forecasters more accurate, on average, than others?'; 'Are some variables more accurately forecast than other variables?'; 'Is the accuracy of forecasts affected by post-forecast policy changes?'. These are some of the questions we attempt to answer in this book.

The forecasts that we analyse are short-run in that the period being forecast varies from the current quarter to one year ahead. We do not concern ourselves with longer run projections such as were involved in the 1965 National Plan[1] (such projections are usually not true forecasts but rather spell out what is implied by the setting of some targets). For the most part the forecasts on which we concentrate are of the major economic aggregates: gross domestic product, total final expenditure, consumption, public expenditure, investment, stockbuilding, exports and imports.

Why are macroeconomic forecasts of the British economy made? The Treasury forecasts are primarily used as an aid to regulating aggregate demand—the general level of economic activity. Demand management has been accepted as the responsibility of successive Governments since Kingsley Wood's 1941 Budget.[2] The National Institute's forecasting was initially undertaken, in 1959, in response to the wish of the then Economic Adviser to the Treasury, Sir Robert Hall, to have an alternative set of projections to the official forecasts provided by an outside and independent body.[3] Quantitative forecasts by OECD have only been published in the last few years; they form part of the annual surveys of all member countries and the implications of the forecasts for macroeconomic policy are stressed.

Explicit quantitative forecasting is not essential for demand management. In the absence of forecasting, macroeconomic policy could, in principle, be generated mechanically by applying simple decision rules which would relate fiscal and monetary changes to past and present states of the economy.[4] To the best of our knowledge such mechanical decision rules have never been applied; this suggests that policymakers prefer to live with the consequences of their forecasts.

An obvious result of bad forecasting is that it is likely to lead to the application of inappropriate demand management policies. If the magnitude of change is underestimated or overestimated then measures aimed at stabilising the economy may be too weak or too strong, the former failing to prevent a cumulative movement and latter over-correcting for it. Failure to correctly predict the direction of change of the economy, the forecasters either missing turning-points or predicting turning-points that never subsequently materialise, are likely to be especially harmful for demand management because the measures applied will then tend to be expansionary when deflation is appropriate and deflationary when expansion is called for. Clearly, then, inaccurate forecasts which encourage active policy intervention may be worse than no forecasting in that the authorities are induced to take policy measures that accentuate fluctuations.[5]

This is not to suggest that perfect forecasting is necessarily always beneficial. It may be possible to forecast future movements of the economy with some accuracy and at the same time to miscalculate the impact of policy intervention so that the net result is worse than if no forecast is made. And it is not only the authorities that may respond to forecasts. The private sector may adjust its planned behaviour in response to announced forecasts, and good forecasters can (at least in principle) take such responses into account in making their forecasts.[6] This raises the interesting question of whether or not an optimum forecast, from the point of view of demand management, is the one that the authorities really believe in, or whether the desired level of aggregate demand may more easily be obtained through judiciously misleading the private sector. Even apart from conscious efforts to use the announcement of forecasts as a policy tool to directly influence the private sector's behaviour, the Government may express in its published forecasts its economic and political targets rather than its objective assessment of future economic developments.

Macroeconomic forecasting has other uses than as an aid to aggregate demand management. Much of the business community needs forecasts of the short-run economic outlook. Fluctuations in the overall level of activity play an important role in the demand for a businessman's products and particular components of aggregate demand are important for different industries. Some sort of forecast of future developments in the level of economic activity are indispensible to a businessman devising his strategies for sales and marketing, investment decisions, takeovers and the like. That is, almost any sort of coherent corporate planning requires some assumptions about future behaviour of the macroeconomic framework in which companies operate. This has led to the creation of economic groups within companies concerned with forecasting the macroeconomic environment. It has also led to the development of regular sets of forecasts with wide circulations: the forecasts derived from the London Business School model, published in *The Sunday Times*, and the forecasts by a team of practising business economists, published in *The Sunday Telegraph*. Just as official forecasts may be aimed at affecting the behaviour of the private sector of the economy, so too may private forecasts be intended to influence official thinking and actions. This is certainly the case with the National Institute's forecasts.[7]

The forecasts made by the Treasury, the National Institute of Economic and Social Research, OECD, the London Business School and *The Sunday Telegraph* have a common feature in that their predictions of total expenditure are constructed from simultaneous predictions of the major individual expenditure components. The forecasting methods used by the forecasters have been well documented and in the rest of this chapter we outline their basic forecasting procedures. Some details of the techniques used for the more disaggregated National Institute forecasts, analysed in Chapter 6, are left to the introductory section of that chapter.

2. The Treasury approach to forecasting

Various accounts of the methods used by the Treasury in making their forecasts of domestic activity have been provided by Treasury economists themselves. The following brief description draws upon these official sources.[8]

The Treasury undertakes, in conjunction with the more important government economic departments, three major forecasting exercises each year, in June-July, October-November and January-February. Forecasts of seasonally adjusted gross domestic product by quarters are built up from forecasts of the major components of total final expenditure (consumers' expenditure, public authorities' current expenditure, gross fixed investment, investment in stocks and exports and imports). The expenditure estimate of GDP at constant factor cost that is obtained for any quarter is converted into a 'compromise estimate' of GDP which is comparable with the 'compromise' series for actual GDP obtained as an average of the three largely independent estimates based on expenditure, income and output data. Half-yearly and annual forecasts are obtained from the quarterly forecasts. Only annual and half-yearly forecasts are published, the latter only since the 1968 Budget. Forecasts are published at Budget time covering eighteen months.

Some components of GDP are taken to be largely exogenous for the forecasting period, that is, largely independent of the other forecast variables; they are not entirely exogenous as they may be revised in the light of the overall picture given by the forecasting exercise. The forecasts of public sector expenditures on goods and services, both on current account and on capital account, are taken from the most recent public expenditure programmes, allowances being made for anticipated deviations from planned expenditures. For private fixed investment, main reliance is placed upon spending plans as obtained in the investment intentions survey of the Department of Trade and Industry (and previously from its predecessors, the Board of Trade and the Ministry of Technology). These are then modified by 'judgement.' Forecasts of private sector housing investment are based on Ministry enquiries and the probable development of monetary variables relevant to the housing market such as the inflow of funds to building societies. Forecasts of exports are obtained from an interdepartmental balance of payments forecasting group; they are essentially demand forecasts based on world economic prospects, there being some disaggregation by area and product.

Variables that are regarded as endogenous, that is, dependent on other forecast variables, are consumers' expenditure, investment in stocks and imports. To obtain consumption forecasts, forecasts are first made of the main components of personal income in current prices, direct taxes and National Insurance contributions; next, personal disposable income is deflated by a forecast price index; a consumption function then relates the volume of consumption to three separate categories of real disposable income (wages and salaries, current grants and other income) and net changes in consumer debt, the coefficients in the consumption function being subject to *a priori* restrictions where free estimation gives what are regarded as implausible answers. Because assumptions concerning GDP are necessary in deriving personal disposable income, and because consumption is a component of GDP, an iterative procedure is used to reach a final figure for consumption. The balance of payments group provides estimates of imports using a combination of regression analysis and interdepartmental expertise. Investment in stocks is estimated on the basis of the level of stocks adjusting towards some ratio of stocks to output 'normal' for the stage of the cycle, the forecast being modified to account for special factors.

The Treasury forecasts, then, have been made within a systematic framework using what might be described as an implicit set of simultaneous equations—a model with unspecified parameters continually subject to modification and development. Judgement, rules of thumb and (increasingly) econometric equations have all played a part. Until recently the forecasts were built up by manual calculation. It was not until the forecasting exercise of June and July 1970 that a formal computerised econometric version of the Treasury's short-term aggregate model was fully operational.

The model in use in the Treasury in May 1972 consisted of about one hundred equations of which about half were behavioural.[9] It is clearly not in a fully developed state; for instance, parameters have not been estimated by a simultaneous estimation technique, and some equations have been estimated by ordinary least squares with no allowance for autocorrelation. However, the more pressing problems have been dealt with and some equations have been estimated using up to fourth order autoregressive schemes. Distributed lags have been widely used. Some coefficients are imposed on the basis of outside information. In general, the model has been designed to produce forecasts of national accounting aggregates, and disaggregation has been undertaken only to improve the quality of the aggregate forecasts. Monetary factors have yet to be integrated into the model.

The development of the Treasury's econometric model is at last bringing the United Kingdom into line with other countries that have, for many years, made use of short-term econometric models in forecasting,[10] although its late entry means, of course, that the British model is still more rudimentary than those of certain other economies. And it remains to be seen just how important the role of the model will be as an aid to forecasting and policy formulation. Nevertheless, the development of the model goes a long way towards meeting the criticism of those who have complained about the unwillingness of the Treasury to make use of quantitative forecasting techniques and have urged it to develop a quantitative model from which the effects of alternative policy measures may be calculated.[11]

3. The National Institute of Economic and Social Research forecasts

The National Institute of Economic and Social Research (NIESR) has fully explained its forecasting methods. Articles in the *National Institute Economic Review* frequently discuss the problems and techniques of forecasting. Our account relies primarily on a book by M. J. C. Surrey,[12] which provides the most comprehensive exposition, while a shorter description has been given by M. J. Artis.[13]

Currently the National Institute publishes a wide range of forecasts. These have been developed over time and earlier forecasts were much less detailed and paid less attention to disaggregation. Disaggregated forecasts for which sufficiently long series are available are analysed in Chapter 6 and the introductory section of that chapter describes the forecasting procedures adopted for personal income and expenditure, investment and the balance of payments. In the present section we concentrate on how the National Institute forecasts gross domestic product and its major components.

At present quarterly, seasonally adjusted, constant price forecasts for a period of twenty-four months ahead are published in each issue of the *National Institute Economic Review*.[14] The February issue of the *Review* regularly includes a major annual survey of the United Kingdom economy and in the May issue the Institute analyses the recently revealed Budget measures. Although the forecasts account for policy changes once announced, for example, the May and subsequent forecasts predict the consequences of the Budget, there is no explicit attempt to forecast policy, the forecasts being based on the assumption that existing measures will remain unchanged.

The first stage of the forecasting procedure involves the construction of estimates of the current economic position and of the recent past from published monthly indicators prior to the publication of official statistics. Some of the relationships between quarterly national accounting aggregates and monthly indicators have been formalised and single equation regression analysis is used.

Exogenous variables are then predicted. On the expenditure side these consist of exports of goods and services, public authorities' current expenditure, public authorities' gross fixed investment and private dwelling investment. Exports are forecast in current prices, primarily using informal methods. The main factors affecting the exports forecast are the likely rates of growth of the industrial countries and the current and prospective exchange positions of less developed countries. Various other factors are taken into account in *ad hoc* fashion. Where possible, use is made of trade forecasts from other national and international research and policy institutions. On the basis of past experience the United Kingdom's share of world trade is taken to be negatively correlated with the rate of expansion of world trade. Export forecasts are then revalued at constant prices. Future public sector consumption is obtained from the official White Paper published at the end of each calendar year and from the Treasury's *Financial Statement* published with the Budget. The Institute has to convert these annual constant-price estimates into quarterly figures on an appropriate price basis. Similar problems are encountered in obtaining appropriate forecasts of public investment from published surveys. Programmes for the public construction of dwellings are checked against information on the number of starts, the number of dwellings under construction and the average construction period. An informal relationship of this kind, combined with data on builders' intentions, is used to derive forecasts of private dwelling investment.

Because of the long time-lags involved the remainder of private sector fixed investment, that is private sector fixed investment excluding dwellings, may be treated as essentially exogenous. Two methods of forecasting are used. Estimates were once obtained from the investment intentions survey used by the Treasury. This still forms the basis for non-manufacturing investment but for manufacturing investment more reliance is now being placed on econometric analysis. A flexible accelerator model is used with change in output, the level of capacity utilisation, or the level of profits serving as the main explanatory variable. The final forecast is normally a compromise between the two methods with the investment intentions survey receiving greater weight the more unusual the economic circumstances.

Exogenous variables on the income side include current grants to persons, National Insurance contributions and changes in personal credit. These forecasts are based on projected past rates of growth on the crucial assumption of unchanged government policy. Minor income components, such as forces' pay and net transfers abroad, are, in the absence of any other qualifying information, projected by extrapolation.

A small aggregate econometric model is next used to generate forecasts of endogenous variables. The model is continually re-estimated and restructured in line with data revisions and on-going research into the relevant relationships, but the version given by Surrey [15] includes ten behavioural equations, three of which are non-linear, and seven identities. There are eleven exogenous variables plus ten intercept adjustment terms to take account of specific, and perhaps transitory, factors that have been left out of the specified relationships. Three equations predict personal income (income from rent and self-employment, income from dividends and net interest receipts, and the wage and salary bill) from their own lagged values, GDP and time, and two relate taxes (the tax on wages and salaries and other personal tax) to incomes, incomes and taxes being expressed in current prices. As movements in personal credit are treated as exogenous the consumption function equation predicts only non-credit consumption; for this a version of the permanent income hypothesis is used. The consumer price index (excluding indirect taxes) is determined by the share of wages and salaries in GDP, import prices and the index lagged. Factor cost adjustment depends on consumer expenditure. The level of stocks equation has an optimum stock-output ratio with distributed lag adjustment together with an allowance for involuntary changes in stockbuilding. Imports of goods and services depend on investment in stocks and total final sales; there is also increasing reliance on a disaggregated approach. The indentities yield forecasts of the consumer price index, real disposable wage income, other real disposable income, consumers' expenditure, total final sales, stockbuilding and gross domestic product. Forecasts of unemployment and employment are obtained outside the model. Residuals from the past performance of the model are examined and projected in the light of extraneous factors which may be expected to distort each normal relationship. The formal imports forecast is adjusted to account for detailed balance of payments analysis. Finally the consistency of a complete set of forecasts is resolved to accord with the forecasters' own judgement of the likely economic future.

In addition to providing detailed explanations of its forecasting methods the National Institute has publicly and critically appraised its forecasts, using approaches rather different to those adopted in this book.[16]

4. Forecasting with the London Business School quarterly econometric model

The forecasts reported in *The Sunday Times* by R. J. Ball and T. Burns are based on the quarterly econometric model developed at the London Business School. This model is now a large one with sixty-eight behavioural equations, sixteen technical equations and seventy identities; earlier versions of the model were much smaller. The following description is of the most recent version at the time of writing.[17]

The model is an expenditure model without industrial disaggregation built around the national and trade accounts. The basic gross domestic product concept employed is an average of expenditure and output although in earlier versions an expenditure estimate was used. Most of the data are seasonally adjusted. The equations are estimated by ordinary least squares. Various forms of distributed lags are employed.

Simple functions explain consumption which is disaggregated only into durables and non-durables (although a disaggregated consumption model is also available); the key explanatory variables are disposable income and new credits. In earlier versions of the model use was made of anticipations data to explain fixed investment but now the neo-classical model is applied to disaggregated fixed investment series. Inventory investment is related to an adjusted output changes series, change in final expenditure and time. Investment in private residential construction is determined by a distributed lag on housing modified by income, price and financial variables. The equations for balance of payments credits include world trade and production, price, exchange rate, trend and other variables; the more disaggregated equations for debits include income, price, production, investment, trend and other variables.

The personal income, employment and unemployment sector is in a state of flux as current economic events demonstrate the inadequacies of the Phillips curve. Various *ad hoc* variables, such as the number unemployed plus the number of employees 'hoarded' are used on empirical rather than theoretical grounds. Prices are determined within the model in a partly disaggregated fashion.

Monetary effects enter the model through private investment and through credit effects on durables. It is assumed that the monetary authorities can exercise direct control over the short-term rate of interest; the long-term rate of interest is determined endogenously by the velocity of circulation, a distributed lag on short rates and inflation expectations. The quantity of money is taken to be exogenous.

There is no comprehensive treatment of the government sector, government current expenditure, government grants and public sector investment being exogenous, and the effect of deficits or surpluses on debt management ignored. However, the model allows for the direct effect of changes in individual tax instruments and allowances on tax liabilities and payments.

Half-yearly forecasts have been presented in the Business News section of *The Sunday Times* three times a year since 1966 and cover three half-years ahead.

5. The Sunday Telegraph forecasts

The forecasts in *The Sunday Telegraph* are the responsibility of James Morrell, who has described the techniques employed in a recent book.[18]

The forecasting process is conducted, as far as possible, in both current and constant prices. Separate estimates are made for factor incomes and total spending and differences in forecast totals are analysed and corrected.

Exports and public expenditure are taken as exogenous. The trend in exports is obtained by studying the relationship between United Kingdom and world exports of manufactures. This is checked by examining the import forecasts of the United Kingdom's major customers; allowance is also made for the pressure of domestic demand. Public spending, capital and current, is built up using information on the components from official sources modified in accordance with changes of government policy and the history of expansions and contractions of such programmes in the past.

Private sector investment is regarded as particularly sensitive to changes in company profits which are derived elsewhere in the model. Dividend declarations, surveys of capital spending intentions, capacity utilisation and the provision of industrial development certificates are also taken into account. Investment in housing is considered separately; liquidity considerations, the flow of funds to building societies and the rate of interest are key variables here.

Forecasts of personal incomes are built up from forecasts of components. By making a variety of assumptions the community's income from employment is derived. A Phillips curve is used in explaining changes in money wage rates. Non-employment incomes are forecast and added in, and gross income is adjusted to give disposable income. The total disposable funds available to the consumer are obtained by adding net changes in credit to disposable income; estimates of saving then yield forecasts of consumer spending. This is matched with a direct forecast of consumer spending using a variety of indicators.

Stocks are forecast using a desired stocks-production ratio with account also being taken of stock-piling by consumers, demand conditions and monetary factors.

Imports are related to the level of final sales and stockbuilding. The relationship is in volume terms and price factors are applied category by category to arrive at value figures.

Estimates are made of unit labour costs which are taken to be a major determinant of total production costs and future price developments. These forecasts of prices and costs lead in turn to forecasts of profit margins.

Cross-checks are made to detect inconsistencies and appropriate re-calculations are made.

The Sunday Telegraph forecasts appear monthly. The forecasts are for half-years and each set of forecasts covers three half-years. In contrast to the other forecasts considered *The Sunday Telegraph* predicts variables in current prices: only total output is forecast in constant prices as well as in current prices. Also, unlike the other forecasts, *The Sunday Telegraph* predictions are not corrected for seasonal variations. *The Sunday Telegraph* forecasts were first published in 1967.

6. OECD forecasting

The Organisation for Economic Co-operation and Development (OECD) provides relatively detailed forecasts for the major OECD countries of which the United Kingdom is one. While account is taken of both official and unofficial forecasts prepared in the United Kingdom the forecasts published are entirely the responsibility of the OECD Economics and Statistics Department.[19] Increasing use is being made by the Department of econometric techniques, especially for forecasting wage and price developments, private consumption and private investment; short-term forecasting models of some of the member countries are also being constructed.

The exogenous components of demand, public consumption, gross fixed investment and exports of goods and services are forecast first. For forecasts of the public sector some use is made of budgetary statements; for investment there is extensive reliance on intentions surveys; exports are initially forecast in the light of past trends. These exogenous elements of aggregate demand, together with information on likely stock changes give a first indication of the future pressure of demand. Relationships describing the potential growth rate of the economy are used to estimate the growth of aggregate supply to set against growth in aggregate demand. An estimate of personal disposable income is then obtained from the forecast pressure of demand and the probable development of incomes as indicated by wage settlements. An assessment of price developments precedes the prediction of real personal consumption. A first forecast of the change in final expenditure is obtained and cyclical variations in import propensities are used to project imports. Similar analyses having been made for other OECD countries, the second and subsequent stages of the forecasting process consist of reiterations to ensure the consistency of foreign trade forecasts of individual countries.

All variables are seasonally adjusted. Domestic variables and aggregates are in constant prices; exports and imports of goods and services are in current prices. Gross domestic product in constant prices is measured in terms of market prices and is a weighted average of expenditure, output and income estimates; any differences between the compromise and expenditure estimates of GDP are allocated at the forecasters' discretion.

Forecasts are made on a half-yearly basis and have been published in *OECD Economic Outlook* since 1967.[20]

Notes

1 *The National Plan* (Cmnd. 2764), H.M.S.O., London, (1965).

2 For discussion of the development of demand management in the United Kingdom, see J. C. R. Dow, *The Management of the British Economy 1945-60*, Cambridge University Press, London (1964).

3 An account of the origins of the National Institute forecasts is given in Lord Roberthall, 'Introduction', *National Institute Economic Review* (November 1969) pp. 3-7.

4 However, such procedures may be shown to imply forecasts arising from the dynamic structure of the economic system.

5 There is some evidence that for the post-war period macroeconomic policy aimed at stabilising the economy has actually proved to be destabilising. However, this is not necessarily the result of bad forecasting. See D. J. Smyth, 'Public finance policy and techniques for economic stability and balanced economic growth', United Kingdom report in *Public Finance Policy and Techniques for Economic Stability and Balanced Economic Growth, Congres de Budapest, Septembre 1964* Institut International de Finances Publiques, La Haye, (1966) pp. 270-97.

[6] It may be shown that if some or all the members of the private sector believe a forecast and use it in planning their economic behaviour instead of relying upon the recent past as a predictor then the magnitude of fluctuations may be increased even if the forecasts are perfectly accurate. See Murray C. Kemp, 'Economic forecasting when the subject of the forecast is influenced by the forecast', *American Economic Review* (June 1962) pp. 492-6; David J. Smyth, 'The effect of public price forecasts on market price variation: a stochastic cobweb example', *American Journal of Agricultural Economics* (February 1973) pp. 83-88 and David J. Smyth, 'The effect of forecasting in a simple stochastic macroeconomic model', *Claremont Economic Papers*, No. 53 (April 1973).

[7] See Roberthall 'Introduction', *op. cit.*

[8] See H. M. Treasury, 'Short-term economic forecasting in the United Kingdom', *Economic Trends* (August 1964) pp. 2-11, reprinted in substantially the same form as Chapter 6 of *Techniques of Economic Forecasting* OECD, Paris (1965) pp. 127-45; James Shepherd, 'Short-term forecasting for the U.K. economy', Chapter 4 in Sir Alec Cairncross, ed. *The Managed Economy*, Basil Blackwell, Oxford (1970) pp. 61-75; A. D. Roy, 'Short-term forecasting for central economic management of the U.K. economy', Chapter 17 in Kenneth Hilton and David F. Heathfield, eds. *The Econometric Study of the United Kingdom*, Macmillan, London (1970). Some specific topics are discussed in H. M. Treasury, 'Econometric research for short-term forecasting', *Economic Trends* (February 1967) pp. 9-15; M. C. Fessey, 'Short-term forecasting of U.K. exports', *Economic Trends* (May 1967) pp. viii-xiii; L. S. Berman and F. Cassell, 'Short-term forecasts of income, expenditure and saving', *Economic Trends* (February 1968) pp. ix-xv. The Treasury's econometric model, as it stood in May 1972, is described in J. R. Shepherd, H. P. Evans and C. J. Riley, 'The Treasury short-term forecasting model', paper presented at the Social Science Research Council Conference on Econometric Model Building in the United Kingdom at the London Business School, July 1972. Some general problems of official forecasting are raised by Sir Alec Cairncross, 'Economic forecasting', *Economic Journal* (December 1969) pp. 797-812.

[9] See J. R. Shepherd, H. P. Evans and C. J. Riley, 'The Treasury short-term forecasting model', *op. cit.*

[10] See OECD *op. cit.*

[11] See, for instance, D. J. Smyth, 'Public finance policy and techniques for economic stability and balanced economic growth', *op. cit.*

[12] M. J. C. Surrey, *The Analysis and Forecasting of the British Economy*, National Institute of Economic and Social Research Occasional Paper 25, Cambridge University Press, London (1971).

[13] M. J. Artis, 'Short-term economic forecasting at N.I.E.S.R.' in Kenneth Hilton and David F. Heathfield *op. cit.* pp. 443-461.

[14] The *Review* is published each February, May, August and November.

[15] M. J. C. Surrey, *op. cit.*

[16] See R. R. Nield and E. A. Shirley, 'Economic review: an assessment of forecasts, 1959-60', *National Institute Economic Review* (May 1961) pp. 12-29; M. C. Kennedy, 'How well does the National Institute forecast'? *National Institute Economic Review* (November 1969) pp. 40-52; and R. L. Major and M. J. C. Surrey, 'Errors in the National Institute forecasts of the balance of payments', *National Institute Economic Review* (May 1970) pp. 35-45.

[17] R. J. Ball, B. Boatwright, T. Burns, P. Lobban and G. Miller, *The London Business School Quarterly Econometric Model of the U.K. Economy*, London Graduate School of Business Studies, Econometric Forecasting Unit, Discussion Paper No. 20. For discussions of earlier versions see R. J. Ball, 'Economic model building for control', *The Advancement of Science* (April 1967); R. J. Ball and T. Burns, 'An econometric approach to short-run analysis of the U.K. economy', *Operational Research Quarterly* (September 1968); R. J. Ball and T. Burns, *Some Recent Experience in Short-term Forecasting*, London Graduate School of Business Studies, Econometric Forecasting Unit, Discussion Paper No. 17 (May 1970). For a comparison of a recent version of the model with selected models for eleven other industrial countries see R. J. Ball, ed. *International Linkage of National Economic Models*, North-Holland, Amsterdam (1973).

[18] James Morrell, ed. *Management Decisions and the Role of Forecasting*, Penguin Books, Harmondsworth (1972).

[19] The statistical concepts and methods applied and the forecasting techniques used by the Economics and Statistics Department of OECD are described in a 'Technical annex' to each issue of *OECD Economic Outlook* (prior to the December 1970 issue this section was called 'Technical Notes'). The account in the text is based on the December 1972 issue, pp. 86-91.

[20] *OECD Economic Outlook* is published twice yearly, in July and December.

2 Techniques of Accuracy Analysis

1. The measurement of forecasting error

In this book we apply some simple econometric techniques to evaluate the accuracy of forecasts. The econometric approach reflects our belief that it is necessary to evaluate forecasts rigorously, consistently and quantitatively. Hence we concentrate on the accuracy of a continuing set of forecasts rather than on a detailed evaluation of particular forecasts taken individually.

Denote the forecast value of a variable by p, the actual value by a, and time periods by subscripts involving t. Then one method of approach would be to examine the divergence between the p_t and a_t series. A disadvantage of this approach is that as most macroeconomic variables grow over time the successive deviations between p_t and a_t would be swamped by trend factors. Further, most macroeconomic forecasting is concerned with the prediction of changes. This suggests that we compare the actual change from time period $t-1$ to time period t, $a_t - a_{t-1}$, with the predicted change for that period, $p_t - a_{t-1}$. However, if the time period is one of some length this procedure does not entirely remove trend elements for the average absolute change in the variable is likely to grow over time. This will especially be the case for variables measured in terms of current prices, and the effect is still likely to be significant for variables expressed in real terms. For instance, gross domestic product at factor cost measured in terms of 1963 prices rose from £19,590 million in 1951 to £32,896 million in 1971 so that a forecast error of, say £100 million in 1951 was relatively as important as an error of £168 million in 1971. Accordingly we shall compare the predicted percentage change in a variable with the actual percentage change in the variable. Thus we define

$$P_t = 100\frac{p_t - a_{t-1}}{a_{t-1}} \tag{2-1}$$

and

$$A_t = 100\frac{a_t - a_{t-1}}{a_{t-1}} \tag{2-2}$$

A hypothetical numerical example together with a graphical representation may help to clarify the techniques we use. Table 2.1 gives twelve successive predicted and actual percentage changes which are plotted in Figure 2.1, A_t being measured on the vertical axis and P_t on the horizontal axis.

Perfect forecasting requires that $P_t = A_t$ for all t, that is, that points lie along a 45° line through the origin. In the north-east and south-west quadrants the sign of P_t is the same as the sign of A_t. Points in these quadrants not on the 45° line of perfect forecasts will represent either overestimation or underestimation of changes and the corresponding regions are indicated. Points in the north-west and south-east quadrants of the scatter diagram represent cases of turning-point errors. In Figure 2.1 it is apparent that in periods 1, 3, 4 and 5 positive changes were underestimated; in periods 2, 6, 10 and 12 positive changes were overestimated; in period 8 the magnitude of a negative change was underestimated; in periods 7 and 9 turning-point errors were made, the predicted change being positive and the actual change being negative so that the change was overestimated; and in period 11 there was perfect prediction.

Clearly it is possible to have a perfect relationship between predicted and actual changes without perfect forecasting, all points in the scatter

Table 2.1

Hypothetical values of predicted and actual percentage changes and prediction error

Period	P_t	A_t	$P_t - A_t$
1	1	2	−1
2	8	4	4
3	5	6	−1
4	6	8	−2
5	4	8	−4
6	2	1	1
7	3	−1	4
8	−1	−3	2
9	1	−2	3
10	3	2	1
11	3	3	0
12	7	5	2

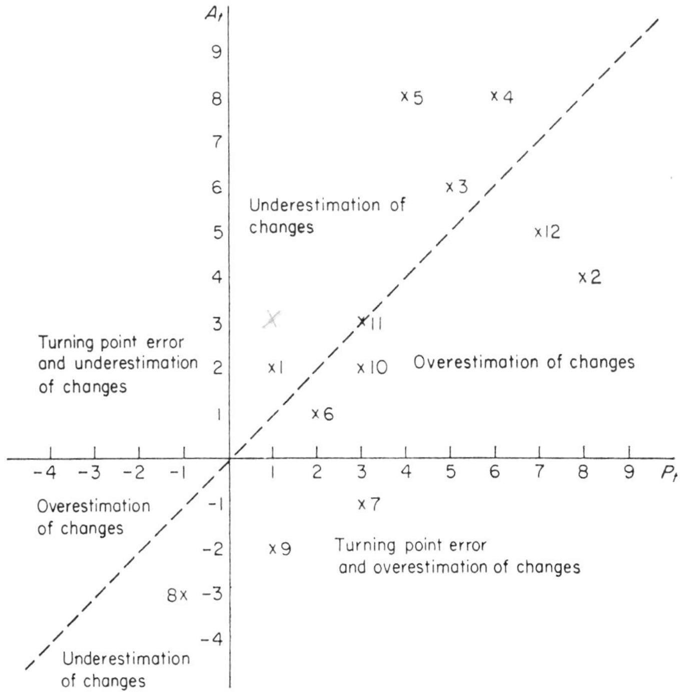

Fig. 2.1 Predictions and realisations: a hypothetical example

diagram falling on a line other than the 45° line, as would be the case if the only points in Figure 2.1 were for periods 3, 4, 9 and 10. Moreover, if the only points we observed were for periods 2, 3, 4, 5 and 12 the estimated correlation coefficient would be negative yet we would not necessarily regard the forecasts for these periods as being bad. Thus we cannot just fit the regression line

$$A_t = \alpha + \beta P_t \qquad (2\text{-}3)$$

and simply use the magnitude of the resulting correlation coefficient as an index of forecasting accuracy. We need a measure of goodness of fit about the 45° line of perfect forecasts. This is provided by looking at the series of values of $P_t - A_t$, the deviations about the 45° line, rather than the deviations about (2-3), the line of best fit. One approach is to calculate $\frac{1}{n} \Sigma |P_t - A_t|$, where n is the number of observations. This gives the mean absolute error of the forecasts and has been used in a number of studies.[1] However, an approach that gives more than proportionate weight to large forecast errors than to small ones, such as the root-mean-square error (RMSE) defined as

$$\text{RMSE} = \sqrt{\frac{1}{n}\Sigma\,(P_t - A_t)^2} \tag{2-4}$$

is to be preferred to the mean absolute error in the same way that the variance is to be preferred as a measure of dispersion to measures based on absolute deviations.[2] The root-mean-square error has the further advantage that it is consistent with the notion of a quadratic loss function.[3]

2. The inequality coefficient and its decomposition

As our measure of predictive accuracy we shall use the standardised root-mean-square error, U, given by

$$U = \frac{\sqrt{\frac{1}{n}\Sigma\,(P_t - A_t)^2}}{\sqrt{\frac{1}{n}\Sigma\,A_t^2}} \tag{2-5}$$

We standardise the root-mean-square error in this way to facilitate comparison of the forecasting accuracy for different variables or different sets of data because a difference between P_t and A_t of a certain magnitude for a variable that normally changes little is more serious than the same error in the prediction of a variable that changes much. By dividing the root-mean-square error by $\sqrt{\frac{1}{n}\Sigma\,A_t^2}$ we are thus adjusting for the normal intensity of change of the variable during the period under consideration.

The coefficient U is Theil's inequality coefficient.[4] In the case of perfect forecasting $U = 0$. As forecasting accuracy deteriorates U rises and U has no upper bound. If a forecaster predicts no change throughout ($P_t = 0$ for all t) then $U = 1$ and clearly a set of forecasts with an inequality coefficient approaching this must be regarded as bad. In the numerical example in Table 2.1 we have $\sqrt{\frac{1}{n}\Sigma\,(P_t - A_t)^2} = 2.466$ and $\sqrt{\frac{1}{n}\Sigma\,A_t^2} =$ $= 4.444$ and hence $U = 0.56$.

Forecasting errors may arise in different ways and, again following Theil, the mean-square error, $\frac{1}{n}\Sigma\,(P_t - A_t)^2$, may be decomposed into three terms each relating to a different type of prediction error. We may write

$$\frac{1}{n}\Sigma\,(P_t - A_t)^2 = (\bar{P} - \bar{A})^2 + (s_P - s_A)^2 + 2(1 - r)s_P s_A \tag{2-6}$$

where $\overline{P}$ and $\overline{A}$ are the means and s_P and s_A are the standard deviations of the P_t and A_t series respectively and r is the correlation coefficient of predicted and actual percentage changes.[5] Dividing both sides of (2-6) by $\frac{1}{n}\Sigma (P_t - A_t)^2$ leads to

$$U^M = \frac{(\overline{P} - \overline{A})^2}{\frac{1}{n}\Sigma (P_t - A_t)^2} \tag{2-7}$$

$$U^S = \frac{(s_P - s_A)^2}{\frac{1}{n}\Sigma (P_t - A_t)^2} \tag{2-8}$$

$$U^C = \frac{2(1 - r)\, s_P s_A}{\frac{1}{n}\Sigma (P_t - A_t)^2} \tag{2-9}$$

and

$$U^M + U^S + U^C = 1 \tag{2-10}$$

U^M is the bias proportion of forecasting error (as measured by the numerator of U) due to underprediction or overprediction of the average change; in the numerical example $U^M = 0.09$ and as $\overline{P}$ is greater than $\overline{A}$ the predicted changes are, on average, too high. U^S is the variance proportion of mean-square error due to underprediction or overprediction of the variance of changes; in the example $U^S = 0.15$ and fluctuations are underestimated as s_P is less than s_A. Finally, U^C, the co-variance proportion, is the proportion of forecasting error that is random; in the example $U^C = 0.76$. If forecasts cannot be perfect then it is desirable that they be free of systematic errors; hence we should like U^M and U^S to be small, errors in the forecasts being predominantly of the unsystematic type, U^C Good forecasters should be able to remove systematic errors with the passage of time.

3. Data revisions

The forecasts have to be made using data available at the time, data that are often subsequently revised. Several alternative estimates of a_t and a_{t-1} are available and it is not obvious whether preliminary estimates available to the forecaster or one of the revised estimates should be used in constructing P_t and A_t. Normally the forecasters make an estimate of $p_t - a_{t-1}$ using the latest revision of a_{t-1} which they publish together with their forecasts. Accordingly we have taken that estimate of a_{t-1} in calculating P_t. In calculating A_t we have used the latest revised data for a_t and a_{t-1} on the grounds that this is what the forecasters are really trying to predict. The procedure adopted is consistent with that of Theil.[6] Experimentation with alternative measures of P_t and A_t suggests that while the choice of a measure may be important for individual observations the use of alternative definitions would not change our general conclusions.[7]

4. Naïve models

It is desirable that the forecasts be evaluated not just in isolation but in conjunction with other forecasts. Accordingly, where possible we have compared the relative accuracy of competing forecasts and also evaluated each set against some naïve predictions. Obvious naïve models to use are those based on the extrapolation of past changes. For the annual forecasts the extrapolative naïve models consist of the previous year's actual percentage change and an average of the percentage changes for the previous three and five years. Denoting these (dummy) predictions by P' we thus have

$$P'_t = A_{t-1} \tag{2-11}$$

$$P'_t = \frac{1}{3} \sum_{i=1}^{3} A_{t-i} \tag{2-12}$$

and

$$P'_t = \frac{1}{5} \sum_{i=1}^{5} A_{t-i} \tag{2-13}$$

where years are indicated by subscripts involving t. For the quarterly forecasts we use the percentage change in the previous quarter, the percentage change in the corresponding quarter of the previous year, and the average percentage change for the previous year. We thus have

$$P'_t = A_{t-1} \tag{2-14}$$

$$P'_t = A_{t-4} \tag{2-15}$$

and

$$P'_t = \frac{1}{4} \sum_{i=1}^{4} A_{t-i} \tag{2-16}$$

where subscripts involving t now indicate quarters. For the half-yearly forecasts we use the percentage change for the previous period, the average for the previous year, and the average for the previous three years. The half-yearly naïve models, are, then

$$P'_t = A_{t-1} \tag{2-17}$$

$$P'_t = \tfrac{1}{2} \sum_{i=1}^{2} A_{t-i} \tag{2-18}$$

and

$$P'_t = \tfrac{1}{6} \sum_{i=1}^{6} A_{t-i} \tag{2-19}$$

where subscripts involving t now indicate half-years. Note that all the quarterly and half-yearly data are seasonally adjusted. For annual, quarterly and half-yearly forecasts we also make use of the average percentage change over the analysis period, $\bar{A}$ so that

$$P'_t = \bar{A} \tag{2-20}$$

This is a more rigorous test than the extrapolative models as in practice the forecasters could not have knowledge of averages based on future periods. However, we interpret this naïve model as representing some long-run or normal average change for the variable and it should be a cause for concern if forecasters do not do as well as this in practice. Finally, we have implicit in our analysis another naïve model for the prediction of no change in all periods, namely

$$P'_t = 0 \tag{2-21}$$

always gives an inequality coefficient of unity.

5. Time series and cross-section analysis

Our procedure is to undertake an accuracy analysis for time series of individual variables and cross-sections of variables for the same time period. The time series analysis permits us to compare the accuracy of forecasts for different variables; the cross-section analysis permits us to investigate whether or not the forecasts have improved over time.

The degree of formalisation of the models of the different forecasters varies considerably. In all the forecasts some variables are forecast exogenously and some endogenously. The forecasts of the endogenous variables depend on the forecasts of the other endogenous variables and/or the forecasts of the exogenous variables, so that the errors in both the endogenous and exogenous variables are interdependent.[8] It follows that overall appraisal of the forecasts will depend on the choice of variables to be studied. Thus it may be argued that main emphasis should be placed on the variable most relevant to domestic economic activity, gross domestic product. But as errors in forecasting components may compensate each other and as it is valuable to see which components are forecast well and which badly (so that effort at improving forecasts may be directed at those variables for which forecasting is worst), the method adopted, that of analysing components as well as totals, does not seem inappropriate.

Because of the interdependence of the forecasts we expect the cross-section inequality coefficients to vary considerably from one forecast period to the next. This is in fact the case.

6. Overestimation, underestimation and turning-point errors

Studies for other countries have often noted a tendency on the part of forecasters to underestimate changes especially when the actual changes are positive.[9] Accordingly when P_t and A_t have the same sign we look to see whether changes are overestimated or underestimated and whether the relative proportions are different from those that would be obtained by chance, the null hypothesis being that underestimates and overestimates are equally likely. The binomial distribution provides a simple way of testing this hypothesis. When P_t and A_t do not have the same sign we regard underestimation of turning-point errors as occurring when A_t is positive and P_t is negative or zero, and overestimation of turning-point errors as occurring when A_t is negative and P_t is positive or zero. If $A_t = 0$ then there is underestimation or overestimation according to whether P_t is negative or positive.

From a policy point of view correctly forecasting the direction of change may be particularly important. For some purposes, such as the successful timing of changes in the direction of policy, it may be more harmful to make a smaller error in prediction and to get the direction of change wrong than to make a larger error but to correctly predict the direction of change. Failure to predict turning-points may cause policy changes to be delayed; the forecasting of turning-points that do not materialise may cause policy to be reserved; in both cases with unfortunate consequences. Accordingly we devote some attention to the investigation of the extent of turning-point errors.[10]

If the sign of P_t is not the same as the sign of A_t then a turning-point error has been made. Note that this classification and analysis is based on rounded data and it is possible that rounding errors may obscure some true turning-points and cause spurious turning-points to be recorded.

As a measure of the overall prevalence of turning-point errors we calculate an index E which is simply the ratio of the total number of turning-point errors to the total number of forecasts. In our example in Table 2.1 there were two turning-point errors and 12 observations so that $E = 0.17$.

Two types of turning-point errors may be distinguished: first, failing to predict a turning-point that actually occurs; secondly, predicting a turning-point which never occurs. Correspondingly, there are two types of correct forecast, successfully predicting a turning-point and successfully predicting no turning-point. To measure the incidence of the first type of turning-point error we calculate E_1, the proportion of turning-points that actually occurred that were missed by the forecasters. The incidence of the second type of turning-point error is estimated by E_2, the proportion of turning-points predicted that are false. In the example of Table 2.1 two turning-points occurred and the forecasters missed one of them so $E_1 = 0.5$; two turning-points were predicted, one of which was false, so $E_2 = 0.5$.

Notes

1 Studies using the mean absolute error include: J. C. R. Dow, *The Management of the British Economy, 1945-60* Cambridge University Press, London (1964); Victor Zarnowitz, *An Appraisal of Short-Term Economic Forecasts* Occasional Paper 104 of the National Bureau of Economic Research, Columbia University Press, New York (1967); Michael K. Evans and Lawrence R. Klein, *The Wharton Econometric Forecasting Model* (2nd enlarged edition) University of Pennsylvania, Philadelphia (1968), Appendix A; Michael K. Evans, *Macroeconomic Activity: Theory, Forecasting and Control* Harper & Row, New York (1969); Geoffrey H. Moore, 'Forecasting short-term economic change', *Journal of the American Statistical Association* (March 1969) pp. 1-22; Herman O. Stekler, *Economic Forecasting* Praeger, New York (1970) and Longman, London (1970); R. L. Major and M. J. C. Surrey, 'Errors in the national institute forecasts of the balance of payments', *National Institute Economic Review* (May 1970) pp. 35-45; M. C. Kennedy, 'How well does

the national institute forecast?' *National Institute Economic Review* (May 1970) pp. 40-52; C. D. Cohen, *British Economic Policy 1960-69* Butterworth, London (1971); Michael K. Evans, Yoel Haitovsky and George I. Treyz, 'An analysis of the forecasting properties of U.S. econometric models' in Bert G. Hickman, ed. *Econometric Models of Cyclical Behavior, Volume II* Number 36 of Studies in Income and Wealth by the Conference on Research in Income and Wealth, National Bureau of Economic Research, New York (1972) pp. 949-1139. Most of these studies used actual changes not percentage changes.

[2] Studies using a mean-square error or root-mean-square error criterion include: C. A. Sims, 'Evaluating short-term macroeconomic forecasts: the Dutch performance', *Review of Economics and Statistics* (May 1967) pp. 225-36; Herman O. Stekler, 'An evaluation of quarterly judgmental economic forecasts', *Journal of Business* (July 1968) pp. 320-39 and *Economic Forecasting, op. cit.*; Jacob Mincer and Victor Zarnowitz, 'The evaluation of economic forecasts', in Jacob Mincer, ed. *Economic Forecasts and Expectations* National Bureau of Economic Research and Columbia University Press, New York (1969) pp. 3-46; Ray C. Fair, *A Short-Run Forecasting Model of the United States Economy* Heath Lexington Books, Lexington, Massachusetts (1971); Lawrence R. Klein, *An Essay on the Theory of Economic Prediction* Markham, Chicago (1971). The Sims study uses percentage changes. Stekler, Fair and Klein use actual changes and Mincer and Zarnowitz use levels.

[3] On the concept of a loss function see Henri Theil, *Applied Economic Forecasting* North-Holland, Amsterdam (1966) pp. 15-19.

[4] A detailed discussion of U is given in Theil, *Applied Economic Forecasting, op. cit.* This inequality coefficient is used in Henri Theil, 'Who forecasts best?' *International Economic Papers* No. 5 (1955) pp. 194-99; *Techniques of Economic Forecasting* OECD, Paris (1965); C. A. Van Den Beld, 'Short-term planning experience in the Netherlands', in Bert G. Hickman, ed. *Quantitative Planning of Economic Policy* The Brookings Institution, Washington D.C. (1965) pp. 134-62; Pieter de Wolff, 'Macroeconomic forecasting', in *Forecasting on a Scientific Basis* proceedings of an International Summer Institute held in Curia, Portugal, September 1966, the NATO Science Committee and the Gulbenkian Foundation, Lisbon (1967); Herman O. Stekler, 'Evaluation of econometric inventory forecasts', *Review of Economics and Statistics* (February 1969) pp. 77-83, and *Economic Forecasting, op. cit.*

Theil earlier used another inequality coefficient in Henri Theil, *Economic Forecasts and Policy* North-Holland, Amsterdam (1961). We shall denote this by V; it is defined as

$$V = \frac{\sqrt{\frac{1}{n}\Sigma (P_t - A_t)^2}}{\sqrt{\frac{1}{n}\Sigma P_t^2} + \sqrt{\frac{1}{n}\Sigma A_t^2}}$$

V is bounded by zero and one. Theil prefers U to V because it is related more directly to the concept of the failure of a forecast and because $\sqrt{\frac{1}{n}\Sigma P_t^2} + \sqrt{\frac{1}{n}\Sigma A_t^2}$ depends on the forecasts and so V is not uniquely determined by mean-square prediction error, given the data on realisations, which is against the idea of a quadratic loss criterion (Theil, *Applied Economic Forecasting*, p. 28, no. 1). The inequality coefficient, V, has been used in a number of studies and in Chapter 8 we shall calculate it for some United Kingdom forecasts in order to extend the sample of countries for which forecasts can be compared. Studies using this older inequality coefficient are: C. Van de Panne, 'De Voorspellingskwaliteit van de Centrale Economische Plannen 1949-56', *De Economist* Jrg. 107 (1959) pp. 91-123; T. G. Ridker, 'An evaluation of the forecasting ability of the Norwegian national budgeting system', *Review of Economics and Statistics* (February 1963) pp. 23-33; D. J. Smyth, 'How well do Australian economists forecast?' *Economic Record* (June 1966) pp. 293-311; H. O. Stekler, 'Forecasting with econometric models: an evaluation', *Econometrica* (July-October 1968) pp. 437-63 and *Economic Forecasting, op. cit.*; D. A. L. Auld, 'Fiscal markmanship in Canada', *Canadian Journal of Economics* (August 1970) pp. 507-11.

5 The decomposition is given in both Theil books referred to above. $\bar{P} = \frac{1}{n}\Sigma P_t$; $\bar{A} = \frac{1}{n}\Sigma A_t$; $s_P = \sqrt{\frac{1}{n}\Sigma (P_t - \bar{P})^2}$; $s_A = \sqrt{\frac{1}{n}\Sigma (A_t - \bar{A})^2}$; $r = \frac{1}{n}\Sigma (P_t - \bar{P})(A_t - \bar{A})/s_P s_A$. In the example, $\bar{P} = 3.50$, $\bar{A} = 2.75$, $s_p = 2.53$, $s_A = 3.49$, $r = 0.74$, $\alpha = -0.82$ (standard error = 1.27) and $\beta = 1.02$ (standard error = 0.29).

6 Theil, *Economic Forecasts and Policy, op. cit.* p. 58.

7 Henri Theil, *Economics and Information Theory* North-Holland, Amsterdam (1967) analyses Dutch forecasts and revised realisations in terms of their information gain. One of us (J. C. K. Ash) hopes, in due course, to report on a similar analysis of United Kingdom data.

8 An example may be of help here. If investment is overestimated, gross domestic product will be overestimated and so, through any consumption function (explicit or implicit) used by the forecasters, consumption will be overestimated as well. Thus the error in investment, gross domestic product and consumption for any forecast period will tend to be in the same direction.

9 See, for instance, Mincer, *op. cit.*, Smyth, *op. cit.*, Stekler, 'An evalua-

tion of quarterly judgemental forecasts' and *Economic Forecasting, op. cit.*, Theil, *Economic Forecasts and Policy* and *Applied Economic Forecasting, op. cit.*, and Zarnowitz, *op. cit.* For Australia, Smyth finds underestimation of positive changes and overestimation of negative changes and provides an explanation for this in terms of pessimism on the part of forecasters.

[10] Turning-point errors are considered in the studies cited in the previous footnote and in R. Fels and C. E. Hinshaw, *Forecasting and Recognizing Business Cycle Turning Points* National Bureau of Economic Research and Columbia University Press, New York (1968).

3 Annual Forecasts

1. Introduction

This chapter evaluates the accuracy of annual forecasts made by the Treasury and the National Institute of Economic and Social Research. The Treasury forecasts which are published at the time of the April Budget comprise real gross domestic product and its major components. The NIESR forecasts, made for the same variables, are published in the February and May issues of the *National Institute Economic Review*.

For the Treasury we have extracted forecasts of the main components of aggregate demand in real terms for the period 1951-1971: consumers' expenditure, public authorities' current expenditure, gross fixed investment, investment in stocks, exports, total final expenditure (the sum of the previous five variables), imports, and gross domestic product (which is total final expenditure minus imports). For each variable we generated a P_t series by taking the forecast percentage change over the actual value of the previous year.[1] For the early years our source for the Treasury forecasts was the annual *Economic Survey*.[2] As the 'fifties progressed so the degree of quantification of forecasts in the *Economic Survey* declined and in 1962 the *Economic Survey* ceased publication. Its successor, the *Economic Report*,[3] was, true to its title, merely a report. For the period 1951-1960 we have made use of J. C. R. Dow's quantifications[4] and from 1961-1967 we have employed the quantifications of forecasts in the Budget Speech published in the *London and Cambridge Economic Bulletin*.[5] The forecasts for the final four years, 1968-1971, are taken directly from the annual *Financial Statement and Budget Report*[6] first issued in 1968. For the transition year between the *Economic Survey* and the *Economic Report*, 1962, we have been unable to find an annual forecast; however, we have been able to calculate the forecast percentage change for the last quarter of 1962 over the corresponding quarter of 1961. For 1966 also only fourth-quarter data are available and a similar calculation has been made here. These fourth-quarter forecasts for 1962 and 1966 are considered in Chapter 4. Actual percentage changes, A_t, were calculated from the *National Income and Expenditure* Blue Books.[7]

It is possible that the forecasts published by the Treasury are merely window-dressing and that they do not represent the predictions on which the Government actually bases its economic policy. However, if the published forecasts are indeed window-dressing, displaying the course the Government would like the economy to take over the calendar year rather than true predictions of the economic future, then our 'accuracy analysis' may shed some light on the Government's effectiveness in implementing its macroeconomic policy. This may be no less interesting than an examination of its forecasting ability.[8]

Another potential criticism of our evaluation of the Treasury forecasts is that many of the forecasts are not fully quantified and so (it may be alleged) their accuracy cannot be examined. We have little sympathy with this view which seeks to protect the Treasury from evaluation and hence criticism. The example of other countries could have been followed and more detailed forecasts published.[9] Failing such detailed predictions the accuracy of official forecasting has to be judged on the basis of the best quantifications that can be made of the forecasts actually published. We welcome the recent re-introduction of quantified forecasts–at the time of the 1968 Budget Speech comprehensive forecasts of the major components of aggregate expenditure, projected as far ahead as the first half of 1969, were published, and since then the Budget data have included forecasts for the period eighteen months ahead. However, as yet this has not led to a continuing series of (revised) forecasts published at regular intervals between Budgets[10] as successive Governments have shown considerable caution in the publication of forecasts. For instance, when one Chancellor of the Exchequer (Mr. Callaghan in 1966) was asked why more information was not provided on balance of payments' forecasts the substance of his reply was that 'it is not usual to publish forecasts of figures for the very good reason that the forecasts are always wrong'.[11] This is surely an unnecessarily defensive attitude.

The National Institute's forecasts of annual changes are available for the period 1963-1971. There are two sets of NIESR forecasts, both published in the *National Institute Economic Review*. The major forecasts are published early in the year in the February issue of the *Review*, earlier than the Treasury forecasts are available. These forecasts are made before the Budget and we have not revised them in any way to attempt to incorporate the effect of Budget changes. In May the National Institute publishes a second set of forecasts and these forecasts take into account Budget changes. Like the Treasury forecasts, the National Institute's forecasts relate to real gross domestic product and its main components. Actual data were extracted from recent volumes of the *Review*. There is no May forecast for 1964 so there are nine observations for the February forecasts and eight for the May forecasts. There are no forecasts for investment in stocks in 1963.

The direct effects of budget changes are incorporated in the Treasury forecasts and the NIESR May forecasts. We have not attempted to allow for any associated multiplier-accelerator reactions additional to those incorporated in the forecasts by the forecasters themselves. Nor are the forecasts adjusted for post-budget changes in fiscal and monetary policy. However, we shall see later that the forecasts are no more inaccurate in years with post-budget changes than in years without such changes, presumably because the time lags with which the economy responds are sufficiently long that measures imposed in the summer or autumn have no significant effects within the current calendar year.

2. Evaluation of the forecasts: time series

Table 3.1 gives the inequality coefficients for the Treasury forecasts and the naïve models for the period 1951-1971. Compared with the naïve models the Treasury forecasters do not fare badly for the Treasury inequality coefficients are consistently lower than their naïve equivalents. The only naïve forecasts that are superior to a series of Treasury predic-

Table 3.1

Inequality coefficients for Treasury and naïve models: annual forecasts, time series 1951-1971

	Treasury	Naïve models			
		A_{t-1}	3-year moving average	5-year moving average	$\bar{A}$
Consumers' expenditure	0.47	0.68	0.75	0.63	0.55
Public authorities' current expenditure	0.72	0.88	0.91	1.22	0.83
Gross fixed investment	0.53	0.93	0.83	0.76	0.68
Investment in stocks	0.96	1.71	1.27	1.08	0.94
Exports	0.56	1.06	1.22	0.98	0.65
Total final expenditure	0.35	0.80	0.69	0.65	0.52
Imports	0.51	1.18	0.94	0.90	0.71
Gross domestic product	0.39	0.71	0.63	0.58	0.51

tions are those generated by the $\bar{A}$ forecast of investment in stocks ($\bar{A}$ is the mean of A_t over the sample period). But it is apparent that the naïve models do not give very good results as inequality coefficients close to or greater than unity are quite common so that reliance on the naïve models as an alternative to genuine forecasting would be unwise.

The most successful naïve predictor of each series is the $\bar{A}$ model. Of course the forecasters would not have $\bar{A}$ available to them when making their forecasts. But the next best naïve model is the five-year moving average model for all series except public authorities' current expenditure and investment in stocks. For the first of these the A_{t-1} model is the best, presumably reflecting short-run stabilisation policy; for the latter the no-change model (for which $U = 1$ always) is superior to the averages. We interpret the $\bar{A}$ and the five-year moving average models as reflecting trend rates of growth that smooth out short-run fluctuations.

Table 3.2 presents a more detailed accuracy analysis of the Treasury forecasts for the period 1951-1971. It gives the inequality coefficients, the partial coefficients, the correlations between P_t and A_t, estimates of α and β in the regression line $A_t = \alpha + \beta P_t$ together with their standard errors, the means of the P_t and A_t series, and the ratios of their standard deviations.

Investment in stocks is the worst forecast series. Its inequality coefficient is 0.96 and bad forecasting is thus indicated for this series (remember that an inequality coefficient of unity is what we would get if we forecasted zero change for each year). It is not surprising that the magnitude of year to year stock changes is not predicted very accurately (the series is notoriously difficult to predict, being volatile with large absolute percentage changes swinging frequently from positive to negative and back again). The next highest inequality coefficient is for public authorities' current spending, with an inequality coefficient of 0.72. The poor forecasting here is surprising for this is the variable for which the Treasury should have the most information and the most power to equate forecasts and realisations. We observe $\bar{P} > \bar{A}$. This overestimation of public authorities' consumption may be due to a variety of political and administrative factors: for example, 'over-bidding' in interdepartmental forward estimates. Furthermore, real constraints may check the planned growth of public expenditure. A final possible explanation is that government spending is planned and fulfilled in money terms, but that rising prices cause actual real expenditure to fall below planned real expenditure. The inequality coefficient for exports is 0.56, followed by fixed investment, 0.53, imports, 0.51, and consumption, 0.47. Gross domestic product is forecast marginally less accurately than total final

Table 3.2

Accuracy analysis of Treasury annual forecasts: time series 1951-1971

	U	U^M	U^S	U^C	r	α	β	SE (α)	SE (β)	$\bar{P}$	$\bar{A}$	s_P/s_A
Consumers' expenditure	0.47	0.12	0.06	0.82	0.64	0.88	0.80	0.52	0.22	1.96	2.45	0.80
Public authorities' current expenditure	0.72	0.08	0.00	0.91	0.67	0.26	0.64	0.68	0.16	2.79	2.04	1.05
Gross fixed investemnt	0.53	0.01	0.17	0.82	0.67	0.54	0.97	1.29	0.25	4.19	4.60	0.69
Investment in stocks	0.96	0.02	0.06	0.92	0.38	36.08	0.50	35.56	0.28	30.26	51.27	0.76
Exports	0.56	0.00	0.02	0.98	0.57	1.39	0.65	1.01	0.22	3.75	3.84	0.88
Total final expenditure	0.35	0.05	0.03	0.92	0.77	0.57	0.88	0.51	0.16	2.65	2.91	0.88
Imports	0.51	0.19	0.12	0.69	0.79	1.23	1.03	0.80	0.19	2.64	3.96	0.77
Gross domestic product	0.39	0.00	0.00	1.00	0.70	0.80	0.69	0.50	0.16	2.64	2.63	1.00

expenditure, the inequality coefficients being 0.39 and 0.35 respectively, apparently because of error in forecasting imports. That the forecasts of gross domestic product and total final expenditure are better than for the components indicates that there have been some offsetting errors.

The partial coefficients do not indicate much systematic forecasting error although there is a tendency to underestimate the average increases as $\bar{P}$ is less than $\bar{A}$ for six of the eight series, and a tendency to underestimate the extent of fluctuations as the variance of the predicted changes is less than the variance of the actual changes for the same six series. The two series that do not conform to the pattern are public authorities' current expenditure and gross domestic product. Bias accounts for more than ten per cent of the error only for imports and consumption where the proportions are nineteen and twelve per cent respectively, and the variance proportion is greater than ten per cent only for gross fixed investment (seventeen per cent) and imports (twelve per cent). The total systematic proportion of forecasting error, measured by $U^M + U^S$, would appear to be important only for imports where U^C ($= 1 - U^M - U^S$) is sixty-nine per cent, and consumer's expenditure and gross fixed investment, both eighty-two per cent. It is interesting to note that systematic error tends to be concentrated in those components of gross domestic product with relatively low U coefficients (consumption, fixed investment and imports) and that those components with relatively high U coefficients (investment in stocks and exports) have high U^C coefficients.

In order to compare the NIESR forecasts with the Treasury forecasts over the same time period we have also undertaken the inequality analysis for the Treasury forecasts for the sub-period 1963-1971. The inequality coefficients for the Treasury forecasts, together with those for the naïve models and NIESR forecasts, are given in Table 3.3. For the shorter period the Treasury fares less well against the naive models. The inequality coefficient for the Treasury forecasts is inferior to those obtained for the three- and five-year moving average and the $\bar{A}$ naïve models for consumers' expenditure, inferior to the five-year average and $\bar{A}$ models for public authorities' current expenditure and imports, and inferior to the no-change ($U = 1$), five-year average, and $\bar{A}$ models for investment in stocks. To some extent this poorer performance by the Treasury vis-à-vis the naïve models is due to higher Treasury inequality coefficients for the shorter period. The inequality coefficient for four series are higher for the 1963-1971 period than for the 1951-1971 period: the increases are public authorities' current expenditure 0.72 to 0.78, gross fixed investment 0.53 to 0.64, investment in stocks 0.96 to 1.04, and imports 0.51 to 0.64. For

Table 3.3

Inequality coefficients for Treasury, NIESR, and naïve models: annual forecasts, time series 1963-1971

	Treasury	NIESR		Naïve models			
		February	May	A_{t-1}	3-year moving average	5-year moving average	$\bar{A}$
Consumers' expenditure	0.45	0.59	0.34	0.54	0.44	0.41	0.41
Public authorities' current expenditure	0.78	0.74	0.73	0.84	0.81	0.72	0.67
Gross fixed investment	0.64	0.63	0.56	1.03	0.81	0.79	0.77
Investment in stocks	1.04	0.57	0.47	1.29	1.15	0.95	0.97
Exports	0.44	0.35	0.45	0.71	0.61	0.56	0.57
Total final expenditure	0.36	0.35	0.42	0.60	0.50	0.39	0.40
Imports	0.64	0.43	0.30	0.77	0.66	0.51	0.48
Gross domestic product	0.29	0.35	0.33	0.53	0.46	0.42	0.43

exports and gross domestic product the coefficients improve from 0.56 to 0.44 and 0.39 to 0.29 respectively; the marked improvement for gross domestic product is, of course, encouraging. The coefficients for consumers' expenditure and total final expenditure are almost the same in the two time periods. However, the major change in the picture is due to a considerable reduction in the inequality coefficients for the naïve models. With the exception of the A_{t-1} and five-year moving average coefficients for gross fixed investment, and the $\bar{A}$ coefficients for gross fixed investment and investment in stocks, the naïve coefficients are all lower for the 1963-1971 period than the corresponding coefficients for the 1951-1971 period. This suggests that for the more recent period the economy has become easier to forecast.

Detailed analysis of the Treasury forecasts for 1963-1971 is given in Table 3.4. The behaviour of some of the partial coefficients is of interest. U^M rises markedly for three series, compared to the coefficients obtained for the longer period, for public authorities' current expenditure (0.08 to 0.24) exports (0.00 to 0.11) and gross domestic product (0.00 to 0.19), and falls markedly for two series, consumption (0.12 to 0.00) and imports (0.19 to 0.03). Instead of having $\bar{P} < \bar{A}$ predominantly, we now have $\bar{P} > \bar{A}$ for five series. The only really marked change for U^S is its rise for exports (from 0.02 to 0.23). For the shorter period $s_P < s_A$ for six series. On balance error has become more systematic as U^C has fallen markedly for public authorities' current expenditure (0.91 to 0.72), exports (0.98 to 0.67) and gross domestic product (1.00 to 0.81); the rises are less marked for consumption (0.82 to 0.92) and imports (0.69 to 0.88).

We turn now to the National Institute forecasts. The NIESR inequality coefficients are compared with those for naïve models in Table 3.3 and the more detailed accuracy analysis is presented in Tables 3.5 and 3.6.

We look first at the February forecasts. The forecasts for consumers' expenditure are inferior to all naïve models except the no-change prediction; the public authorities' current expenditure forecasts are inferior to the five-year moving average and $\bar{A}$ models; for the other series the NIESR February forecasts outperform all the naïve models. Nevertheless the inequality coefficients for the NIESR February forecasts are quite high. In descending order the coefficients are: public authorities' current expenditure, 0.74, gross fixed investment, 0.63, consumers' expenditure, 0.59, investment in stocks, 0.57, imports, 0.43, and exports, total final expenditure, and gross domestic product all 0.35. As total final expenditure and gross domestic product are forecast better than the individual components there are presumably offsetting errors in the forecasts. Bias coefficients in excess of ten per cent are found for imports (0.29), public

Table 3.4

Accuracy analysis of Treasury annual forecasts: time series 1963-1971

	U	U^M	U^S	U^C	r	α	β	SE (α)	SE (β)	$\bar{P}$	$\bar{A}$	s_P/s_A
Consumers' expenditure	0.45	0.00	0.08	0.92	0.69	1.03	0.55	0.58	0.22	2.20	2.23	1.25
Public authorities' current expenditure	0.78	0.24	0.05	0.72	0.32	0.70	0.43	1.54	0.48	2.94	1.97	0.74
Gross fixed investment	0.64	0.02	0.16	0.82	0.59	0.00	0.87	2.56	0.46	4.53	3.94	0.68
Investment in stocks	1.04	0.04	0.05	0.92	0.58	1.60	0.47	33.43	0.25	44.13	22.50	1.23
Exports	0.44	0.11	0.23	0.67	0.57	1.03	0.97	2.56	0.53	4.48	5.37	0.72
Total final expenditure	0.36	0.01	0.03	0.97	0.68	0.58	0.77	1.04	0.32	2.98	2.88	0.88
Imports	0.64	0.03	0.09	0.88	0.46	1.82	0.64	2.00	0.47	3.36	3.97	0.72
Gross domestic product	0.29	0.19	0.01	0.81	0.83	0.30	0.78	0.65	0.20	2.96	2.60	0.76

authorities' current expenditure (0.17) and consumers' expenditure (0.15). Only exports, with a U^S of 0.29, has a variance coefficient greater than ten per cent. There is no systematic pattern between $\bar{P}$ and $\bar{A}$ or between s_P and s_A for the set of variables. Systematic error is greatest for exports ($U^M + U^S = 0.33$) followed by imports (0.30), consumers' expenditure (0.24), public authorities' current expenditure (0.19), and gross domestic product (0.16).

The May forecasts incorporate the effects of the Budget changes. For six series the inequality coefficients are lower than for the corresponding February forecasts, a marked reduction being noted for consumption (down from 0.59 to 0.34), imports (0.43 to 0.30) and investment in stocks (0.57 to 0.47). Increases are noted for exports (up from 0.35 to 0.45) and total final expenditure (0.35 to 0.42). The May forecasts are superior to the naïve models except that the NIESR inequality coefficients for public authorities' current expenditure and total final expenditure are higher than for the five-year moving average and the $\bar{A}$ naïve models.

Examining the partial coefficients, we find the marked changes in U^M consist of an increase for total final expenditure (up from 0.00 to 0.09) and decreases for imports and gross domestic product (down from 0.09 to 0.01 and from 0.09 to 0.00 respectively). U^S is higher for public authorities' current expenditure (0.02 to 0.10), investment in stocks (0.02 to 0.36), total final expenditure (0.04 to 0.21) and imports (0.01 to 0.18), and markedly lower for consumers' expenditure (0.09 to 0.00) and exports (0.29 to 0.07). The net effect is that there is a marked rise in

Table 3.5

Accuracy analysis of NIESR annual forecasts (February): times series 1963-1971

	U	U^M	U^S	U^C
Consumers' expenditure	0.59	0.15	0.09	0.77
Public authorities' current expenditure	0.74	0.17	0.02	0.81
Gross fixed investment	0.63	0.01	0.06	0.92
Investment in stocks	0.57	0.00	0.02	0.98
Exports	0.35	0.04	0.29	0.67
Total final expenditure	0.35	0.00	0.04	0.96
Imports	0.43	0.29	0.01	0.70
Gross domestic product	0.35	0.07	0.09	0.84

systematic error for public authorities' current expenditure ($U^M + U^S$ up from 0.19 to 0.30), investment in stocks (0.02 to 0.38), total final expenditure (0.04 to 0.30) and marked falls in systematic error for exports ($U^M + U^S$ down from 0.33 to 0.09) imports (0.30 to 0.19) and gross domestic product (0.16 to 0.05). There is again no consistent pattern in the relation between $\bar{P}$ and $\bar{A}$ or between s_P and s_A.

The forecasting procedures of both the Treasury and the National Institute are such that consumers' expenditure, investment in stocks, and imports are treated as endogenous, and public authorities' current expenditure, gross fixed investment, and exports as largely exogenous. The average inequality coefficients for the endogenous and exogenous components are, respectively: Treasury, 1951-1971, 0.65 and 0.60; Treasury, 1963-1971, 0.71 and 0.62; NIESR February, 1963-1971, 0.53 and 0.57; NIESR May, 1963-1971, 0.37 and 0.58. The difference between the means is significant at the five per cent level for the NIESR May forecasts; the other differences are not significant.

Of the endogenous variables the National Institute's forecasts of investment in stocks and imports are much superior to those of the Treasury. The National Institute forecasts these within its small aggregate econometric model and its relative success here may reflect accumulated expertise in econometric analysis compared to the more *ad hoc* approach adopted by the Treasury.

Turning now to the exogenous variables, we have already commented that it is surprising that the Treasury forecasts of public authorities' current expenditure are not better. The inaccuracy of the NIESR forecasts

Table 3.5 (continued)

r	α	β	SE (α)	SE (β)	$\bar{P}$	$\bar{A}$	s_P/s_A
0.44	1.87	0.31	0.57	0.24	1.82	2.43	1.42
0.10	1.75	0.13	1.43	0.46	2.90	2.12	0.77
0.63	0.46	0.79	2.18	0.37	4.33	3.88	0.80
0.81	8.10	0.88	33.17	0.26	37.38	41.00	0.92
0.75	–0.46	1.19	2.06	0.40	4.78	5.22	0.63
0.67	1.38	0.57	0.80	0.24	3.01	3.09	1.18
0.71	2.45	0.66	1.10	0.25	3.56	4.81	1.08
0.79	0.76	0.64	0.61	0.19	2.83	2.15	1.23

for the same variable may merely reflect the inaccuracy of the Treasury forecasts. Also not well forecast by both NIESR and the Treasury is gross fixed investment. This may be accounted for by the considerable reliance placed upon the investment intentions survey by both sets of forecasters. D. J. Smyth and G. Briscoe have shown that manufacturing investment is not well forecast directly by the anticipatory series. Realisation functions using the anticipatory data in conjunction with forecast demand changes, measured by changes in capacity utilisation or in gross domestic product, provide reasonable forecasts of actual investment but are inferior to non-anticipatory models using capacity variables.[12]

3. Evaluation of the forecasts: cross-section

So far we have been considering the accuracy of forecasts for time series of gross domestic product and its components. We now turn to the question of how the accuracy of forecasts has varied over time. Our procedure here is to compare P_t and A_t for different variables in the same year. We deliberately omit observations for changes in stocks as the scale of this variable is rather different to that of the other variables (because of the large percentage changes) and if it were included it would dominate the results.[13] We are left with seven observations for each year so that coefficients for individual years must be treated with some reserve, especially as the observations for different series are not strictly independent; for instance, an error in the forecast for exports will affect the forecast for

Table 3.6

Accuracy analysis of NIESR annual forecasts (May): time series 1963-1971

	U	U^M	U^S	U^C
Consumers' expenditure	0.34	0.19	0.00	0.81
Public authorities' current expenditure	0.73	0.20	0.10	0.70
Gross fixed investment	0.56	0.00	0.05	0.95
Investment in stocks	0.47	0.02	0.36	0.62
Exports	0.45	0.02	0.07	0.91
Total final expenditure	0.42	0.09	0.21	0.70
Imports	0.30	0.01	0.18	0.81
Gross domestic product	0.33	0.00	0.05	0.95

gross domestic product and hence also that for consumption. Nevertheless, the cross-section inequality coefficients should be useful in helping us see if there are systematic changes in the accuracy of the forecasts over time.

Table 3.7 presents the summary inequality coefficients for the Treasury and the National Institute together with the coefficients for the naïve models. There are no Treasury forecasts for 1962 and 1966 as for those years the Treasury only made fourth-quarter predictions, not forecasts for the whole year. There was no NIESR forecast in May 1964.

There is considerable variation in the inequality coefficients from year to year. There is probably a two-fold explanation for this. First, some years are more difficult to forecast than others. Secondly, there is the interdependence of errors referred to above. For some years the naïve models are very bad indeed, in particular 1952, 1958 and 1962. However, in six of the nineteen years at least one naïve model outperforms the Treasury and in no less than five years, over a shorter time span, both the NIESR February and May forecasts are inferior to a naïve model.

Table 3.8 gives some summary statistics for the cross-section forecasts; Tables 3.9, 3.10 and 3.11 show the more detailed analysis. There is no evidence of upward or downward trends in U and U^C over time for either the Treasury or the National Institute as none of the correlation coefficients reported in Table 3.8 are significant at the ten per cent level. For the Treasury forecast $\bar{P}$ is less than $\bar{A}$ for six of the nineteen years. Making use of the binomial cumulative distribution function, the probability of obtaining six or fewer observations for which $\bar{P}$ is less than $\bar{A}$ is 0.084 if the null hypothesis is that $\bar{P} < \bar{A}$ and $\bar{P} > \bar{A}$ are equally likely. Only three

Table 3.6 (continued)

r	α	β	SE (α)	SE (β)	$\bar{P}$	$\bar{A}$	s_P/s_A
0.74	0.99	0.71	0.58	0.25	2.04	2.43	1.04
−0.05	2.36	−0.08	1.99	0.65	2.94	2.12	0.63
0.72	0.54	0.85	1.81	0.31	3,93	3.88	0.85
0.90	1.83	1.26	25.21	0.26	31.00	41.00	0.49
0.54	1.80	0.70	2.26	0.42	4.86	5.22	0.77
0.73	1.36	0.49	0.70	0.17	3.51	3.09	1.49
0.87	1.66	0.68	0.83	0.15	4.66	4.81	1.28
0.77	0.87	0.66	0.61	0.21	2.58	2.57	1.17

Table 3.7

Inequality coefficients for Treasury, NIESR and naïve models: annual forecasts, cross-section 1951-1971

	Treasury	NIESR		Naïve models			
		February	May	A_{t-1}	3-year moving average	5-year moving average	$\bar{A}$
1951	0.59			1.62	1.95		0.84
1952	0.57			1.28	1.49	2.34	1.33
1953	0.34			1.39	0.82	0.60	0.48
1954	0.76			0.42	0.70	0.50	0.36
1955	0.44			0.58	0.84	0.75	0.57
1956	0.37			1.66	1.38	1.01	0.78
1957	0.43			0.51	0.59	0.58	0.59
1958	0.78			1.52	1.95	2.35	2.05
1959	0.51			0.97	0.71	0.48	0.36
1960	0.35			0.37	0.66	0.61	0.55
1961	0.39			1.33	0.75	0.71	0.58
1962				2.26	2.36	1.70	1.37
1963	0.76	0.54	0.42	0.66	0.56	0.51	0.45
1964	0.33	0.20		0.75	0.73	0.57	0.63
1965	0.65	0.67	0.53	2.03	0.72	0.82	0.49
1966		0.18	0.30	0.38	0.91	0.66	0.47
1967	0.84	0.93	0.86	0.65	0.49	0.50	0.49
1968	0.48	0.44	0.21	0.84	0.67	0.61	0.58
1969	0.56	0.70	0.74	0.71	0.75	0.97	0.85
1970	0.25	0.47	0.31	0.70	0.23	0.24	0.36
1971	0.47	0.52	0.64	0.49	0.71	0.54	0.71

of the nineteen values of s_P/s_A for the Treasury forecasts are greater than one, and if the null hypothesis is that $s_P < s_A$ and $s_P > s_A$ are equally likely then the probability of so few observations with s_P/s_A greater than one is 0.002. This last result provides substantial evidence that year by year the Treasury underestimates the variation in changes between variables. For the National Institute, on the other hand, there is no significant pattern between $\bar{P}$ and $\bar{A}$ or s_P and s_A.

We also tested to see if there were significant time trends in the inequality coefficients for the naïve models. The correlation coefficients obtained were negative, indicating improved forecasting by the naïve models over time, but the coefficients were not significant at the five per cent level. However, it will be recalled from section 2 of the present chapter that the inequality coefficients for the naïve models were markedly smaller for the more recent period, 1963-1971, than for the full period, 1951-1971. Accordingly, we divided the cross-section inequality coefficients into two time periods, 1951-1962, and 1963-1971, calculated the means for the two periods, and tested to see if they were significantly different. The means are (1951-1962 period given first): A_{t-1}, 1.16 and 0.80; three-year moving average, 1.18 and 0.64; five-year moving average, 1.06 and 0.60; $\bar{A}$, 0.82 and 0.56. In all cases the means are lower for the more recent period; for the five-year moving average the difference between means is significant at the one per cent level; for the three-year moving average the difference is significant at the five per cent level; the other two differences are not significant at the five per cent level. Note that for the $\bar{A}$ series the same predicted changes were used each year, and this probably accounts for its lack of significance, whereas slowly changing average values over time were picked up by the moving average series models. These results support our previous finding that the economy has become somewhat easier to forecast in recent years. Thus the finding that Treasury forecasts have not improved over time is somewhat disturbing; for the period 1951-1962 the mean U for the Treasury is 0.48, for the 1963-1971 period it is higher, 0.54 (the difference not being significant at the five per cent level). We can only conclude that, relative to the difficulty of forecasting the economy measured by the goodness of fit of the naïve models, the Treasury forecasts have worsened.

Table 3.8

Summary statistics for cross-section analysis: Treasury and NIESR annual forecasts

	Treasury 1951-71	Treasury 1963-71	NIESR (Feb.) 1963-71	NIESR (May) 1963-71
Mean U	0.52	0.54	0.52	0.50
Standard deviation of U	0.17	0.19	0.22	0.21
Highest U	0.84	0.84	0.93	0.86
Lowest U	0.25	0.25	0.18	0.21
Correlation of U with time	−0.06	−0.41	0.20	0.15
Mean U^C	0.55	0.55	0.62	0.65
Standard deviation of U^C	0.24	0.21	0.22	0.13
Highest U^C	0.98	0.91	0.93	0.86
Lowest U^C	0.13	0.20	0.20	0.30
Correlation of U^C with time	0.14	0.23	0.41	0.17
Proportion $\bar{P} < \bar{A}$	0.68	0.63	0.44	0.67
Proportion $s_P < s_A$	0.84	0.88	0.50	0.50

4. Post-budget policy changes and the accuracy of forecasts

A possible objection to our analysis thus far is that we are evaluating forecasts based on the assumption of unchanged policy against outcomes which are at least partially determined by post-budget changes in fiscal and monetary policy. We may test to see if such a criticism is valid. Consider those years included in our analysis in which there occurred major post-budget changes in the policy variables. In 1955 restrictions were imposed in July on hire purchase, bank credit and public investment, and in October there was a supplementary, deflationary Budget. September 1957 occasioned a two per cent rise in Bank Rate, together with the imposition of ceilings on bank advances and public investment. In 1958 there were four post-budget changes in Bank Rate, whilst in the summer and autumn of that year restrictions on consumer credit and public investment were removed. Major deflationary measures were taken after the April Budgets of both 1960 and 1961. A November Budget and the introduction of the import surcharge followed the General Election of 1964,

Table 3.9

Accuracy analysis of Treasury annual forecasts: cross-section 1951-1971

	U	U^M	U^S	U^C	r	α
1951	0.59	0.14	0.22	0.64	0.86	0.49
1952	0.57	0.00	0.25	0.75	0.83	0.14
1953	0.34	0.37	0.08	0.55	0.76	1.33
1954	0.76	0.78	0.06	0.17	0.43	3.51
1955	0.44	0.09	0.60	0.31	0.84	−2.17
1956	0.37	0.07	0.32	0.61	0.94	0.30
1957	0.43	0.41	0.23	0.36	0.89	0.41
1958	0.78	0.02	0.16	0.82	0.63	0.21
1959	0.51	0.86	0.01	0.13	0.88	2.29
1960	0.35	0.04	0.28	0.69	0.65	−0.17
1961	0.39	0.01	0.01	0.98	0.81	0.37
1962						
1963	0.76	0.56	0.00	0.44	−0.53	6.84
1964	0.33	0.09	0.72	0.20	0.94	−4.00
1965	0.65	0.00	0.45	0.55	0.69	1.78
1966						
1967	0.84	0.18	0.05	0.77	−0.31	4.36
1968	0.48	0.20	0.15	0.65	0.68	1.22
1969	0.56	0.01	0.54	0.44	0.81	−0.86
1970	0.25	0.28	0.31	0.41	0.90	−1.58
1971	0.47	0.00	0.09	0.91	0.59	0.53

and the effects of these policies were reinforced by the April 1965 Budget together with additional adjustments later that year to limit credit and curb domestic expenditure. The restrictive 'July measures' of 1966 were designed to counter a run of confidence on the pound, the devaluation of which in November 1967 was accompanied by another major deflationary package. Hence for these nine years we might expect the cross-section U coefficient to be (unfairly) large. We do not have a Treasury estimate for 1966 but for the other eight years the mean U is 0.53 compared with a mean of 0.51 for the eleven years without post-budget measures. For the NIESR May forecasts the mean value of U is 0.56 in the years with, and 0.46 in the years without, subsequent intervention. For the years in which post-budget measures were imposed we might also expect forecasting errors to be more systematic, that is U^C to be smaller than usual, but this is not the case. The mean values of U^C in years with and without the measures are 0.59 and 0.52 respectively for the Treasury forecasts, and 0.57 and 0.70 for the NIESR May forecasts. None of these differences are significant at the five per cent level.[14]

Table 3.9 (continued)

β	SE (α)	SE (β)	$\bar{P}$	$\bar{A}$	s_P/s_A
0.63	1.03	0.17	3.94	2.96	1.37
1.16	1.20	0.35	–0.27	–0.17	0.72
0.99	1.82	0.38	4.36	5.63	0.77
0.78	1.20	0.74	1.24	4.47	0.55
1.80	2.11	0.53	3.63	4.37	0.47
0.73	0.38	0.12	2.00	1.76	1.29
1.29	0.53	0.29	1.27	2.04	0.69
0.92	0.59	0.51	0.06	0.26	0.68
1.00	0.67	0.25	2.16	4.44	0.88
1.11	3.53	0.58	5.86	6.31	0.59
0.85	1.26	0.27	3.66	3.47	0.95
–0.62	2.49	0.45	5.50	3.44	0.85
1.82	1.91	0.31	5.74	6.51	0.52
0.35	0.58	0.16	2.54	2.66	1.97
–0.47	1.61	0.64	1.99	3.43	0.66
1.00	1.96	0.48	3.37	4.60	0.68
1.59	1.30	0.52	1.89	2.13	0.51
1.31	1.04	0.28	3.59	3.13	0.69
0.78	1.45	0.48	2.69	2.61	0.76

5. Evaluation of the forecasts: underestimation, overestimation and turning-point errors

Tables 3.12, 3.13, and 3.14 classify forecasts and outcomes by whether or not the forecasts were underestimates or overestimates of actual changes and by whether or not turning-point errors were involved.

Theil and a number of other investigators[15] have noted a tendency for forecasters to underestimate changes, especially positive changes. Looking at Table 3.12 there is evidence of such underestimation for the Treasury forecasts. Of the total of 152 Treasury forecasts, seventy-four are underestimates, fifty are overestimates, twenty-three represent turning-point

Table 3.10

Accuracy analysis of NIESR annual forecasts (February): cross section 1963-1971

	U	U^M	U^S	U^C	r	α
1963	0.54	0.07	0.02	0.91	–0.12	3.74
1964	0.20	0.13	0.71	0.16	0.98	–3.46
1965	0.67	0.24	0.17	0.59	0.57	1.39
1966	0.18	0.31	0.29	0.41	0.91	0.74
1967	0.93	0.32	0.03	0.65	–0.30	3.97
1968	0.44	0.36	0.07	0.57	0.80	1.49
1969	0.70	0.12	0.25	0.63	0.64	–1.21
1970	0.47	0.05	0.12	0.84	0.39	1.08
1971	0.52	0.00	0.13	0.87	0.42	1.05

Table 3.11

Accuracy analysis of NIESR annual forecasts (May): cross-section 1963-1971

	U	U^M	U^S	U^C	r	α
1963	0.42	0.21	0.00	0.79	0.32	2.61
1964						
1965	0.53	0.33	0.17	0.50	0.75	0.88
1966	0.30	0.33	0.16	0.51	0.71	1.13
1967	0.86	0.24	0.06	0.71	–0.31	4.26
1968	0.21	0.00	0.32	0.68	0.95	–0.79
1969	0.74	0.02	0.44	0.53	0.52	–1.04
1970	0.31	0.12	0.28	0.61	0.80	–1.15
1971	0.64	0.13	0.00	0.87	0.45	1.84

errors and for the remaining five forecasts the (rounded) P_t is equal to the (rounded) A_t. On the null hypothesis that overestimation and underestimation are equally likely then the probability that as many as seventy-four of the 124 forecasts in which the sign was correctly predicted (and $P_t \neq A_t$) should be underestimated is, using the normal approximation to the binomial, 0.02. During the period of our analysis most of the macro-economic variables grew from year to year and of the positive changes the Treasury underestimated sixty-five and overestimated forty-four. Again the probability of this by chance is 0.02. The Treasury underestimated negative changes nine times and overestimated them six times, a difference that is insignificant. Turning-points were underestimated three times and

Table 3.10 (continued)

β	SE (α)	SE (β)	$\bar{P}$	$\bar{A}$	s_P/s_A
−0.10	1.18	0.36	2.93	3.44	1.20
1.41	0.85	0.11	7.10	6.51	0.70
0.35	0.94	0.23	3.63	2.66	1.63
0.64	0.38	0.13	2.76	2.50	1.42
−0.43	1.26	0.61	1.26	3.43	0.70
1.00	1.37	0.33	3.10	4.60	0.80
1.09	2.11	0.59	3.01	2.06	0.58
0.58	2.27	0.62	3.50	3.13	0.67
0.63	1.74	0.61	2.59	2.69	0.66

Table 3.11 (continued)

β	SE (α)	SE (β)	$\bar{P}$	$\bar{A}$	s_P/s_A
0.31	1.20	0.40	2.74	3.44	1.00
0.50	0.80	0.20	3.56	2.66	1.50
0.47	0.64	0.21	2.94	2.50	1.51
−0.48	1.50	0.66	1.71	3.43	0.65
1.18	0.94	0.18	4.56	4.60	0.81
1.24	2.58	0.90	2.50	2.06	0.42
1.22	1.48	0.40	3.50	3.13	0.66
0.44	1.04	0.39	1.94	2.69	1.00

overestimated three times. The Treasury persistently underestimated consumers' expenditure, total final expenditure and imports, and tended to overestimate public authorities' current expenditure. This confirms our earlier analysis for the Treasury forecasts where we commonly found $\bar{P} < \bar{A}$, and $s_P < s_A$. The evidence for conservative behaviour on the part of the Treasury forecasters is thus very strong.

Of the National Institute's seventy-one February forecasts thirty were underestimates, thirty-three overestimates, six were turning-point errors and for two $P_t = A_t$. The corresponding figures for the sixty-three May forecasts are: underestimates, thirty; overestimates, twenty-seven; turning-point errors, six. Clearly there is no overall underestimation or overestimation of changes with these NIESR forecasts although six out of

Table 3.12

Underestimation, overestimation and turning-point errors: Treasury annual forecasts 1951-1971

	Positive change		
	Under-estimation (1)	Over-estimation (2)	$P_t = A_t$ (3)
Consumers' expenditure	10	5	2
Public authorities' current expenditure	4	9	0
Gross fixed investment	8	7	0
Investment in stocks	4	2	0
Exports	8	6	1
Total final expenditure	12	5	0
Imports	10	3	0
Gross domestic product	9	7	1
Total	65	44	4

	Underestimation of turning-point errors (10)	Overestimation of turning-point errors (11)
Consumers' expenditure	0	1
Public authorities' current expenditure	1	3
Gross fixed investment	2	2
Investment in stocks	3	2
Exports	1	2
Total final expenditure	1	0
Imports	3	1
Gross domestic product	0	1
Total	11	12

eight increases are underestimated for both consumption and imports in the May forecasts.

Thus far in this chapter we have discussed the performance of the forecasters in predicting the magnitude of the percentage changes in the actual series. We now evaluate their success in forecasting the sign of A_t. For some purposes, such as the successful timing of policy measures, it may be more useful to correctly forecast the direction of change even at the expense of a larger absolute error than might be obtained with a forecast that was closer numerically but which wrongly predicted the sign of the actual change. Failure to predict turning-points may cause policy changes to be delayed and the prediction of spurious turning-points may cause unnecessary policy reversals; both of these may have destabilising effects

Table 3.12 (continued)

Negative change			Turning-point errors	Total no. of observations	E
Under-estimation	Over-estimation	$P_t = A_t$			
(4)	(5)	(6)	(7)	(8)	(9)
1	0	0	1	19	0.05
1	1	0	4	19	0.21
0	0	0	4	19	0.21
4	3	1	5	19	0.26
0	1	0	3	19	0.16
1	0	0	1	19	0.05
1	1	0	4	19	0.21
1	0	0	1	19	0.05
9	6	1	23	152	0.15

A_t no turning-point		A_t turning-point		E_1	E_2
P_t no turning-point	P_t turning-point	P_t no turning-point	P_t turning-point		
(12)	(13)	(14)	(15)	(16)	(17)
16	1	0	2	0.00	0.33
14	1	3	1	0.75	0.50
14	2	2	1	0.67	0.67
1	4	3	11	0.21	0.27
13	2	1	3	0.25	0.40
16	1	0	2	0.00	0.33
10	3	1	5	0.17	0.38
15	0	1	3	0.25	0.00
99	14	11	28	0.28	0.33

on the economy. We class a forecast as a turning-point error if P_t and A_t have opposite signs. Turning-point errors are listed in column 7 of Tables 3.12, 3.13 and 3.14 and analysed in columns 9-17.

Of the Treasury forecasts, twenty-three are turning-point errors: investment in stocks registers five turning-point errors, public authorities' current expenditure, gross fixed investment and imports each have four, exports three, and the other series one each. For the shorter period 1963-1971, the National Institute has six turning-point errors for both its February and May forecasts and in each case half of these are for gross fixed investment. It is noteworthy that the National Institute makes only one turning-point error in forecasting investment in stocks. For the same time period the Treasury makes nine turning-point errors, three being for

Table 3.13

Underestimation, overestimation and turning-point errors: NIESR (February) annual forecasts 1963-1971

	Positive change		
	Under-estimation (1)	Over-estimation (2)	$P_t = A_t$ (3)
Consumers' expenditure	2	5	0
Public authorities' current expenditure	3	5	0
Gross fixed investment	3	3	0
Investment in stocks	2	1	0
Exports	5	4	0
Total final expenditure	4	5	0
Imports	5	4	0
Gross domestic product	2	5	0
Total	26	32	0

	Underestimation of turning-point errors (10)	Overestimation of turning-point errors (11)
Consumers' expenditure	2	0
Public authorities' current expenditure	0	1
Gross fixed investment	1	2
Investment in stocks	0	0
Exports	0	0
Total final expenditure	0	0
Imports	0	0
Gross domestic product	0	0
Total	3	3

gross fixed investment and three for investment in stocks.

Some summary statistics that are helpful in analysing turning-point errors are presented in Tables 3.12, 3.13 and 3.14. E is the proportion of forecasts that involve turning-point errors, E_1 is the proportion of turning-points missed by the forecasters, and E_2 is the proportion of predicted turning-points that proved false.

Fifteen per cent of the Treasury forecasts were turning-point errors. It is somewhat surprising that the Treasury forecasts featured more turning-points than did the actual outcomes. Thirty-three per cent of forecast turning-points were not realised; twenty-eight per cent of actual turning-points were not predicted. Looking at the breakdown of the Treasury forecasts by variable we note once again the disappointing forecasts of

Table 3.13 (continued)

Negative change					
Under-estimation (4)	Over-estimation (5)	$P_t = A_t$ (6)	Turning-point errors (7)	Total no. of observations (8)	E (9)
0	0	0	2	9	0.22
0	0	0	1	9	0.11
0	0	0	3	9	0.33
4	1	0	0	8	0.00
0	0	0	0	9	0.00
0	0	0	0	9	0.00
0	0	0	0	9	0.00
0	0	2	0	9	0.00
4	1	2	6	71	0.08

A_t no turning-point		A_t turning-point			
P_t no turning-point (12)	P_t turning-point (13)	P_t no turning-point (14)	P_t turning-point (15)	E_1 (16)	E_2 (17)
7	2	0	0	—	1.00
7	0	1	1	0.50	0.00
5	1	2	1	0.67	0.33
5	0	0	3	0.00	0.00
9	0	0	0	—	—
9	0	0	0	—	—
9	0	0	0	—	—
9	0	0	0	—	—
59	3	3	6	0.33	0.33

public authorities' current expenditure as three out of four turning-points are missed. These results, taken in conjunction with the classification of turning-point errors given in columns 10 and 11, lead us to conclude that the Government has some difficulty in foreseeing cutbacks or stagnation in its own current expenditure. The Treasury record for investment in stocks appears rather better from the turning-point analysis than from the inequality analysis; fourteen actual turning-points are recorded, of which all but three are successfully predicted. But there are four turning-point errors of the second type for investment in stocks, the Treasury being too willing to predict reversals. Exports have an E_1 value of 0.25 and an E_2 value of 0.40, the corresponding figures for imports being 0.17 and 0.38. These E_1 proportions are quite good; most actual turning-points are correctly forecast. On the other hand, recalling that increases and turning-

Table 3.14

Underestimation, overestimation and turning-point errors: NIESR (May) annual forecasts 1963-1971

	Positive change		
	Under-estimation (1)	Over-estimation (2)	$P_t = A_t$ (3)
Consumers' expenditure	6	2	0
Public authorities' current expenditure	2	5	0
Gross fixed investment	2	3	0
Investment in stocks	2	0	0
Exports	5	3	0
Total final expenditure	3	5	0
Imports	6	2	0
Gross domestic product	2	5	0
Total	28	25	0

	Underestimation of turning-point errors (10)	Overestimation of turning-point errors (11)
Consumers' expenditure	0	0
Public authorities' current expenditure	0	1
Gross fixed investment	1	2
Investment in stocks	0	1
Exports	0	0
Total final expenditure	0	0
Imports	0	0
Gross domestic product	1	0
Total	2	4

points in imports are markedly underestimated, the E_2 values apparently reflect optimistic balance of payments forecasters in the Treasury looking for downturns in expenditure on imports and upturns in exports which do not subsequently take place. Note also the commendable zero values of E_1 for consumers' expenditure and total final expenditure (although it must be mentioned that there were only two actual turning-points for each of these variables) and of E_2 for gross domestic product.

There are too few turning-point errors in the shorter NIESR series to give much point to a variable by variable analysis. The overall values of the coefficients for February and May respectively are: E, 0.08 and 0.10; E_1, 0.33 and 0.35; E_2, 0.33 and 0.35. Apart from a tendency, noted earlier, to underestimate import growth in the May forecasts there is no further evidence (from turning-point analysis) of undue balance of payments optimism.

Table 3.14 (continued)

Negative change					
Under-estimation (4)	Over-estimation (5)	$P_t = A_t$ (6)	Turning-point errors (7)	Total no. of observations (8)	E (9)
0	0	0	0	8	0.00
0	0	0	1	8	0.13
0	0	0	3	8	0.38
2	2	0	1	7	0.14
0	0	0	0	8	0.00
0	0	0	0	8	0.00
0	0	0	0	8	0.00
0	0	0	1	8	0.13
2	2	0	6	63	0.10

A_t no turning-point		A_t turning-point			
P_t no turning-point (12)	P_t turning-point (13)	P_t no turning-point (14)	P_t turning-point (15)	E_1 (16)	E_2 (17)
8	0	0	0	—	—
7	0	1	0	1.00	—
4	1	2	1	0.67	0.50
3	1	0	3	0.00	0.25
8	0	0	0	—	—
8	0	0	0	—	—
8	0	0	0	—	—
7	1	0	0	—	1.00
53	3	3	4	0.35	0.35

6. Evaluation of the forecasts: who forecasts best?

We have analysed the Treasury and National Institute forecasts in the preceding sections. The obvious question to ask now is 'Who forecasts best: the Treasury or the National Institute?' To make comparison between the Treasury and NIESR forecasts we must clearly limit our attention to the 1963-1971 period common to both groups of forecasters.

We first look at the time series results in Table 3.3. The Treasury forecasts are inferior to the NIESR February forecasts for six of the variables, and inferior to the NIESR May forecasts for five of the variables. However, the Treasury forecasts of the key gross domestic product variable are superior to the corresponding NIESR forecasts. The series for which both the February and May National Institute forecasts are better than the Treasury forecasts are public authorities' current expenditure, gross fixed investment, investment in stocks and imports, the National Institute's superiority being most marked for the last two variables.

We next compare the U^C coefficients from Tables 3.4, 3.5 and 3.6. The Treasury makes more systematic error in its forecasts than the National Institute for five variables and less for two (for exports the two values of U^C are the same). But when the NIESR May forecasts replace their February counterparts the results are reversed; the Treasury errors are less systematic for five of the eight variables.

We turn now to the cross-section results. The summary information in Table 3.8 indicates that there is little to choose between the U and U^C coefficients for the different forecasts. Examining the years for which forecasts were made by both the Treasury and NIESR, the Treasury inequality coefficient is less than the NIESR February coefficient for five of the eight years, and less than the NIESR May coefficient for four of the seven years. It is interesting to note that over the most recent five years, 1967-1971, the Treasury forecasts were more accurate four times out of five.

Finally we look at the analysis of turning-point errors. For the period 1963-1971, fourteen per cent of the Treasury forecasts were turning-point errors but only eight per cent of the NIESR February forecasts and ten per cent of the May forecasts were. Moreover the values of E_1 and E_2 for the Treasury, 0.40 and 0.63 respectively, were higher than the corresponding values for the NIESR forecasts which were both 0.33 for NIESR February, and 0.35 and 0.35 for NIESR May.

On balance, then, there is little difference in the accuracy of the Treasury and NIESR forecasts with preference perhaps going to the National Institute. As the forecasts are made at different times it is commendable that the NIESR February forecasts are as accurate as the Treasury forecasts made later with the Budget; equally it is regrettable that a significant improvement in the NIESR forecasts between February and May cannot be reported, for in May the National Institute can make use of the information contained in the Budget and, compared with February, has an additional quarter's data to use in its calculations.

7. Conclusions

Section 6 has compared the forecasting performance of the Treasury and the National Institute. We now summarise the remainder of the results of this chapter.

(1) The predictive accuracy of the Treasury and NIESR forecasts varies considerably between variables (time series) and between years (cross-section). So too does the extent to which the mean and variance of changes are wrongly estimated.

(2) The naïve models are not a reliable alternative to genuine economic forecasting. Both the Treasury and NIESR forecasts are superior to the naïve models whether the comparison is based on time series or cross-sectional analysis.

(3) The Treasury's forecasts of total final expenditure and gross domestic product are quite good in terms of the prediction of size and sign of the annual percentage change in actual outcomes. Its poor performance in predicting the magnitude of investment in stocks is offset to some extent by its partial success in predicting turning-points for this volatile series.

(4) For some variables and some years the accuracy of the National Institute's forecasts either do not improve or deteriorate between February and May. The Institute's best (May) forecasts are for imports and gross domestic product. Investment in stocks is forecast more accurately than gross fixed investment and public authorities' current expenditure.

(5) Treasury and NIESR forecasts of public authorities' current expenditure are relatively poor. Mean predicted change is larger than the corresponding actual figure. Increases in public expenditure are overestimated, and turning-point errors are committed when public expenditure declines.

(6) Forecasts of the balance of payments tend to be unduly optimistic, increases in imports being frequently underestimated.

(7) The Treasury forecasters reveal a marked conservative propensity to underestimate the magnitude of changes and fluctuations, and the variation in changes between variables.

(8) Approximately two-thirds of all turning-points are correctly forecast by the Treasury and the National Institute. The Treasury is quite successful in predicting turning-points in consumers' expenditure, investment in stocks, total final expenditure, imports and gross domestic product, but less so for the other variables. The National Institute forecasts turning-points well except for gross fixed investment. The forecasters predict spurious turning-points at least as often as they miss actual turning-points.
(9) Post-budget policy changes subsequent to the publication of forecasts do not impair their accuracy, presumably as a result of the economy's lagged response to expansionary or contractionary stimuli.
(10) There is no evidence of any improvements in predictive accuracy over time for either the Treasury or National Institute forecasts, nor that the proportion of systematic error has been reduced. If the performance of the naïve models is used to judge the ease or difficulty of the task of forecasting the British economy then the economy was easier to forecast in the 1963-1971 period than in the 1951-1962 period. Hence the relative forecasting performance of the Treasury has declined.

Notes

[1] As explained in Chapter 2, the estimate of the actual value of a variable for time period $t-1$ that was available to the forecaster at the time he made the forecast was used in the calculation of P_t.
[2] H. M. Treasury, *Economic Survey* H.M.S.O., London.
[3] Central Statistical Office, *Economic Report*, issued as an annual supplement to *Economic Trends*, H.M.S.O., London.
[4] J. C. R. Dow, *The Management of the British Economy 1945-60* Cambridge University Press, London (1964).
[5] *London and Cambridge Economic Bulletin* issued as a supplement to *The Times Review of Industry and Technology*.
[6] H. M. Treasury, *Financial Statement and Budget Report* H.M.S.O., London.
[7] Central Statistical Office, *National Income and Expenditure 1969* H.M.S.O., London (1969), and *National Income and Expenditure 1972* H.M.S.O., London (1972).
[8] There is evidence that post-war economic policy aimed at stabilising the economy has actually proved destabilising, see D. J. Smyth, 'Public finance policy and techniques for economic stability and balanced economic growth', United Kingdom report in *Public Finance Policy and Techni-*

ques for Economic Stability and Balanced Economic Growth, Congres de Budapest, Septembre 1964, Institut International de Finances Publiques, La Haye (1966) pp. 270-97. This is not necessarily the result of bad forecasting: policies may have been deficient, and political factors may have inhibited the application of appropriate stabilisation measures.

[9] For instance, the Netherlands, U.S.A., Sweden and France. See *Techniques of Economic Forecasting* OECD, Paris (1965).

[10] See House of Commons, *Parliamentary Debates* Vol. 767, Cols. 217-8 and 233-4, H.M.S.O., London (1968).

[11] House of Commons, *Parliamentary Debates* Vol. 737, Col. 671, H.M.S.O., London (1966).

[12] D. J. Smyth and G. Briscoe, 'Investment plans and realisations in United Kingdom manufacturing', *Economica* (August 1969) pp. 277-94.

[13] Compare the $\bar{P}$ and $\bar{A}$ for investment in stocks in Tables 3.2, 3.4, 3.5 and 3.6 with those for other variables.

[14] A similar analysis for the NIESR February forecasts would not provide a satisfactory test of the hypothesis relating to post-budget measures because the forecasts are made before the Budget so that both Budget and post-budget measures would operate to invalidate the forecasts; years with post-budget measures are often also years with important Budget changes. In view of this it is surprising that for the February forecasts the mean value of U is lower in years with post-budget measures (0.49) than in the remaining years (0.53). However, mean U^C is 0.36 in years with the measures and 0.76 in the years without, and the difference between these means is significant at the five per cent level.

[15] See the references cited in footnote 9 of Chapter 2.

4 Fourth Quarter Forecasts

1. Introduction

The previous chapter analysed annual macroeconomic forecasts made by the Treasury and the NIESR, but as the NIESR annual forecasts only started in 1963, and no annual forecast appeared in May 1964, only nine observations were available for our evaluation of the February, and eight for the May, forecasts. Some years earlier, in 1959, the NIESR commenced publishing, in the February and May issues of the *National Institute Economic Review*, predictions of gross domestic product for the fourth quarter of the year, and in the present chapter we analyse the accuracy of these more numerous forecasts. Also considered are the fourth quarter forecasts made by the Treasury for the two years, 1962 and 1966, in which no annual forecasts were published.

We analyse the same eight variables as in the previous chapter using both time series and cross-sections. The forecasts are for the last quarter of the year in which the forecast is being made and are related by the National Institute (and the Treasury) to the last quarter of the previous year. We thus calculate P_t as the predicted percentage change for the fourth quarter of the year over the fourth quarter of the previous year; correspondingly A_t is calculated as the actual percentage change for the fourth quarter of the year over the fourth quarter of the previous year. The NIESR predictions are from the February and May issues of the *National Institute Economic Review*. The actual value of the fourth quarter of the previous year used in calculating a value of P_t is the estimate published in the same issue of the *Review* from which the forecasts were extracted as this is the estimate that was available to the forecasters. There is no May forecast in 1964. The A_t series were calculated using data published in the most recent volumes of the *Review*. These series for fourth quarter outcomes were used in the construction of the naïve models: the naïve models are as in the previous chapter except that they are based on fourth quarters instead of whole years. The Treasury forecasts for 1962 and 1966 have been calculated in the same way as the NIESR forecasts, the data being taken from sources given in Chapter 3.

2. Evaluation of the forecasts: time series

Table 4.1 gives the time series inequality coefficients for the NIESR forecasts and the naïve models. It is readily apparent that the February forecasts are not very satisfactory; the inequality coefficients range from a low of 0.55 for consumers' expenditure to a high of 0.98 for investment in stocks. The only forecasts that are not outperformed by one or more of the naïve models are those for exports and imports. For the non-balance of payments series the $\bar{A}$ model performs as well or better than the February forecasts for all variables and the five-year moving average model is superior to the NIESR forecasts for four variables.

The National Institute's fourth quarter forecasts improve considerably between February and May, probably reflecting their incorporation of policy changes in the Budget. The fall in the inequality coefficients is most marked for the two investment series, U being down from 0.83 to 0.56 for fixed investment and from 0.98 to 0.64 for investment in stocks. Other decreases of note are for consumption (from 0.55 to 0.46), total final expenditure (0.56 to 0.43), imports (0.60 to 0.54), and an important decrease in U from 0.64 to 0.42 for gross domestic product. But the May

Table 4.1.
Inequality coefficients for NIESR and naïve models: time series 1959-1971

	NIESR		Naïve models			
	February	May	A_{t-1}	3-year moving average	5-year moving average	$\bar{A}$
Consumers' expenditure	0.55	0.46	0.68	0.64	0.52	0.50
Public authorities' current expenditure	0.73	0.78	0.86	0.87	0.78	0.50
Gross fixed investment	0.83	0.56	1.10	0.91	0.76	0.75
Investment in stocks	0.98	0.64	1.50	1.19	1.08	0.98
Exports	0.74	0.70	1.35	1.02	0.92	0.85
Total final expenditure	0.56	0.43	0.70	0.75	0.55	0.53
Imports	0.60	0.54	1.11	0.98	0.80	0.73
Gross domestic product	0.64	0.42	0.82	0.71	0.56	0.55

forecasts for public authorities' current expenditure, presumably influenced by the Government's statement of its own planned spending in the Budget speech, are worse than those made in February as U rises from 0.73 to 0.78. The comparison of the May forecasts with the naïve models is much more favourable than the February forecasts as, except for public authorities' current expenditure, all the naïve models are inferior to the May forecasts.

A more detailed accuracy analysis of the forecasts is presented in Tables 4.2 and 4.3. Overall, bias is absent from the forecasts except for consumers' expenditure ($U^M = 0.33$ and $\bar{P} < \bar{A}$) and total final expenditure ($U^M = 0.12$ and $\bar{P} < \bar{A}$); this is removed in the May forecasts where the highest U^M is 0.06 for consumers' expenditure. In the February forecasts there is a marked tendency to underestimate fluctuations with $s_P < s_A$ for all variables except public authorities' current expenditure (for which $s_P = s_A$), the variance proportion, U^S, being 0.72 for exports, 0.43 for investment in stocks, 0.37 for imports, 0.36 for total final expenditure, 0.27 for gross domestic product, 0.18 for gross fixed investment and 0.11 for consumers' expenditure. However, the variance proportion for the May forecasts is even higher for five variables, and the increase is marked for the two investment series ($U^S = 0.32$ and 0.65 for fixed and stocks investment respectively), and imports ($U^S = 0.54$), the increase being more moderate for consumers' expenditure and total final expenditure ($U^S = 0.16$ and 0.42 respectively). The only marked decline is for gross domestic product (to 0.18). Again $s_P < s_A$ except for the public authorities' series. As a result of the large variance proportion, systematic error is quite high (U^C quite low) for all February and May variables except public authorities' current expenditure. Systematic error is most marked for exports ($U^C = 0.28$ in February and 0.30 in May) and investment in stocks (0.58 in February and 0.35 in May).

The endogenous variables (consumption, investment in stocks and imports) are forecast slightly better than the exogenous variables (public expenditure, fixed investment and exports) in both February and May but the differences between the means are not significant at the five per cent level.

3. Evaluation of the forecasts: cross-section

Cross-section inequality coefficients for the NIESR and Treasury fourth quarter forecasts and the corresponding naïve models are presented in Table 4.4. As before, the investment in stocks variable has been excluded.

It is again apparent that the NIESR February forecasts are not very good although they are outperformed by one or more of the naïve models in only five years (1959, 1960, 1963, 1964 and 1970). Over the last seven years the forecasters are consistently more accurate, except in 1970 which is the year with the lowest NIESR inequality coefficient; the success of the $\bar{A}$ and moving average models in that year suggest that it was a time when growth was on trend.

The forecasts improve from February to May in eight years and regress in four years; however the difference between the mean inequality coefficients (0.72 for the February forecasts and 0.66 for the May forecasts) is not significant at the five per cent level. The May forecasts outperform the naïve models, except in 1963 (when the $\bar{A}$ model is better), 1966 (the A_{t-1} model), and 1970 (the five-year moving average and $\bar{A}$ models).

Table 4.2

Accuracy analysis of NIESR forecasts (February): time series 1959-1971

	U	U^M	U^S	U^C
Consumers' expenditure	0.55	0.33	0.11	0.56
Public authorities' current expenditure	0.73	0.00	0.00	1.00
Gross fixed investment	0.83	0.03	0.18	0.80
Investment in stocks	0.98	0.00	0.43	0.58
Exports	0.74	0.00	0.72	0.28
Total final expenditure	0.56	0.12	0.36	0.52
Imports	0.60	0.03	0.37	0.60
Gross domestic product	0.64	0.06	0.27	0.67

Table 4.3

Accuracy analysis of NIESR forecasts (May): time series 1959-1971

	U	U^M	U^S	U^C
Consumers' expenditure	0.46	0.06	0.16	0.78
Public authorities' current expenditure	0.78	0.02	0.00	0.98
Gross fixed investment	0.56	0.02	0.32	0.66
Investment in stocks	0.64	0.00	0.65	0.35
Exports	0.70	0.00	0.70	0.30
Total final expenditure	0.43	0.04	0.42	0.54
Imports	0.54	0.00	0.54	0.46
Gross domestic product	0.42	0.00	0.18	0.82

For the years 1962 and 1966 fourth quarter forecasts were made by the Treasury. The inequality coefficients obtained are 0.89 and 1.19 for 1962 and 1966 respectively. These inequality coefficients are markedly higher than those obtained for both the February and May forecasts by the National Institute, the Treasury inequality coefficient for 1966 being higher than any of the NIESR coefficients in Table 4.4.

There is no evidence of either the February or the May forecasts by the National Institute improving or worsening with time. The correlations between the U coefficients and time are not significant at the five per cent level, and when the period 1959-1971 is divided into two and the means for the years 1966-1971 are compared with the means for the years 1959-1965 they are found not to differ significantly at the five per cent level. Similar results are obtained for the naïve models. We thus conclude

Table 4.2 (continued)

r	α	β	SE(α)	SE(β)	$\bar{P}$	$\bar{A}$	s_P/s_A
0.46	1.48	0.73	0.87	0.42	1.77	2.77	0.63
0.01	2.68	0.01	0.93	0.28	2.82	2.71	1.00
0.07	4.06	0.13	2.58	0.58	3.59	4.51	0.54
0.19	24.96	0.54	80.60	0.85	42.38	47.76	0.35
0.60	−5.65	2.25	4.50	0.91	4.53	4.55	0.27
0.21	1.94	0.57	2.22.	0.80	2.65	3.43	0.37
0.61	−0.08	1.20	2.27	0.50	3.99	4.70	0.51
−0.10	3.64	−0.26	1.94	0.75	2.47	3.01	0.38

Table 4.3 (continued)

r	α	β	SE (α)	SE (β)	$\bar{P}$	$\bar{A}$	s_P/s_A
0.47	0.98	0.75	1.09	0.42	2.41	2.78	0.62
−0.19	3.29	−0.19	1.02	0.30	3.02	2.71	1.00
0.68	−0.25	1.18	1.89	0.38	4.02	4.51	0.58
0.85	−33.82	1.77	42.06	0.34	46.00	47.76	0.48
0.67	−4.76	2.15	3.52	0.72	4.32	4.55	0.31
0.61	−0.57	1.30	1.65	0.51	3.07	3.43	0.47
0.73	−2.78	1.59	2.35	0.45	4.69	4.70	0.46
0.64	0.24	0.95	1.10	0.34	2.92	3.01	0.67

Table 4.4
Inequality coefficients for NIESR, Treasury and naïve models: cross-section 1959-1971.

	NIESR		Treasury	Naïve models			
	February	May		A_{t-1}	3-year moving average	5-year moving average	$\bar{A}$
1959	0.81	0.48		0.64	0.76	0.63	0.50
1960	0.61	0.46		0.66	0.54	0.67	0.55
1961	0.74	0.81		1.66	1.76	1.29	1.16
1962	0.67	0.73	0.89	1.64	1.16	0.92	0.95
1963	0.70	0.56		0.90	0.69	0.58	0.53
1964	0.55			0.29	0.48	0.38	0.48
1965	0.67	0.58		1.60	1.20	0.88	0.68
1966	0.84	0.99	1.19	0.89	1.93	1.42	1.49
1967	0.90	0.84		1.23	0.99	0.93	0.91
1968	0.64	0.57		1.30	0.96	0.86	0.76
1969	0.80	0.67		1.93	0.86	0.97	0.99
1970	0.39	0.42		0.88	0.30	0.48	0.38
1971	0.99	0.81		1.40	1.88	1.12	1.09

that fourth quarter forecasting has become neither harder nor easier with the passage of time, and that the accuracy of the forecasts has neither improved nor deteriorated.

We also tested to see if the mean inequality coefficients were significantly different in those years with post-budget measures. The difference was not significant at the five per cent level. Nor was there a significant difference between the mean values of U^C.

The data presented by M. C. Kennedy[1] can be used to shed additional light on the extent to which forecasts (and forecasting analysis) are invalidated by the effects of unforeseen policy changes. Kennedy calculates predicted and actual constant price, fourth quarter absolute changes in gross domestic product and its components for the period 1959-1967, and also quantifies the effects in the fourth quarter of post-forecast policy adjustments. The forecasts are those published in February; policy changes are announced in the Spring Budget as well as later in the year. Thus using Kennedy's detailed quantifications, it is possible to calculate

Table 4.5

Policy effects on the accuracy of NIESR fourth quarter forecasts (February) 1959-1967

	U_0	U_1	U_2
Consumers' expenditure	0.65	0.48	0.47
Imports of goods and services	0.58	0.52	0.46
Adjustment to factor cost	0.87	0.75	0.69
Gross domestic product at factor cost	1.04	0.47	0.50

inequality coefficients for the forecasts which ignore altogether the effects of subsequent policies, U_0, which are adjusted for the effects of Budget measures only, U_1, and which account for Budget and post-budget policy changes, U_2. Forecasts of consumers' expenditure, imports, factor cost adjustment and gross domestic product are examined in this way, for these are the variables on which policy changes will have their most immediate impact. Our results are shown in Table 4.5.

The coefficients confirm our view that Budgetary changes may well have a significant effect on fourth quarter outcomes; Budget-adjusted U_1 is always less than unadjusted U_0, so that accuracy is improved by about twenty-five per cent on average by this adjustment. But there is no comparable reduction in observed forecasting error when the predictions are further adjusted for post-budget changes. On average, U_2 is only four per cent lower than U_1, while the adjustment to gross domestic product forecasts for post-budget policies results in accuracy which is actually inferior to that of forecasts adjusted only for budgetary measures. On the basis of this evidence there seems to be little harm in ignoring the effects of policy changes announced in the second half of the year when evaluating the accuracy of short-run NIESR forecasts.

Tables 4.6 and 4.7 provide more details of the accuracy analysis of the cross-section forecasts.[2] The importance of bias and variance error varies from year to year. There is no significant tendency for $\bar{P}$ to be less than or to exceed $\bar{A}$. However, the variance is underestimated in every year in the February forecasts and is underestimated in ten out of twelve years in the May forecasts. The probabilities of obtaining by pure chance such high proportions of forecasts which under-predict the variance of outcomes are 0.0001 and 0.016 respectively. There is no significant pattern in U^C over time.

Table 4.6

Accuracy analysis of NIESR fourth quarter forecasts (February): cross-section 1959-1971

	U	U^M	U^S	U^C	r	α
1959	0.81	0.68	0.08	0.24	0.10	5.78
1960	0.61	0.18	0.14	0.68	0.37	0.74
1961	0.74	0.30	0.22	0.48	0.75	−2.08
1962	0.67	0.08	0.12	0.80	0.43	0.47
1963	0.70	0.34	0.15	0.51	−0.57	12.01
1964	0.55	0.01	0.02	0.97	0.27	3.85
1965	0.67	0.05	0.03	0.92	−0.09	2.95
1966	0.84	0.38	0.19	0.43	0.71	−1.75
1967	0.90	0.01	0.47	0.53	0.11	2.25
1968	0.64	0.35	0.58	0.07	0.93	−1.26
1969	0.80	0.10	0.21	0.69	0.48	−0.50
1970	0.39	0.52	0.39	0.09	0.95	−0.84
1971	0.99	0.02	0.06	0.92	−0.56	4.04

Table 4.7

Accuracy analysis of NIESR fourth quarter forecasts (May): cross-section 1959-1971

	U	U^M	U^S	U^C	r	α
1959	0.48	0.78	0.18	0.04	0.95	0.34
1960	0.46	0.13	0.26	0.61	0.66	−1.34
1961	0.81	0.53	0.21	0.26	0.83	−3.50
1962	0.73	0.13	0.00	0.87	0.50	0.76
1963	0.56	0.16	0.17	0.68	−0.10	7.82
1964						
1965	0.60	0.03	0.03	0.94	0.18	1.95
1966	0.99	0.31	0.42	0.27	0.49	−2.95
1967	0.84	0.01	0.51	0.48	0.31	0.66
1968	0.57	0.17	0.73	0.10	0.92	−5.04
1969	0.67	0.00	0.54	0.46	0.67	−1.33
1970	0.42	0.22	0.69	0.08	0.91	−4.72
1971	0.81	0.04	0.00	0.96	0.34	1.21

Table 4.6 (continued)

β	SE (α)	SE (β)	$\bar{P}$	$\bar{A}$	s_P/s_A
0.20	1.97	0.94	1.59	6.10	0.50
0.62	3.67	0.69	5.09	3.87	0.60
1.21	1.68	0.47	2.87	1.40	0.62
0.64	2.05	0.61	3.03	2.40	0.67
−1.43	3.59	0.92	3.69	6.73	0.40
0.31	2.86	0.51	5.01	5.41	0.87
−0.11	1.85	0.57	3.06	2.60	0.82
1.17	1.45	0.52	2.36	1.00	0.61
0.36	4.82	1.46	2.73	3.23	0.31
2.68	2.00	0.49	3.10	7.04	0.35
0.84	0.24	0.07	3.01	2.01	0.57
1.82	0.78	0.27	2.61	3.91	0.52
−0.86	1.52	0.57	2.39	2.00	0.65

Table 4.7 (continued)

β	SE (α)	SE (β)	$\bar{P}$	$\bar{A}$	s_P/s_A
1.79	0.97	0.27	3.21	6.10	0.53
1.12	2.80	0.57	4.64	3.87	0.59
1.38	1.69	0.42	3.54	1.40	0.60
0.50	1.53	0.39	3.26	2.40	1.00
−0.22	4.90	0.92	5.07	6.73	0.45
0.22	1.72	0.55	2.91	2.60	0.82
1.61	3.27	1.28	2.46	1.00	0.30
0.98	4.36	1.34	2.63	3.23	0.32
2.65	2.70	0.51	4.56	7.04	0.35
1.58	0.19	0.08	2.11	2.01	0.42
2.86	1.78	0.57	3.01	3.91	0.32
0.32	1.22	0.39	2.44	2.00	1.06

4. Evaluation of the forecasts: underestimation, overestimation and turning-point errors

Tables 4.8 and 4.9 classify the forecasts by whether they are underestimates or overestimates of actual changes, and provide an analysis of turning-points. Sixteen of the February forecasts are turning-point errors; of the remainder, fifty-two are underestimates, thirty-five are overestimates and for one the (rounded) values of P_t and A_t are equal. Fifteen of the May forecasts are turning-point errors; of the remainder, fifty are underestimates and thirty-one are overestimates. The probabilities of obtaining by chance such a high proportion of the institute's forecasts that are

Table 4.8

Underestimation, overestimation and turning-point errors: NIESR (February) fourth quarter forecasts 1959-1971

	Positive change		
	Under-estimation (1)	Over-estimation (2)	$P_t = A_t$ (3)
Consumers' expenditure	8	4	0
Public authorities' current expenditure	6	5	1
Gross fixed investment	5	3	0
Investment in stocks	3	2	0
Exports	6	6	0
Total final expenditure	7	6	0
Imports	9	2	0
Gross domestic product	6	7	0
Total	50	35	1

	Underestimation of turning-point errors (10)	Overestimation of turning-point errors (11)
Consumers' expenditure	1	0
Public authorities' current expenditure	0	1
Gross fixed investment	2	3
Investment in stocks	2	4
Exports	0	1
Total final expenditure	0	0
Imports	0	2
Gross domestic product	0	0
Total	5	11

underestimates are 0.03 and 0.02 for February and May respectively. If negative changes are eliminated these probabilities become 0.05 and 0.04 respectively. These results are consistent with the inequality coefficient analysis where we observed a marked tendency to underestimate the magnitude of fluctuations.

Fifteen per cent of the February forecasts and sixteen per cent of the May forecasts are turning-point errors. Turning-point errors are predominantly concentrated in the two investment series; between them, these two series account for approximately two-thirds of all the turning-point errors. The forecasters both missed turning-points (E_1 = 0.50 for the February forecasts and 0.42 for the May forecasts) and predicted spurious turning-points (E_2 = 0.44 and 0.39 for the February and May forecasts respectively).

Table 4.8 (continued)

Negative change					
Under-estimation (4)	Over-estimation (5)	$P_t = A_t$ (6)	Turning-point errors (7)	Total no. of observations (8)	E (9)
0	0	0	1	13	0.08
0	0	0	1	13	0.08
0	0	0	5	13	0.38
2	0	0	6	13	0.46
0	0	0	1	13	0.08
0	0	0	0	13	0.00
0	0	0	2	13	0.15
0	0	0	0	13	0.00
2	0	0	16	104	0.15

A_t no turning-point		A_t turning-point			
P_t no turning-point (12)	P_t turning-point (13)	P_t no turning-point (14)	P_t turning-point (15)	E_1 (16)	E_2 (17)
12	1	0	0	—	1.00
10	0	1	2	0.33	0.00
7	2	3	1	0.75	0.67
4	4	2	3	0.40	0.57
11	0	1	1	0.50	0.00
13	0	0	0	—	—
9	0	2	2	0.50	0.00
13	0	0	0	—	—
79	7	9	9	0.50	0.44

5. Fourth quarter versus annual forecasts

The National Institute is more successful at forecasting whole years than fourth quarters. This is clear from a comparison of time series inequality coefficients (Tables 3.3 and 4.1), cross-section inequality coefficients (Tables 3.7 and 4.4) and turning-points (Tables 3.13 and 4.8, and Tables 3.14 and 4.9). None of the May annual time series forecasts are inferior to the corresponding fourth quarter forecasts, and only two of the February forecasts are worse (those for consumers' expenditure and public authorities' current expenditure). For only two years do the cross-section forecasts for the fourth quarter have lower inequality coefficients than their full-year counterparts, the years being 1967 and 1970 for the

Table 4.9

Underestimation, overestimation and turning-point errors: NIESR (May) fourth quarter forecasts 1959-1971

	Positive change		
	Under-estimation (1)	Over-estimation (2)	$P_t = A_t$ (3)
Consumers' expenditure	6	5	0
Public authorities' current expenditure	6	5	0
Gross fixed investment	4	4	0
Investment in stocks	4	0	0
Exports	7	4	0
Total final expenditure	7	5	0
Imports	9	1	0
Gross domestic product	4	7	0
Total	47	31	0

	Underestimation of turning-point errors (10)	Overestimation of turning-point errors (11)
Consumers' expenditure	1	0
Public authorities' current expenditure	0	1
Gross fixed investment	1	3
Investment in stocks	3	2
Exports	0	1
Total final expenditure	0	0
Imports	0	2
Gross domestic product	1	0
Total	6	9

February forecasts, and 1967 and 1969 for the May forecasts. Fifteen per cent of the fourth quarter forecasts made in February and sixteen per cent of the fourth quarter forecasts made in May are turning-point errors; the corresponding annual percentages are eight and ten respectively. The values of E_1 for the fourth quarter February and May forecasts are 0.50 and 0.42 respectively; for the annual forecasts they are 0.33 and 0.35 respectively. The values of E_2 for the fourth quarter February and May forecasts are 0.44 and 0.39 respectively; for the annual forecasts, 0.33 and 0.35.

These results are not surprising as there are a number of reasons why we might expect it to be harder to forecast the last quarter than the whole year. The fourth quarter is forecast some months ahead whereas the an-

Table 4.9 (continued)

Negative change			Turning-point errors	Total no. of observations	E
Under-estimation (4)	Over-estimation (5)	$P_t = A_t$ (6)	(7)	(8)	(9)
0	0	0	1	12	0.08
0	0	0	1	12	0.08
0	0	0	4	12	0.33
3	0	0	5	12	0.42
0	0	0	1	12	0.08
0	0	0	0	12	0.00
0	0	0	2	12	0.17
0	0	0	1	12	0.08
3	0	0	15	96	0.16

A_t no turning-point		A_t turning-point		E_1	E_2
P_t no turning-point (12)	P_t turning-point (13)	P_t no turning-point (14)	P_t turning-point (15)	(16)	(17)
11	1	0	0	—	1.00
9	0	1	2	0.33	0.00
7	1	3	1	0.75	0.50
2	4	1	5	0.17	0.44
10	0	1	1	0.50	0.00
12	0	0	0	—	—
8	0	2	2	0.50	0.00
11	1	0	0	—	1.00
70	7	8	11	0.42	0.39

nual forecasts are made some way into the year. With fourth quarter forecasting it is necessary to predict seasonal variations in aggregate expenditure. The accuracy of quarterly forecasts will be critically sensitive to the specification of lag structures in the implicit or explicit forecasting models used. Finally, there is more scope for errors to offset each other with annual forecasts than with quarterly forecasts.

The naïve models further provide evidence that fourth quarter forecasting is indeed the more difficult. For the time series twenty-nine out of thirty-two *U* coefficients for naïve models in Table 3.3 are lower than the corresponding values in Table 4.1, and only three are higher; thirty-nine of the cross-section *U* coefficients in Table 3.7 are lower than their counterparts in Table 4.4, eleven are higher, and two are the same.

6. Conclusions

(1) Consistent with its annual forecasting performance, the National Institute's success at predicting fourth quarter activity varies considerably between variables and years.
(2) The February forecasts compare unfavourably with the naïve models, except those for exports and imports.
(3) In most respects the forecasts improve markedly between February and May; this improvement is most evident for the two investment series. The May forecasts fare well against the naïve models.
(4) Overall, bias is absent from the forecasts although there is a marked tendency to underestimate fluctuations.
(5) There is no significant difference in the accuracy with which endogenous and exogenous variables are forecast.
(6) Almost one forecast in six involves a turning-point error. The forecasters miss between four and five out of every ten actual turning-points, and about two out of five predicted turning-points are spurious.
(7) The fourth quarter forecasts are less accurate than the National Institute's annual forecasts, but they are also more difficult to make.
(8) There is no evidence of improvement in forecasting accuracy over time. As indicated by the naïve models, the task of making fourth quarter forecasts has become neither harder nor easier.
(9) The accuracy of May forecasts for the fourth quarter does not appear to be significantly reduced by post-budget policy measures. On the other hand, February forecasts of some items of national expenditure in the fourth quarter may well be invalidated by the Budget.
(10) In the two years where a comparison is possible, the Treasury

fourth quarter forecasts are clearly less accurate than the National Institute's.

Notes

[1] M. C. Kennedy, 'How well does The National Institute forecast?' *National Institute Economic Review* (November 1969) pp. 40-52.

[2] Corresponding details for the 1962 and 1966 Treasury forecasts, respectively, are: $U = 0.89$, 1.19; $U^M = 0.23$, 0.34; $U^S = 0.03$, 0.33; $U^C = 0.75$, 0.33; $r = 0.19$, -0.05; $\alpha = 1.49$, 1.60; $\beta = 0.24$, -0.21; $SE(\alpha) = 2.35$, 5.07; $SE(\beta) = 0.56$, 1.74; $\bar{P} = 3.80$, 2.84; $\bar{A} = 2.40$, 1.00; $s_P/s_A = 0.79$, 0.24.

5 NIESR Quarterly Forecasts: Gross Domestic Product and its Major Components

1. Introduction

Chapter 3 examined the annual forecasts by the Treasury and the National Institute of Economic and Social Research, and Chapter 4 dealt with fourth quarter forecasts. However, considerable detail on time paths of economic aggregates is obscured by the use of annual or fourth quarter data especially if cycles are short or, in a growing economy, the downswing phases are short-lived and the troughs shallow. If macroeconomic policy is based on forecasting, rather than on decision rules, as would seem to be the case in the United Kingdom, then its effective implementation requires fairly precise forecasting of the timing of fluctuations. (We have already observed that postwar measures aimed at stabilising the economy may actually prove to have been destabilising because they were applied too late.[1]) It is thus important to examine the accuracy of quarterly and half-yearly forecasts. In 1965 the National Institute commenced publishing a series of quarterly forecasts of gross domestic product and its major components, which we evaluate in this chapter; a further analysis of the National Institute's disaggregated quarterly forecasts of some of these expenditures, together with other related variables, is provided in Chapter 6. Half-yearly forecasts made by various teams of economists, including the National Institute, are assessed in Chapter 7.

The NIESR forecasts examined in this chapter start with the first quarter of 1965 and end with the fourth quarter of 1970. Throughout the chapter the quarter of a year will be denoted by lower case Roman numerals after the year; for instance, 1968(iii) means the third quarter of 1968.

The forecast variables dealt with are consumers' expenditure, public authorities' current spending, gross fixed investment, exports of goods and services, total final expenditure excluding stockbuilding (the sum of the previous four items), stockbuilding (investment in stocks), imports of goods and services, adjustment to factor cost and gross domestic product (the sum of total final expenditure including stockbuilding, less imports and the factor cost adjustment). GDP is the compromise factor cost estimate calculated as the arithmetic average of three largely independent estimates, namely real output, real expenditure and real income. All the forecasts are in constant prices and seasonally adjusted.

Each quarterly issue of the *National Institute Economic Review* contains revised forecasts of GDP and its components, but to keep the analysis manageable only two sets of forecasts will be considered here. Our first set of predictions, denoted by $P1$, consists of a series of twenty-four forecasts published in the quarters to which the forecasts refer. For example, for the period 1969(ii) to 1970(i) we extracted second quarter 1969 forecasts from the May 1969 *Economic Review* and calculated $P1_{69(ii)} = [p_{69(ii)} - a_{69(i)}]/a_{69(i)}$, third quarter 1969 forecasts from the August 1969 issue and calculated $P1_{69(iii)} = [p_{69(iii)} - a_{69(ii)}]/a_{69(ii)}$, fourth quarter 1969 forecasts from the November 1969 issue and calculated $P1_{69(iv)} = [p_{69(iv)} - a_{69(iii)}]/a_{69(iii)}$ and first quarter 1970 forecasts from the February 1970 issue and calculated $P1_{70(i)} = [p_{70(i)} - a_{69(iv)}]/a_{69(iv)}$. The actual values used are those available at the time of the forecast, thus the value of $a_{69(i)}$ used in calculating $P1_{69(ii)}$ is the estimate of $a_{69(i)}$ in the May 1969 *Economic Review*. For the period in the example above the outcomes to which the predictions were compared are respectively, $A_{69(ii)} = [a_{69(ii)} - a_{69(i)}]/a_{69(i)}$, $A_{69(iii)} = [a_{69(iii)} - a_{69(ii)}]/a_{69(ii)}$, $A_{69(iv)} = [a_{69(iv)} - a_{69(iii)}]/a_{69(iii)}$ and $A_{70(i)} = [a_{70(i)} - a_{69(iv)}]/a_{69(iv)}$. The actual values used for the outcomes are the latest revisions that could be obtained from the *Economic Review*.

Clearly $P1$ predictions should show NIESR quarterly forecasting at its best as at least a month of the forecast quarter has elapsed by the time of publication of a forecast. However, it may be objected that the $P1$ forecasts are hardly relevant to demand management or business decision making for the months predicted simply because of their proximity to the outcome and that they should be viewed as estimates of the current economic position rather than as genuine forecasts of the course of events. Accordingly, we also analyse predictions for more extended time periods. To do this we take the forecasts in the May issue of the *Review*. We choose this set of forecasts as they have incorporated in them the policy changes newly announced in the April Budgets. From each May issue of the *Review* we calculated the forecast percentage changes on a rolling quarterly basis giving us, as with the $P1$ forecasts, a set of twenty-four predictions. We denote this series of predictions by $P2$. To illustrate: from the May 1969 *Review* we calculated $P2_{69(ii)} = [p_{69(ii)} - a_{69(i)}]/a_{69(i)}$, $P2_{69(iii)} = [p_{69(iii)} - p_{69(ii)}]/p_{69(ii)}$, $P2_{69(iv)} = [p_{69(iv)} - p_{69(iii)}]/p_{69(iii)}$ and $P2_{70(i)} = [p_{70(i)} - p_{69(iv)}]/p_{69(iv)}$. We compared these with the respective values for $A_{69\,(ii)}$, $A_{69\,(iii)}$, $A_{69\,(iv)}$ and $A_{70\,(i)}$ given above. Note that for the second quarter the *P*1 and *P*2 forecasts are identical (in the example above $P1_{69\,(ii)} = P2_{69\,(ii)}$) but for other quarters they differ. The *P*2 forecasts for the third and fourth quarters of the same year and the first quarter of the following year are made one, two, and three quarters earlier, respectively, whereas the *P*1 forecasts are made in the current quarter. In the *P*2 series the percentage changes for the third and fourth quarters of the current year and the first quarter of the succeeding year are necessarily based not on actual values (which being in the future could not be known to the forecasters) but on the forecasters' own predictions.

Comparison of the *P*2 series with the corresponding actual percentage change series thus provides a fairly stiff test of predictive accuracy. Consider *P*2 forecasts for the first quarter of any year. The relevant predicted changes are those between the forecast values for the first quarter in question and the forecast values for the preceding fourth quarter, that is, changes between two sets of forecast values predicted ten and seven months in advance. *P*1 percentage changes are in principle less hazardous as the bases of the forecast changes are always the previous quarters' outcomes (as published with the forecasts, not as subsequently revised). But given the lag in the publication of official statistics of anything from one month (unemployment, vacancies, exports and imports) to nine months (employment) and the continual revision of published data for several years after the event, the quarterly forecaster's quantification of the current position and immediate past may at best be only marginally less tenuous than his forecast of the immediate future.

Although both sets of forecast are made on the assumption of unchanged government policy none of the forecasts have been adjusted by us for post-budget policy changes. The time lag between publication and outcome is obviously so short as to make such adjustment unnecessary for the *P*1 forecasts. The *P*2 forecasts include the effects of the Budget but not of any subsequent fiscal and monetary measures. Any apparent difference in accuracy between the *P*1 and *P*2 forecasts may partly reflect such policy influences. However, we saw in Chapters 3 and 4 that there is no evidence that the accuracy of annual and fourth quarter forecasts is significantly impaired by policy changes implemented after the forecasts were published (even though their final impact on economic activity is often substantial). We shall see later that analysis of the quarterly forecasts yields a similar conclusion.

The forecasts are compared with five naïve models. Three are extrapolative, being the actual percentage change in the previous quarter, the actual percentage change in the corresponding quarter of the previous year, and the average percentage change over the previous year, A_{t-1}, A_{t-4}, and $\frac{1}{4}\sum_{i=1}^{4} A_{t-i}$ respectively. The other two naïve models are the mean actual percentage change for the period 1965(i)-1970(iv), $\bar{A}$, and the no-change assumption which always gives an inequality coefficient of 1.

2. Evaluation of the forecasts: time series

The time series inequality coefficients for the two sets of forecasts and for the naïve models are given in Table 5.1.

For the most part both the *P*1 and *P*2 forecasts outperform the naïve models. However, the *P*1 and *P*2 forecasts of gross fixed investment are inferior to both the $\bar{A}$ and no-change models, and the *P*1 and *P*2 forecasts of gross domestic product and the *P*2 forecasts for exports are outperformed by the $\bar{A}$ model; in addition, the $\bar{A}$ model gives the same inequality coefficient as the *P*1 forecasts for public authorities' current expenditure, and the four-quarter moving average the same value as is obtained for

Table 5.1
Inequality coefficients for NIESR *P*1 and *P*2 forecasts and naïve models: time series 1965(i)-1970(iv)

	*P*1	*P*2	A_{t-1}	A_{t-4}	4-quarter moving average	$\bar{A}$
Consumers' expenditure	0.83	0.90	1.53	1.53	1.17	0.96
Public authorities' current spending	0.95	0.94	1.40	1.29	1.05	0.95
Gross fixed investment	1.09	1.03	1.63	1.40	1.11	0.97
Exports of goods and services	0.54	0.91	1.50	1.35	1.12	0.97
Total final expenditure excluding stockbuilding	0.66	0.84	1.69	1.45	1.09	0.94
Stockbuilding	0.91	0.99	1.78	1.49	1.14	1.00
Imports of goods and services	0.67	0.92	1.63	1.39	1.08	0.95
Adjustment to factor cost	0.86	0.91	1.49	1.35	1.15	0.99
Gross domestic product: compromise estimate at factor cost	0.86	0.89	1.35	0.95	0.89	0.81

the $P2$ forecasts of gross domestic product. Moreover, it is readily apparent that the naïve models forecast very badly: all but two of the coefficients for the A_{t-1}, A_{t-4} and four-quarter moving average models in Table 5.1 are greater than one, the two exceptions being for gross domestic product.

While there is considerable variation in the accuracy with which different series are forecast it is clear that neither the $P1$ nor the $P2$ forecasts are very good. Six of the $P1$ series have inequality coefficients in excess of 0.80 and the lowest value is 0.54. As expected the $P2$ forecasts are inferior to the $P1$ forecasts, the only exception being public authorities' current spending. The deterioration in inequality coefficients is most marked (both absolutely and relatively) for those variables for which the $P1$ forecasts perform best: exports, imports and total final expenditure excluding stockbuilding. For the $P2$ forecasts seven of the nine inequality coefficients are greater than 0.90 and the lowest coefficient is 0.84.

The worst forecast variable for both $P1$ and $P2$ is gross fixed investment for which both inequality coefficients are greater than one whereas all the inequality coefficients for the other $P1$ and $P2$ variables are less than one. Reference to Tables 5.2 and 5.3 later in this chapter will indicate that it is the only variable for which predicted and actual percentage changes are negatively correlated. We have already suggested, in Chapter 3, that poor forecasting of gross fixed investment may be due to over-reliance on investment intentions data which have been shown to be inferior to capacity accelerator models in explaining manufacturing investment.[2]

The high inequality value, 0.95, for public authorities' current spending is not altogether unexpected. The NIESR forecasts lean heavily on official public expenditure surveys, and we saw in Chapter 3 that the Treasury's own performance in predicting government expenditure is unimpressive.

Nor is it surprising that stockbuilding is one of the worst forecast variables; the series is volatile and most of the discrepancy between the sum of the expenditure components and the compromise gross domestic product total is treated as unrecorded stockholding.[3] Stockbuilding is forecast within the aggregate econometric model primarily according to the predicted levels of other endogenous variables. Two other closely related endogenous variables, consumers' expenditure and factor cost adjustment, have relatively high inequality coefficients for the $P1$ series (0.83 and 0.86 respectively) but the increase in the coefficients for the $P2$ series (to 0.90 and 0.91 respectively) is not very marked.

The lowest inequality coefficients for the individual components of gross domestic product for the $P1$ forecasts are exports (0.54) and imports (0.67). This is probably accounted for by the availability of actual balance of payments data with a lag of only one month. The deterioration in accuracy of these forecasts for the $P2$ series, where the base of the forecasts (except for the second quarter of the year) consists of forecasts rather than reasonably reliable actual estimates, confirms this. The $P2$ inequality coefficient for exports is 0.91, that for imports is 0.92.

At 0.84 the inequality coefficient for total final expenditure excluding stockbuilding is lower than for any of its components for the $P2$ series and its value of 0.66 for the $P1$ series is bettered only by that for exports. Some offsetting errors are thus indicated. The inequality coefficient for gross domestic product is 0.86 for the $P1$ series; the $P2$ coefficient, 0.89, is only marginally higher. It is, of course, disappointing that the forecasts of gross domestic product are not more accurate both because the accuracy of the GDP forecasts reflects the performance of the complete NIESR model and because of the importance of GDP forecasts for policy making.

The average inequality coefficients for the endogenous variables are slightly lower than the average for the exogenous variables for both the $P1$ and $P2$ series but the differences are not significant at the five per cent level.

More detailed accuracy analyses of the $P1$ forecasts are presented in Table 5.2. Bias is greater than five per cent only for consumers' expenditure and imports for both of which U^M equals 0.11 as average changes are underestimated. Except for consumer's expenditure, misforecasting variance is a more important source of error than bias. The variance proportion is eighty-eight per cent for public authorities' current spending and ten per cent or less only for consumers' expenditure and stockbuilding. The ratio s_P/s_A is less than one for all variables so fluctuations are consistently underpredicted. Systematic error is most marked for public authorities' current spending ($U^C = 0.12$) and least obvious in the case of inventory investment ($U^C = 0.86$). Less than twenty per cent of the error in the consumers' expenditure and gross domestic product series is systematic. Whereas U was rather large for GDP presumably partly as a result of accumulated total error in its components it appears that U^C is large because systematic errors offset each other. The reverse seems to be the case for total final expenditure excluding stockbuilding where U^C is relatively low as well as U, even though the bias proportion of consumers' expenditure is offset elsewhere. There is less systematic error on average for the variables forecast within the econometric model than for the exogenous variables but the difference is not significant at the five per cent level.

Table 5.3 gives detailed results for the accuracy analysis of the $P2$ fore-

Table 5.2

Accuracy analysis of NIESR *P*1 forecasts: time series 1965(i)-1970(iv)

	U	U^M	U^S	U^C	r	α	β	SE (α)	SE (β)	$\bar{P}$	$\bar{A}$	s_P/s_A
Consumers' expenditure	0.83	0.11	0.08	0.82	0.60	0.42	0.79	0.25	0.22	0.01	0.43	0.77
Public authorities' current spending	0.95	0.01	0.88	0.12	0.07	0.19	1.05	2.39	3.44	0.68	0.90	0.06
Gross fixed investment	1.09	0.01	0.29	0.70	–0.12	0.90	–0.32	0.73	0.54	0.90	0.62	0.42
Exports of goods and services	0.54	0.02	0.24	0.74	0.84	–0.71	1.16	0.66	0.16	1.83	1.42	0.82
Total final expenditure excluding stockbuilding	0.66	0.00	0.38	0.62	0.73	–0.09	1.29	0.26	0.26	0.50	0.55	0.58
Stockbuilding	0.91	0.04	0.10	0.86	0.49	–20.95	0.70	27.66	0.26	16.54	–9.40	0.71
Imports of goods and services	0.67	0.11	0.24	0.66	0.75	0.69	1.15	0.45	0.21	0.33	1.07	0.67
Adjustment to factor cost	0.86	0.05	0.22	0.73	0.53	0.73	0.89	0.67	0.31	–0.18	0.57	0.59
Gross domestic product: compromise estimate at factor cost	0.86	0.01	0.18	0.81	0.19	0.41	0.34	0.26	0.38	0.51	0.59	0.53

Table 5.3

Accuracy analysis of NIESR *P*2 forecasts: time series 1965(i)-1970(iv)

	U	U^M	U^S	U^C	r	α	β	SE (α)	SE (β)	$\bar{P}$	$\bar{A}$	s_P/s_A
Consumers' expenditure	0.90	0.06	0.10	0.85	0.48	0.36	0.68	0.28	0.26	0.10	0.43	0.71
Public authorities' current spending	0.94	0.01	0.91	0.08	0.29	−2.40	5.32	2.41	3.77	0.62	0.90	0.07
Gross fixed investment	1.03	0.02	0.52	0.46	−0.09	1.00	−0.39	1.04	0.90	0.98	0.62	0.22
Exports of goods and serviees	0.91	0.01	0.72	0.28	0.38	−0.42	1.91	1.40	0.99	0.97	1.42	0.21
Total final expenditure excluding stockbuilding	0.84	0.01	0.37	0.63	0.46	0.11	0.99	0.34	0.41	0.45	0.55	0.46
Stockbuilding	0.99	0.04	0.22	0.74	0.32	−22.04	0.60	30.83	0.38	21.22	−9.40	0.53
Imports of goods and services	0.92	0.02	0.38	0.60	0.30	0.60	0.75	0.73	0.51	0.63	1.07	0.40
Adjustment to factor cost	0.91	0.04	0.26	0.70	0.44	0.64	0.83	0.70	0.36	−0.08	0.57	0.52
Gross domestic product: compromise estimate at factor cost	0.89	0.00	0.25	0.75	0.01	0.57	0.03	0.35	0.47	0.65	0.59	0.40

casts. The partial inequality coefficients show that bias comprises a very small proportion of total $P2$ forecasting error. Consumers' expenditure and imports, which registered the highest U^M values for the $P1$ forecasts, have U^M statistics reduced to 0.06 and 0.02 respectively although these improvements in the bias proportion are not reflected in lower inequality coefficients. Only for fixed and inventory investment is the average actual percentage change overestimated. The variance proportion is quite high for most variables, the lowest value of U^S being 0.10 for consumers' expenditure. The U^S values usually show marked increases compared with those obtained for the $P1$ series. U^S rises from 0.29 to 0.52 for fixed investment, from 0.24 to 0.72 for exports, from 0.10 to 0.22 for stockbuilding, from 0.24 to 0.38 for imports and from 0.18 to 0.25 for GDP. For all variables the variance is underforecast. Due to these increases the total systematic error is usually higher with the $P2$ chained series than the corresponding current-period $P1$ forecasts, except for consumers' expenditure and stockbuilding. It is notable that systematic error is much more marked for those variables determined exogenously, public authorities' current spending (U^C = 0.08), gross fixed investment (0.46) and exports (0.28) than for those determined endogenously within the econometric model, consumers' expenditure (U^C = 0.85), stockbuilding (0.74) imports (0.60) and factor cost adjustment (0.70). The mean values for the exogenous and endogenous variables are 0.27 and 0.73 respectively and the difference between the means is easily significant at the five per cent level.

3. Evaluation of the forecasts: cross-section

Table 5.4 presents cross-section inequality coefficients for the $P1$ and $P2$ forecasts and for the naïve models. As in Chapters 3 and 4 stockbuilding has been excluded from the cross-sections as the scale of this variable is different from that of the other GDP components and it would therefore tend to dominate the results.[4] The factor cost adjustment variable is included. All variables are weighted equally.

The naïve models mostly generate rather bad cross-section forecasts. When the naïve models are ranked by the mean values of their inequality coefficients, the $\bar{A}$ model performs best (average U = 0.98) followed by the no-change model (1.00), and then in order the four-quarter moving average (1.13), A_{t-4} (1.55) and A_{t-1} (1.61) models.

There is considerable variation in the inequality coefficients obtained for the forecasts. The $P1$ coefficients range between a minimum of 0.42 in 1968(i) and a maximum of 1.57 in 1970(iv) with mean value 0.87. The smallest $P2$ coefficient is 0.50 in 1969(iii) and the largest is 1.36 in

Table 5.4

Inequality coefficients for NIESR $P1$ and $P2$ forecasts and naïve models: cross-section 1965(i)-1970(iv)

		$P1$	$P2$	A_{t-1}	A_{t-4}	4-quarter moving average	$\bar{A}$
1965	(i)	0.77	0.93	0.87	1.20	0.94	0.96
	(ii)	0.78	0.78	1.56	1.02	1.23	1.06
	(iii)	0.63	0.83	2.50	1.06	0.98	0.71
	(iv)	0.58	0.74	1.45	0.80	0.83	0.78
1966	(i)	0.82	0.84	1.02	0.93	0.99	0.90
	(ii)	1.28	1.28	1.75	1.99	1.34	1.33
	(iii)	0.90	0.81	1.68	0.64	0.94	0.75
	(iv)	0.68	1.14	1.59	1.00	1.04	1.09
1967	(i)	0.84	0.86	1.20	1.01	0.99	0.90
	(ii)	1.21	1.21	2.25	1.12	1.29	1.00
	(iii)	0.81	1.07	2.05	2.40	1.88	1.29
	(iv)	0.93	1.08	1.10	1.69	1.04	1.09
1968	(i)	0.42	0.92	1.30	0.99	1.06	0.92
	(ii)	0.59	0.59	3.29	1.53	1.49	1.21
	(iii)	0.87	0.96	1.95	1.22	0.79	0.80
	(iv)	0.50	0.57	1.67	2.41	0.94	0.76
1969	(i)	1.16	1.36	1.86	5.52	2.16	1.33
	(ii)	0.80	0.80	1.43	2.12	0.98	0.78
	(iii)	0.51	0.50	0.76	1.12	0.43	0.61
	(iv)	1.21	0.80	1.92	1.78	1.19	0.86
1970	(i)	1.48	1.32	1.04	0.98	1.05	1.21
	(ii)	0.75	0.75	1.34	1.16	1.01	0.84
	(iii)	0.92	0.98	1.93	1.15	0.97	1.01
	(iv)	1.57	1.18	1.14	2.43	1.51	1.27

1969(i), the mean value being 0.93. Note that because second quarter forecasts for $P1$ and $P2$ are the same, the $P1$ and $P2$ second quarter inequality coefficients are indentical. For thirteen of the remaining eighteen quarters the $P1$ inequality coefficients are less than the corresponding $P2$ coefficients, a proportion which is significant at the five per cent level. It is of interest that four of the five quarters for which the inequality coefficient for $P2$ is less than that for $P1$ are in the period 1969(iii)-1970(iv).

The $P1$ forecasts are less accurate than at least one of the naïve models in eight quarters; the $P2$ forecasts are similarly inferior on thirteen occasions. Six of the $P1$ forecasts and eight of the $P2$ forecasts have inequality coefficients in excess of one. The mean $P1$ coefficient is significantly different from one at the five per cent level, the mean $P2$ coefficient is not. The $P2$ forecasts, then, are not significantly more accurate than the no-change model. Moreover, neither the $P1$ nor the $P2$ forecasts are significantly better than the $\bar{A}$ naïve model at the five per cent level. Both NIESR quarterly series are less accurate than the corresponding annual and fourth quarter forecasts considered in Chapters 3 and 4, the mean annual cross-section coefficients being 0.52 and 0.50 for the February and May forecasts respectively and the mean fourth quarter coefficients being 0.72 and 0.66 respectively.

Table 5.5 provides a detailed accuracy analysis of the $P1$ series. Six quarters have inequality coefficients greater than one: 1966(ii), 1967(ii), 1969(i), 1969(iv), 1970(i) and 1970(iv). Inspection of the partial inequality coefficients and the raw percentage change data suggests that the most common instance of a quarter being badly forecast was when the forecasters missed a downturn in the general level of economic activity: this was the case in 1969(i), although the turning-point in consumers' expenditure was correctly forecast (underestimated) and 1970(i) and 1970(iv), when reductions in government expenditure, total final expenditure and factor cost adjustment were forecast as increases, and modest increments in the other variables were overestimated. For these three quarters U^M, the bias proportion, is at least forty-five per cent, $\bar{P}$ is positive and $\bar{A}$ negative. In 1967(ii) the Institute predicted a downswing which never occurred: $U^M = 0.42$, $\bar{P} = -1.10$, $\bar{A} = 1.13$. Only government spending was forecast to increase, but this was the sole component of GDP which actually fell in that quarter. Errors in the 1966(ii) and 1969(iv) forecasts were primarily nonsystematic, though in the latter quarter there is evidence of overestimating the growth rate, particularly of exports, while small downturns in government expenditure and gross fixed investment were predicted as substantial increases. For the remaining quarters, systematic error, especially bias, averages higher than for the time-series analysis. The mean value of $(U^M + U^S)$ over all quarters is 0.51. U^M is greater than fifty per cent for the first two quarters of 1968, when first an upswing and then a downturn were underestimated, but the variance proportion is small for these quarters, and their inequality coefficients are the best of the cross-section results. Similarly, the four quarters for which U^C is greater than fifty per cent, 1965(ii), 1966(i), 1966(iv) and 1969(iii), are forecast with below average inaccuracy, so that high systematic error is associated with poor overall accuracy only when the Institute wrongly forecasts turning-points. Excepting these turning-point errors, and the rather badly forecast quarters 1966(ii), 1966(iii) and 1969(iv), the means and variances of the quarterly cross-section outcomes are underpredicted.

Significance tests on the differences in mean U for the four quarters do

Table 5.5

Accuracy analysis of NIESR *P*1 forecasts: cross-section 1965(i)-1970(iv)

	U	U^M	U^S	U^C	r	α	β	SE (α)	SE (β)	$\bar{P}$	$\bar{A}$	s_P/s_A
1965 (i)	0.77	0.15	0.44	0.41	0.63	0.51	1.50	0.74	0.76	0.43	1.15	0.41
(ii)	0.78	0.32	0.57	0.11	0.90	–2.40	2.41	0.72	0.48	0.43	–1.38	0.37
(iii)	0.63	0.12	0.00	0.88	0.52	1.11	0.52	0.64	0.35	1.29	1.78	1.00
(iv)	0.58	0.11	0.14	0.75	0.62	0.31	0.90	0.42	0.46	0.68	0.93	0.69
1966 (i)	0.82	0.09	0.66	0.26	0.29	0.10	1.56	1.75	2.14	0.75	1.29	0.17
(ii)	1.28	0.00	0.07	0.92	0.17	–1.16	0.12	0.76	0.28	–1.15	–1.30	1.41
(iii)	0.90	0.11	0.19	0.71	0.63	1.49	0.41	0.67	0.20	1.13	1.95	1.56
(iv)	0.68	0.02	0.77	0.22	0.87	0.17	2.23	0.56	0.52	–0.33	–0.55	0.39
1967 (i)	0.84	0.21	0.37	0.42	0.34	2.35	0.94	2.27	1.07	1.29	3.56	0.36
(ii)	1.21	0.42	0.23	0.35	0.16	1.62	0.44	1.60	1.01	–1.10	1.13	0.38
(iii)	0.81	0.19	0.03	0.79	0.69	–0.54	0.80	0.50	0.34	0.28	–0.33	0.87
(iv)	0.93	0.12	0.45	0.44	0.49	–1.31	1.31	1.40	0.95	0.83	–0.23	0.37
1968 (i)	0.42	0.73	0.00	0.27	0.95	3.02	0.98	0.82	0.13	2.76	5.73	0.97
(ii)	0.59	0.65	0.01	0.34	0.82	–1.84	0.74	0.48	0.21	–1.18	–2.71	1.10
(iii)	0.87	0.35	0.19	0.46	0.25	1.89	0.53	1.01	0.85	0.60	2.21	0.48
(iv)	0.50	0.27	0.01	0.72	0.77	0.56	0.83	0.36	0.28	0.80	1.23	0.92
1969 (i)	1.16	0.46	0.01	0.53	0.23	–1.18	0.26	0.48	0.45	0.16	–1.14	0.87
(ii)	0.80	0.30	0.32	0.38	0.47	1.01	1.19	0.85	0.91	0.55	1.66	0.40
(iii)	0.51	0.03	0.52	0.45	0.67	–0.47	1.56	0.84	0.71	1.10	1.24	0.43
(iv)	1.21	0.26	0.02	0.73	–0.03	0.52	–0.04	0.56	0.50	0.99	0.49	0.67
1970 (i)	1.48	0.45	0.06	0.49	0.08	–0.52	0.13	0.85	0.64	1.01	–0.39	0.63
(ii)	0.75	0.44	0.38	0.18	0.37	0.90	1.64	1.67	1.67	0.91	2.40	0.22
(iii)	0.92	0.01	0.31	0.69	0.30	0.27	0.66	0.77	0.84	0.46	0.58	0.47
(iv)	1.57	0.47	0.16	0.38	–0.23	0.54	–0.61	1.20	1.04	1.08	–0.11	0.39

not reveal that any one quarter is less successfully forecast than any other at the five per cent significance level. However, mean U^C is 0.38 for second quarter forecasts and 0.66 for third quarter forecasts, a difference which is significant at the five per cent level.

Detailed accuracy analysis for the *P*2 series is provided in Table 5.6. Six of the eight *P*2 inequality coefficients greater than one, those for 1966(iv), 1967(iii), 1967(iv), 1969(i), 1970(i) and 1970(iv), refer to quarters in which decreases in the GDP components were predicted as increases, and often in which the forecasters markedly underestimated the variance of changes in the components. For example, in the fourth quarter of 1970 public authorities' current spending fell by 1.3 per cent and factor cost adjustment by 2.4 per cent; gross fixed investment and GDP increased by 0.8 and 0.5 per cent respectively. All the forecast changes however were positive, within the range 0.5 to 0.9 per cent. Of the remaining two quarters with inequality coefficients greater than one, the forecasters predicted a spurious recession in the second quarter of 1967, and underestimated the actual downturn in the second quarter of 1966. The best forecast quarter is 1969(iii) with an inequality coefficient of 0.50. A high proportion of the *P*2 forecasting error is systematic: $(U^M + U^S)$ averages sixty-five per cent, and exceeds ninety per cent in 1968(i) and 1970(iv). U^C on the other hand is larger than ninety per cent only in 1966(ii). Bias is most marked in 1968(ii), a quarter in which the Institute under-forecast the extent of a general downturn, and in the first quarters of 1969 and 1970, when turning-point errors were committed, again with respect to downturns. For quarters in which $\bar{P}$ and $\bar{A}$ have the same sign, the average actual change is underestimated. Under-forecasting the variance of the variables accounts for much of the *P*2 error. In ten quarters U^S is more than 0.50; this statistic averages 0.38 and the average would be much higher if it were not for relatively good variance forecasting in the period 1968(ii)-1970(i).

Since the *P*2 forecasts are published in May of each year and predict onwards to the first quarter of the following year, it might be expected that the quality of the forecasts would deteriorate over the predicted four quarters and especially that the second quarter *P*2 forecasts, which are finalised in that same quarter, would be superior, in terms of low U and high U^C, to first quarter forecasts. There is little evidence of this. The average values of the inequality coefficient are 1.04, 0.90, 0.86, 0.92 and the averages of U^C are 0.26, 0.38, 0.37, 0.38 for quarters one through four respectively. Accuracy is worst and systematic error highest for the first quarter of each year, and third quarter forecasts,not second quarter forecasts, are most accurate. None of the differences in means are signifi-

Table 5.6

Accuracy analysis of NIESR *P*2 forecasts: cross-section 1965(i)-1970(iv)

	U	U^M	U^S	U^C	r	α	β	SE (α)	SE (β)	$\bar{P}$	$\bar{A}$	s_P/s_A
1965 (i)	0.93	0.01	0.66	0.34	–0.31	3.95	–2.13	3.61	2.68	1.31	1.15	0.13
(ii)	0.78	0.32	0.57	0.11	0.90	–2.40	2.41	0.73	0.48	0.43	–1.38	0.37
(iii)	0.83	0.31	0.21	0.48	–0.29	2.39	–0.81	0.97	1.08	0.76	1.78	0.38
(iv)	0.74	0.02	0.49	0.49	–0.02	0.97	–0.06	1.26	1.53	0.79	0.93	0.20
1966 (i)	0.84	0.03	0.45	0.52	0.09	1.01	0.28	1.46	1.32	0.96	1.29	0.33
(ii)	1.28	0.00	0.07	0.92	0.17	–1.16	0.12	0.76	0.28	–1.15	–1.30	1.41
(iii)	0.81	0.26	0.54	0.20	0.21	0.95	1.25	2.08	2.40	0.80	1.95	0.14
(iv)	1.14	0.24	0.57	0.20	–0.07	–0.01	–0.06	3.22	3.24	0.94	–0.55	0.14
1967 (i)	0.86	0.27	0.60	0.13	0.51	0.52	3.25	2.66	2.23	0.94	3.56	0.16
(ii)	1.21	0.42	0.23	0.35	0.16	1.62	0.45	1.60	1.10	–1.10	1.13	0.38
(iii)	1.07	0.28	0.51	0.21	0.45	–1.63	2.05	1.21	1.64	0.64	–0.33	0.22
(iv)	1.08	0.07	0.73	0.20	–0.51	4.66	–6.74	3.51	4.59	0.73	–0.23	0.08
1968 (i)	0.92	0.43	0.55	0.02	0.68	–5.72	15.27	5.40	6.81	0.75	5.73	0.04
(ii)	0.59	0.65	0.01	0.34	0.82	–1.84	0.74	0.48	0.21	–1.18	–2.71	1.10
(iii)	0.96	0.36	0.10	0.54	0.11	2.13	0.20	0.95	0.72	0.43	2.21	0.55
(iv)	0.57	0.15	0.06	0.80	0.61	0.55	0.78	0.49	0.41	0.88	1.23	0.80
1969 (i)	1.36	0.69	0.16	0.16	–0.08	–0.91	–0.32	1.23	1.59	0.71	–1.14	0.25
(ii)	0.80	0.30	0.32	0.38	0.47	1.01	1.19	0.85	0.91	0.54	1.66	0.40
(iii)	0.50	0.20	0.34	0.46	0.74	0.05	1.36	0.53	0.50	0.88	1.24	0.54
(iv)	0.80	0.12	0.33	0.55	0.34	–0.09	0.81	0.69	0.90	0.71	0.49	0.44
1970 (i)	1.32	0.50	0.11	0.38	0.33	–0.96	0.62	0.84	0.72	0.93	–0.39	0.55
(ii)	0.75	0.44	0.38	0.18	0.37	0.90	1.64	1.67	1.67	0.91	2.40	0.22
(iii)	0.98	0.00	0.66	0.34	–0.12	1.05	0.76	1.72	2.52	0.63	0.58	0.17
(iv)	1.18	0.40	0.55	0.05	0.71	–4.19	5.72	1.70	2.34	0.71	–0.11	0.11

cant at the five per cent level.

On a cross-section basis the $P2$ series usually predicts rather less accurately and with substantially more variance error than the $P1$ series. Cross-sectional bias is on average the same for the two series. $P2$ forecasts better in terms of a lower inequality coefficient in 1966(iii), 1969(iii), 1969(iv), 1970(i) and 1970(iv), and in terms of reduced systematic error in 1966(i), 1968(iii), 1968(iv), and 1969(iii), for most of which quarters the relevant $P1$ results are poor. Significance tests on the differences in $P1$ and $P2$ mean values of U and U^C for the four quarters reveal that only in the third quarter is $P2$ significantly more liable to systematic error: the difference for that quarter is significant at the one per cent level; the other differences are not significant at the five per cent level.

In order to see if there has been a general improvement or deterioration in the Institute's forecasts the cross-section inequality coefficients and U^C coefficients were correlated against time. Improved accuracy would result in a negative correlation between U and time, and reduced systematic error would yield a positive time correlation for U^C. For $P1$ the time correlation coefficient was 0.33 for U, and -0.07 for U^C; these results are not significant at the five per cent level. Similar correlations were calculated for each of the four quarters, and in the main the correlation coefficients were not significant. However there is evidence that the accuracy of fourth quarter $P1$ forecasts has deteriorated: the correlation between time and the fourth quarter U statistic is 0.79, which is significant at the five per cent level. Time correlations of 0.06 and -0.10 over all $P2$ observations for U and U^C respectively are not significant, and the only quarter which yielded a significant result was the first, where the correlation for U is 0.81. Analysis of the time correlation of the U statistic was also carried out for the naïve models. If the inequality coefficients for naïve forecasting improved over time then in some sense forecasting has become easier, which in turn should be reflected in improved predictive accuracy of the NIESR forecasts. The correlations between cross-section inequality coefficients and time for the A_{t-4}, four-quarter moving average and $\bar{A}$ models were positive and insignificant; the correlations were negative and insignificant for A_{t-1}. Finally for each quarter the ratio of the $P1$ inequality coefficient to the lowest naïve U was calculated and this ratio correlated with time. A similar procedure was followed for $P2$. The object of this exercise was to see if the forecasters' performance had improved or deteriorated with respect to the best results that could be achieved by naïve forecasts. The correlation coefficients were positive and not significant. Overall we conclude that there is no evidence that forecasts have improved; rather that for at least two quarters ($P1$, first quarter, and $P2$ second quarter) forecasting accuracy has deteriorated.

The cross-section analysis may be used to investigate the effects on the accuracy of the $P2$ series of major policy changes occurring after the May forecasts were published. In July of 1965 and 1966, measures were taken aimed at strengthening the balance of payments and reducing speculative pressure on sterling, which may have invalidated the $P2$ forecasts for the third and fourth quarters of 1965 and 1966 and the first quarters of 1966 and 1967. $P2$ forecasts of 1968(i) did not take into account the November 1967 devaluation package. Likewise, the forecasts for the first quarter of 1969 did not include the effects of credit restrictions, the activation of the fiscal regulator and the introduction of the imports deposits scheme in November of the preceding year. Thus there are eight quarters for which the cross-section inequality coefficients may be unfairly large and the non-systematic proportion of forecasting error, U^C, relatively low. The mean value of U for these quarters is 0.94 against 0.93 for the remainder. Mean U^C for quarters with post-forecast policy change is 0.28 against 0.38 for quarters with unchanged policy. Neither difference is significant at the five per cent level. Note that $P2$ forecasts are most likely to be invalidated in the first quarter, which averages the highest U statistic and for which the inequality coefficient increases over time. But again there is no significant difference for either U or U^C between those years with and without policy measures, and in fact U is lower on average in years with post-forecast measures than in years without. We thus conclude that the May forecasts seem remarkably resilient to subsequent policy changes.

4. Evaluation of the forecasts: underestimation, overestimation, turning-point errors and the dating of fluctuations

Tables 5.7 and 5.8 classify forecasts and outcomes by whether or not the forecasts were underestimates or overestimates of actual changes and by whether or not turning-point errors were involved.

Both sets of forecasts tend to underestimate actual changes. Of a total of 216 $P1$ forecasts, ninety-two are underestimates, forty-five are overestimates, sixty-nine are turning-point errors, and for the remaining ten pairs of observations the (rounded) P_t is equal to the (rounded) A_t. The figures are similar for $P2$: ninety-nine underestimates, forty-one overestimates, seventy-two turning-point errors and four perfectly accurate forecasts. For $P1$, sixty-eight actual increases were underestimated and thirty-six overestimated; for $P2$ there are eighty-four underestimates of increases and thirty-seven overestimates. Underestimation also characterises negative actual changes for which there are fewer observations. Twenty-four out of thirty-three decreases are underestimated by $P1$ and fifteen out of nineteen by $P2$.[5] All the proportions cited would be obtained by chance less than five per cent of the time. Underestimation is a feature of all the series except the $P1$ series for stockbuilding. The overall picture of conservative forecasting indicated by the inequality analysis is, therefore, confirmed. With conservative forecasting we might expect the percentage forecasting error to increase with the absolute magnitude of the outcome. The correlation between $|(P_t - A_t)/A_t|$ and $|A_t|$ for all pairs of observations (excluding stockbuilding) which are not turning-point errors is −0.17 for $P1$ which is (just) significant at the five per cent level and −0.14 for $P2$ which is not significant at the five per cent level. If the absolute value of the proportionate error and the absolute value of the outcome are transformed into logarithms and the correlations repeated the coefficients obtained are −0.27 for $P1$ and −0.23 for $P2$ both of which are significant at the one per cent level. Thus contrary to the conservative hypothesis, forecasting error decreases with the absolute size of the outcome but at a diminishing rate. However, linear correlations of errors and outcomes for subsamples of the data reveal a strong negative correlation for small actual changes together with a positive correlation as the actual changes become larger. For example, for $|A_t| \leqslant 0.50$ the correlation is - 0.57 for $P1$ and −0.73 for $P2$, both these correlation coefficients being significant at the one per cent level; for $|A_t| \geqslant 0.50$ the correlation is 0.07 for $P1$ (not significant at the five per cent level) and 0.37 for $P2$ (significant at the one per cent level). These results suggest that the forecasters are threshold sensitive, especially in their May forecasts. Small actual changes, less than one half of one per cent, are difficult to perceive and at least as difficult to predict as large outcomes which are conservatively underestimated. Forecasting error declines sharply as the perception threshold is approached from below and thereafter the correlation with A_t is weaker but positive.

Turning-point errors are listed in column 7 of Tables 5.7 and 5.8 and analysed in columns 9-17. Approximately one-third of both the $P1$ and $P2$ forecasts are turning-point errors. For both sets of forecasts the gross fixed investment series is most subject to turning-point error with over fifty per cent of the forecasts predicting the wrong sign. Total final expenditure excluding stockbuilding and gross domestic product are the only two series for which the May forecasts contain fewer turning-point errors than the $P1$ forecasts. The majority of turning-point errors are overestimates; this is most marked for the $P2$ series where the difference between overestimates and underestimates is significant at the five per cent level; the difference for *P*1 is not significant at this level. For the *P*2 series upturns in consumers' expenditure, stockbuilding, imports and factor cost adjustment are frequently forecast with incorrect signs. The proportion of actual turning-points missed by the forecasters, E_1, is 0.38 for *P*1 and 0.43 for *P*2. For P_1 the highest E_1 values are for gross domestic product and public authorities' current spending, for both of which over fifty per cent of actual turning-points (usually downturns) are missed, and the lowest E_1 value is for imports for which all but one of twelve

Table 5.7

Underestimation, overestimation and turning-point errors: NIESR *P*1 forecasts 1965(i)-1970(iv)

	Positive change		
	Under-estimation (1)	Over-estimation (2)	$P_t = A_t$ (3)
Consumers' expenditure	8	3	1
Public authorities' current spending	9	5	2
Gross fixed investment	5	3	0
Exports of goods and services	9	5	2
Total final expenditure excluding stockbuilding	8	5	1
Stockbuilding	4	4	0
Imports of goods and services	7	4	1
Adjustment to factor cost	9	2	0
Gross domestic product: compromise estimate at factor cost	9	5	3
Total	68	36	10

	Underestimation of turning-point errors (10)	Overestimation of turning-point errors (11)
Consumers' expenditure	5	1
Public authorities' current spending	0	8
Gross fixed investment	3	10
Exports of goods and services	0	6
Total final expenditure excluding stockbuilding	2	6
Stockbuilding	5	2
Imports of goods and services	6	0
Adjustment to factor cost	5	3
Gross domestic product: compromise estimate at factor cost	3	4
Total	29	40

turning-points are correctly predicted. For $P2$ the coefficient E_1 is 0.50 or greater for public authorities' current spending, gross fixed investment and gross domestic product. The proportion of forecast turning-points that subsequently prove to be spurious, E_2, is 0.28 for the $P1$ forecasts and 0.27 for the $P2$ forecasts. For the $P1$ forecasts, the largest values of E_2 are for the gross fixed investment and gross domestic product series (both have E_2 = 0.40) and the lowest is for total final expenditure excluding stocks (only one of the nine turning-points forecast proved spurious). The coefficient for stockbuilding is also low, E_2 = 0.14, which is commendable

Table 5.7 (continued)

Negative change					
Under-estimation (4)	Over-estimation (5)	$P_t = A_t$ (6)	Turning-point errors (7)	Total no. of observations (8)	E (9)
5	1	0	6	24	0.29
0	0	0	8	24	0.33
2	1	0	13	24	0.54
2	0	0	6	24	0.25
1	1	0	8	24	0.33
4	5	0	7	24	0.29
6	0	0	6	24	0.25
4	1	0	8	24	0.33
0	0	0	7	24	0.29
24	9	0	69	216	0.32

A_t no turning-point		A_t turning-point			
P_t no turning-point (12)	P_t turning-point (13)	P_t no turning-point (14)	P_t turning-point (15)	E_1 (16)	E_2 (17)
11	3	3	7	0.30	0.30
11	2	6	5	0.55	0.29
2	6	7	9	0.44	0.40
10	2	4	8	0.33	0.20
8	1	7	8	0.47	0.11
5	2	5	12	0.29	0.14
7	5	1	11	0.08	0.31
9	4	4	7	0.36	0.36
14	2	5	3	0.63	0.40
77	27	42	70	0.38	0.28

in view of the volatility of this series. For the $P2$ forecasts the largest value of E_2 is for gross fixed investment (0.43); for total final expenditure excluding stockbuilding all eight predictions of turning-points proved correct. The only $P1$ or $P2$ series for which E_2 is greater than E_1 is $P1$ imports; here the forecasters erroneously and optimistically expected the level of imports to fall in five quarters.

It may be objected that the above analysis of turning-points is too demanding, especially for the multi-period chained $P2$ series inasmuch as it requires a forecaster either to date a fluctuation exactly or to commit a

Table 5.8

Underestimation, overestimation and turning-point errors: NIESR $P2$ forecasts 1965(i)-1970(iv)

	Positive change		
	Under-estimation (1)	Over-estimation (2)	$P_t = A_t$ (3)
Consumers' expenditure	11	3	0
Public authorities' current spending	11	5	0
Gross fixed investment	7	1	2
Exports of goods and services	9	7	0
Total final expenditure excluding stockbuilding	10	5	0
Stockbuilding	4	3	0
Imports of goods and services	11	3	1
Adjustment to factor cost	11	2	0
Gross domestic product: compromise estimate at factor cost	10	8	1
Total	84	37	4

	Underestimation of turning-point errors (10)	Overestimation of turning-point errors (11)
Consumers' expenditure	3	4
Public authorities' current spending	0	8
Gross fixed investment	1	13
Exports of goods and services	0	6
Total final expenditure excluding stockbuilding	1	6
Stockbuilding	6	5
Imports of goods and services	3	3
Adjustment to factor cost	3	5
Gross domestic product: compromise estimate at factor cost	1	4
Total	18	54

turning-point error. Credit should be given for predicting an actual turning-point, even though the forecast fluctuation leads or lags the outcome by, say, a quarter. Some of the E_2 errors may fall into this category. On the other hand the preceding results may in some instances give too sanguine a view of the Institute's ability to predict turning-points. Consider the following hypothetical fluctuation comprising three values of A_t with successive signs (+ – +) which is forecast as (+ + +). The observation-by-observation analysis would reveal one turning-point error, misforecasting the downturn. If however the three actual outcomes are taken together as

Table 5.8 (continued)

Negative change					
Under-estimation (4)	Over-estimation (5)	$P_t = A_t$ (6)	Turning-point errors (7)	Total no. of observations (8)	E (9)
2	1	0	7	24	0.29
0	0	0	8	24	0.33
0	0	0	14	24	0.58
2	0	0	6	24	0.25
1	1	0	7	24	0.29
5	1	0	11	24	0.46
3	0	0	6	24	0.25
2	1	0	8	24	0.33
0	0	0	5	24	0.21
15	4	0	72	216	0.33

A_t no turning-point		A_t turning-point			
P_t no turning-point (12)	P_t turning-point (13)	P_t no turning-point (14)	P_t turning-point (15)	E_1 (16)	E_2 (17)
11	3	4	6	0.40	0.33
11	2	6	5	0.55	0.29
2	6	8	8	0.50	0.43
10	2	4	8	0.33	0.20
9	0	7	8	0.47	0.00
2	5	6	11	0.35	0.31
10	2	4	8	0.33	0.20
10	3	5	6	0.45	0.33
15	1	4	4	0.50	0.20
80	24	48	64	0.43	0.27

one complete fluctuation it could be argued that the forecasters have made two turning-point errors: by apparently forecasting three quarters of steady growth they have missed the peak (first/second pair of observations) and the trough (second/third pair of observations). This will be the case if, when making the third forecast, the forecasters failed to recognise that a downturn had occurred in the second quarter. Of course, provided the forecasters had recognised the downturn before predicting a positive change for the third quarter it would only be right to charge them one turning-point error (+, – in the second quarter): the trough is now explicitly forecast.

Table 5.9 attempts to account for some of these objections. There are a total of fifty actual fluctuations. A fluctuation includes a downturn or peak (+ –) and an upturn or trough (– +); thus there are 100 turning-points in the sense of columns 14 and 15 of Tables 5.7 and 5.8. Twelve of the turning-points in the earlier tables are excluded from Table 5.9 as the relevant fluctuations were incomplete in the period 1965(i)-1970(iv). The fluctuations are classified by GDP component and by quarter according to whether the two sets of Institute forecasts correctly predicted the date of the downturns and upturns, predicted them with a lead or a lag, or did not predict them at all. All but seven of the leads and lags misdate a turning-point by only one quarter; of these seven, six are leads or lags of two quarters and one is a three quarter lead.

Of fifty downturns, *P*1 forecasts only fourteen correctly, eleven at least one quarter early (lead), two at least one quarter late (lag) and twenty-three downturns are missed. However, *P*1 predicts all but eight of the upturns, half of the upturns being correctly timed. When one is forecasting the current quarter in a period characterised by steady growth it is clearly easier to recognise a downturn after the event than it is to identify an impending peak.[6] Thus it is somewhat surprising that in general the National Institute is more likely to predict a downturn too early than too late and an upturn too late rather than too early.

The *P*2 chained forecasts are less successful than the *P*1 forecasts. Over half the downturns are not forecast at all, even given the generous allowance for dating. Upturns are hardly forecast any better; two less are correctly dated but four more are predicted, albeit with a lag.

The detailed analysis for individual series in Table 5.9 must be used with care because of the limited number of observations. However, the stricter criteria employed for successful turning-point prediction together with our more flexible approach to timing indicates that the earlier E_1 values are rather too lenient for *P*2 forecasts of public authorities' current spending, gross fixed investment, exports, total final expenditure exclud-

Table 5.9

Dating of fluctuations: NIESR *P*1 and *P*2 forecasts 1965(i)-1970(iv)

	*P*1								*P*2								Total number of downturns	Total number of upturns
	Downturns				Upturns				Downturns				Upturns					
	Not forecast	Date correct	Lead	Lag	Not forecast	Date correct	Lead	Lag	Not forecast	Date correct	Lead	Lag	Not forecast	Date correct	Lead	Lag		
Consumers' expenditure	2	2	1	0	2	1	1	1	1	3	0	1	1	1	1	2	5	5
Public authorities' current spending	4	0	0	0	0	2	0	2	4	0	0	0	4	0	0	0	4	4
Gross fixed investment	6	0	2	0	2	4	1	1	7	0	1	0	6	1	1	0	8	8
Exports of goods and services	3	2	0	0	1	3	1	0	3	2	0	0	3	1	1	0	5	5
Total final expenditure excluding stockbuilding	3	2	1	0	1	4	1	0	3	2	0	1	3	2	0	1	6	6
Stockbuilding	1	4	2	1	1	5	0	2	2	2	3	1	1	4	1	2	8	8
Imports of goods and services	0	2	3	0	0	4	0	1	1	2	2	0	1	2	1	1	5	5
Adjustment to factor cost	1	2	2	0	1	1	1	2	1	3	0	1	1	1	1	2	5	5
Gross domestic product: compromise estimate at factor cost	3	0	0	1	0	1	0	3	4	0	0	0	4	0	0	0	4	4
Quarter (i)	8	1	2	1	2	7	1	1	8	0	0	4	5	1	5	0	12	11
(ii)	10	10	3	1	2	2	3	6	11	12	1	0	6	2	1	4	24	13
(iii)	2	2	3	0	4	11	0	3	2	2	3	0	9	6	0	3	7	18
(iv)	3	1	3	0	0	5	1	2	5	0	2	0	4	3	0	1	7	8
Column total	23	14	11	2	8	25	5	12	26	14	6	4	24	12	6	8	50	50
Column total as a proportion of total fluctuations	0.46	0.28	0.22	0.04	0.16	0.50	0.10	0.24	0.52	0.28	0.12	0.08	0.48	0.24	0.12	0.16		
Column total for fluctuations six months or longer	5	5	1	0	1	6	2	2	5	4	2	0	4	1	5	1	11	11

ing stockbuilding and gross domestic product, and too harsh for *P*1 forecasts of stockbuilding and gross domestic product, and for both series' predictions of factor cost adjustment. It is noteworthy that *P*1 never misses fluctuations (up or down) in imports, or upturns in gross domestic product and public authorities' current spending even though none of the peaks in the latter variable are ever predicted. Conversely, fluctuations in gross domestic product and public authorities' current spending are never forecast by *P*2.

The cross-sectional analysis of fluctuation timing is similarly constrained by the limited number of observations, but it does reveal that most peaks occur in the first and second quarters of each year and hence, since downturns rarely persist longer than three months, that most troughs are observed in the second and third quarters. This bunching of fluctuations in the first half of the year helps to explain why *P*2 cross-section inequality coefficients do not deteriorate monotonically from second to first quarter as one might expect, and why there is only slender evidence of policy changes impairing the accuracy of prior forecasts. In Section 3 of the present chapter we saw that the most common cause of a quarter being badly forecast was that a general downturn in demand was misforecast: for the *P*2 series the intrinsic problems of multi-period chain forecasting are aggravated by having to recognise frequent peaks in the immediate past (first quarter) and to predict their imminent occurrence in the second quarter. Fortunately for the forecasters, if not for the success of policy measures, it appears that the economy's lagged response to policy changes is such that most May forecasts of the third and fourth quarters are not invalidated.[7] (Recall that the second quarter of each year is a current period forecast for both *P*1 and *P*2 which cannot be falsified by 'unexpected' policies, while inasmuch as there is any difference in inter-quarter accuracy both forecasts yield the highest average cross-section *U* statistic in the first quarter).

The cross-section scores in Table 5.9 emphasise again the superiority with which *P*1 predicts troughs over peaks: most successfully forecast by *P*1 are fourth quarter upswings, none of which are completely mistimed, and at least half of which are correctly dated. *P*1's worst performance is with first quarter downturns: the majority are not forecast at all, and only two out of twelve are correctly dated. As noted earlier, the *P*2 forecasts do not exhibit much overall improvement between downturns and upturns, although there is greater variability in the dating of observations. First and fourth quarter peaks are forecast particularly badly: thirteen out of nineteen downturns are not forecast at all, two fourth quarter downturns are timed to lead the outcome, and the remaining four lagged predictions of first quarter peaks represent *ex post* recognition of the event the following May. Approximately half of all upturns are predicted by *P*2, irrespective of quarter, but it is interesting that troughs are more accurately dated the later in the year they occur.

The majority of fluctuations enumerated in Table 5.9 are short and shallow. Ignoring or mistiming a small one quarter downturn may not be considered a serious error; indeed in some circumstances it might be advantageous for policy to be based on forecasts which inadvertently smooth out a sequence of short, small oscillations. Thus some attention should be directed towards the Institute's success in predicting longer cycles; this is examined in the final row of Table 5.9. Eleven of the fifty fluctuations lasted for six months or longer: dating them from peak to trough they are consumers' expenditure, 1966(ii)-1967(i); public authorities' current spending, 1968(ii)-1969(i); gross fixed investment, 1965(ii)-1965(iv), 1967(iii)-1968(i), 1968(ii)-1968(iv), 1969(i)-1969(iii) and 1969(iv)-1970(ii); exports of goods and services, 1967(ii)-1968(i); stockbuilding, 1965(iii)-1966(i) and 1969(ii)-1969(iv); factor cost adjustment 1966(ii)-1967(i). Both sets of forecasts ignore five of the eleven downturns and correctly time all but one or two of the remainder; seven cycles peak in the second quarter when *P*1 = *P*2, hence the similar performance of the two forecasts. Troughs are well predicted by *P*1, six correctly dated, two leads and two lags. *P*2 misses four troughs and forecasts five upturns too early. *P*1 and *P*2 frequently misforecast major downturns; however current period forecasts have a clear advantage in predicting the duration of a recession, which, if detected at all by the multi-period *P*2 forecast, is typically underestimated.

5. Conclusions

Time-series, cross-section and observation-by-observation analyses indicate a wide variation in the accuracy with which the National Institute forecasts the magnitude and sign of quarterly changes in GDP and its constituents. Our analysis supports the following conclusions concerning the performance of the NIESR short-term macroeconomic forecasts.

(1) The naïve models generate poor forecasts. Judged by the size of inequality coefficients, which for the naïve predictions are typically greater than unity, the genuine forecasts, especially *P*1, are clearly superior. Nevertheless it is disconcerting that one or more of the naïve models is at least as accurate as the Institute's forecasts of public authorities' current

spending, gross fixed investment and GDP, and in the cross-section analysis, at least as accurate for eight quarters predicted by *P*1 and thirteen quarters by *P*2.

(2) Of the individual GDP components, current period changes in exports and imports of goods and services are most accurately forecast. This may partly be due to the early availability of official balance of payments statistics. Fluctuations in imports are particularly well forecast by *P*1: none are missed altogether and most are correctly dated, although forecast downturns are consistently too shallow. When the Institute does commit a turning-point error it is usually by predicting a spurious fall in the level of imports. Turning-point errors in forecasting exports on the other hand are overestimated, either missing a downturn or prematurely predicting a recovery.

(3) Worst forecast (by both *P*1 and *P*2) are quarterly changes in gross fixed investment, stockbuilding and public authorities' current spending. Gross fixed investment is the only series for which the inequality coefficient is greater than unity, i.e. the forecasts are less accurate than the continual prediction of no change. Sixteen of the twenty-four actual changes in fixed investment are turning-points: *P*1 commits thirteen and *P*2 fourteen turning-point errors, usually either by not forecasting downturns, which even if forecast are incorrectly dated, or by underestimating the duration of a recession. By contrast, the high inequality coefficients for stockbuilding are at least partially offset by the lack of systematic forecasting error, and by the forecasters' relative success in predicting and timing fluctuations in this volatile series. Forecasts of public authorities' current spending markedly underestimate the variance of actual changes. Increases are underestimated, and downturns are never correctly timed, although *P*1 predicts troughs either accurately or with a lag. *P*2 gives no warning at all of peaks or troughs in public expenditure.

(4) Gross domestic product is forecast better than its components by *P*2, but (non-systematic) errors accumulate in the *P*1 forecasts, even though overall *P*1 accuracy marginally improves on May. That this improvement is no greater is surprising. The current period GDP forecasts show a higher proportion of undetected and spurious turning-points if timing is ignored: the E_1 proportion is sixty-three per cent, the highest of any *P*1 or *P*2 series. When timing is accounted for, the *P*1 forecasts appear to improve: troughs are always forecast, albeit frequently with a lag. Nevertheless, downturns in GDP are rarely anticipated by either set of forecasts.

(5) Most of the error in forecasting GDP and its components is non-systematic. Consumers' expenditure, stockbuilding and GDP itself are

notably free of bias or variance error. For all variables except consumers' expenditure the variance proportion is highest, accounting for an average twenty-nine per cent of total *P*1 error and forty-one per cent of *P*2 error, and reaching a maximum of ninety-one per cent of the *P*2 error in predicting changes in public authorities' current spending. The variance of outcomes is always underestimated.

(6) The worst forecast quarters are those in which the forecasters miss or underrate a downturn in economic activity. On these occasions systematic error, especially bias, is also high. Otherwise the cross-section errors are predominantly non-systematic, although the error proportions vary considerably between quarters.

(7) Downturns tend to be bunched in the first and particularly the second quarters of each year. Upturns are more evenly spread throughout the year, though since most fluctuations rarely persisted beyond three months the largest number of troughs occurred in the third quarter. There appears to be no difference in the total accuracy with which *P*1 forecasts each quarter, but rather more systematic error is committed in forecasts of the second quarter. All eight troughs recorded in the fourth quarter were predicted by *P*1, and five of them were accurately dated. Although troughs are also more accurately dated later in the year by *P*2, the May forecasters are seldom able to predict peaks in the forthcoming fourth and first quarters. Consequently the average *P*2 inequality coefficient is highest for the first quarter, but not significantly so.

(8) There is no evidence that predictive accuracy improved or systematic error was reduced during the period here studied. On the contrary, it appears that current period forecasts of the fourth quarter, and May forecasts of the first quarter have deteriorated.

(9) The majority of actual changes are underpredicted, irrespective of sign. However, for small actual changes, less than a half per cent, the proportionate forecasting error falls markedly as the size of the outcome increases; thereafter the size of error and outcome vary directly but more moderately.

(10) Approximately one third of all pairs of observations, P_t, A_t, are turning-point errors. The forecasters predict spurious turning-points less frequently than they miss actual turning-points. Current period forecasts predict troughs much better than peaks; when turning-points are mistimed, downturns are usually forecast with a lead and upturns with a lag of one quarter. Half of all peaks and troughs are missed by *P*2, a quarter are correctly dated and the remainder mistimed. Both sets of forecasts have similar difficulty predicting the onset of a more major recession, the duration of which is often underestimated in May.

(11) In general the May forecasts are less accurate and more subject to systematic error than current period forecasts. However, there are some exceptions: marginally lower *P*2 inequality coefficients for public authorities' current spending and gross fixed investment, and more substantial improvement over *P*1 for five quarters. Although the variance proportion is usually much higher for *P*2, total systematic error is slightly reduced for consumers' expenditure, total final expenditure and four quarters. *P*2 systematic error is significantly higher in the third quarter of each year. As noted in (9) above, the May forecasts are less successful at predicting and timing fluctuations: even so, *P*2 predicts a smaller proportion of spurious turning-points in total final expenditure, imports, factor cost adjustment and GDP. On reflection, it is not so much remarkable that the May, multi-period, chained forecasts are inferior to the current quarter predictions when evaluated by the same quite stringent criteria, but rather that there is not an even larger discrepancy in the accuracy of the two sets of forecasts, particularly in the NIESR forecasts of GDP itself.
(12) The effect on forecasting accuracy of post-May policy changes is negligible; *P*2 accuracy in the relevant quarters is no worse than usual. In certain specific instances the May forecasts of a particular variable (e.g. exports, 1968(i)) was invalidated; overall it is not obvious that the higher *P*2 time series and cross-section inequality coefficients are primarily due to unforeseen policy adjustments. If the impact of policy changes is lagged, the effects of mid-year or late-year changes may not begin to be felt until some time in the first half of the following year. Noting that most policy adjustments were deflationary, and that downturns most frequently occurred in the second quarter, it is questionable whether the assessment of the Institute's May forecasts here reported would have been more favourable had the data been first corrected for post-forecast policies. But this point can only be resolved by further empirical research.

Notes

[1] See D. J. Smyth, 'Public finance policy and techniques for economic stability and balanced economic growth', United Kingdom report in *Public Finance Policy and Techniques for Economic Stability and Balanced Economic Growth, Congres de Budapest, Septembre 1964* Institut International de Finances Publiques, La Haye (1966) pp. 270-97.
[2] D. J. Smyth and G. Briscoe, 'Investment plans and realizations in United Kingdom manufacturing', *Economica* (August 1969) pp. 277-94.
[3] M. J. C. Surrey, *The Analysis and Forecasting of the British Economy*,

National Institute of Economic and Social Research, Occasional Paper 25, Cambridge University Press, London (1971) p. 97.

[4] $\bar{A}$ is –9.40 for stockbuilding and 0.59 for gross domestic product.

[5] The *P*1 and *P*2 totals for positive and negative actual changes recorded in columns 1-6 in Tables 5.7 and 5.8 differ as they refer to changes which are not turning-point errors.

[6] This is supported for United States forecasts in R. Fels and C. E. Hinshaw, *Forecasting and Recognizing Business Cycle Turning Points*, National Bureau of Economic Research and Columbia University Press, New York (1968).

[7] One of the fourth quarter peaks, missed altogether by *P*2, may well have been policy induced; this was the fall in imports in 1966(iv) following the 'July measures'. There was a similar downturn in imports in the fourth quarter of the previous year but the NIESR *P*1 forecasts anticipated this with a one quarter lead in spite of unforeseen government intervention in the summer.

6 Quarterly Forecasting: Personal Income and Expenditure, Gross Fixed Investment and Balance of Payments on Current Account

1. Introduction

In Chapter 5 we evaluated the National Institute's success at predicting quarterly changes in gross domestic product and its components. Supporting these aggregated forecasts are detailed sub-forecasts of a large number of variables which either contribute directly to national income, expenditure and product, or which are instrumental to the determination and estimation of the general level of British economic activity. The present chapter concerns the accuracy of NIESR quarterly forecasts of personal income and expenditure, gross fixed investment, and the balance of payments on current account, which are published in the *Economic Review* at the same time as the gross domestic product forecasts.

Predictions of personal income and expenditure are integral to the Institute's complete forecasting procedure.[1] Some of the income and expenditure components are endogenous to the small, aggregate econometric model used in conjunction with other methods for forecasting at the NIESR. Of the eighteen variables listed below in Table 6.1, wages and salaries and other personal income are determined by the level of gross domestic product and their own lagged values. Other personal income comprises income from rent, self-employment and dividends, and net interest receipts. Income from rent and self-employment is more stable than dividend income and net interest receipts, and in their respective log-linear forecasting equations income from dividends and net interest receipts has an elasticity coefficient on lagged gross domestic product fourteen times as large as that of income from rent and self-employment. Direct taxes are functions of the various types of income. (The equations for the wage and salary bill, and for taxes on wages and salaries also include time trends.) The consumers' price index is related to the exogenous indirect tax component of consumer prices, and to an index excluding indirect taxes, which is determined by the proportion of labour costs, the wage and salary bill, in gross domestic product, and by import prices and an autoregressive term. Real personal disposable income is made up of real disposable wage and salary income, and other real disposable income, i.e. endogenous and exogenous money income, adjusted for employers' contributions to private superannuation schemes, for employees' National Insurance contributions, and for direct taxation, all deflated by the consumer price index. Consumers' expenditure is forecast from real income, the real credit effect, and lagged real non-credit consumption.

Employment forecasts are obtained outside the model. The equilibrium level of employment is estimated from projected gross domestic product, labour supply, normal working hours and a time trend. Actual employment adjusts to the discrepancy between current equilibrium and outcome in the previous quarter; this response is slower for higher levels of disequilibrium. Changes in wage rates and average earnings have been forecast individually from the proportion of workers receiving wage increases, normal hours data and indices of retail prices and capacity utilisation. However, since 1966 these relationships have not proved satisfactory and consequently the Institute now derives exogenous forecasts of wage rates from, *inter alia*, the likely effects of official (prices and incomes) policy, and aggregate forecasts of the wage and salary bill from the gross product relationship mentioned earlier. Forces' pay and current grants from authorities to persons are forecast from official published data. Net insurance contributions comprise employers' contributions to private pension schemes less employees' National Insurance contributions: 'the first is a very trend-like series while the second changes sharply when contribution rates are changed . . . [the] balance is treated as an exogenous element.'[2] Also exogenous is the credit effect, forecast on the assumption of unchanged policy towards private hire purchase and bank debt.[3] Net transfers abroad, a small item, is obtained from the Institute's balance of payments forecast.

Gross fixed investment is forecast outside the National Institute's econometric model.[4] Public sector non-dwelling investment is forecast exogenously from published information on the government's investment plans. Single-equation estimates, using the number of starts as the principal argument, assist the forecasting of public and private sector housing; starts, however, are predicted either from official plans or, in the case of the private sector, by informal methods. Private non-dwelling investment, comprising capital formation by manufacturing industry and other private industries (construction, transport, agriculture, mining, distribution and other services) is forecast from econometric relationships involving lagged changes in gross domestic product, capacity utilisation, capital goods production, time, profits and cost of capital. Capacity utilisation, the GDP accelerator and profits are all close substitutes for forecasting purposes, due to their observed inter-correlation over time. Whichever is actually used as explanatory variable, the Institute estimates that a five quarter lag is on average required to induce a change in investment. (This incidentally helps to confirm us in our view that post-budget policy changes usually do not invalidate the May forecasts of the ensuing four quarters.) The Department of Trade and Industry's quarterly survey of investment intentions provides an additional source of information for the NIESR forecasters, whose final forecast of private non-dwelling investment 'is likely to represent a compromise between the two methods, with the investment intentions data receiving greater weight the more distinctive the current economic situation is compared with past experience.'[5]

Our earlier analysis of the quarterly gross domestic product forecasts revealed that, for current period forecasts, exports and imports of goods and services are among the more accurately predicted macroeconomic variables. However the *P*2 forecasts of changes in the current balance of payments are only marginally more accurate than naïve predictions of no change. The concluding sections of this chapter examine in some detail the forecasts of balance of payments on current account;[6] in the context of controlling the United Kingdom economy it is obviously of considerable importance that balance of payments forecasts be reasonably accurate.

The National Institute treats exports of goods as an exogenous expenditure item, which in the main is forecast by informal methods. Econometric models of exports of manufactures to industrial countries, exports to primary producing countries and total exports of goods have been estimated, but tend not to forecast well outside the estimation period. An autocorrelated log-linear relationship between the total value of United Kingdom exports of goods and an index of industrial countries' manufacturing production (and the ratio of this index to its linear trend) is used to make a central forecast.[7] Otherwise, the current value of United Kingdom exports are forecast informally on the basis of likely overseas growth rates and foreign exchange reserves, export orders and industry's own predictions, plus any special temporary factors. Informal forecasts of export prices are obtained from estimates of domestic and import costs. Again, formal work in this area has not proved to be very successful. Imports are forecast more objectively. Within the aggregate econometric model, imports of goods and services, valued at constant prices, are related separately to the forecast level of stockbuilding and the forecast level of total final sales (excluding stockbuilding). In other empirical relationships, import coefficients have been estimated for each of the individual categories of final sales but the implied import elasticities were inconsistent with input-output data, hence their suppression in favour of the simpler relationship involving aggregated expenditure.[8] Changes in the prices of non-food agricultural products, non-ferrous metals, food, basic materials and fuels are forecast by a combination of informal methods and crude statistical relationships, and weighted to calculate the NIESR price forecast for imported goods. The price of imported services is obtained primarily by extrapolation from past trends. Once the invisible component of total imports is distinguished, the imports forecast can be revalued in current prices. The invisible items on the current balance of payments comprise exports and imports of services, net property income and net transfers: they are forecast by the usual mixture of trend-extrapolation and judgement.

The performance of the NIESR forecasts of income and expenditure, fixed investment and balance of payments is evaluated from the first quarter of 1965 to the last quarter of 1970. The analysis for income and expenditure and fixed investment is entirely in quarterly terms. However, quarterly forecasts of the balance of payments on current account were not published until 1969, before which the forecasts referred to the half-year. Thus we examine forecasts for twelve half-years, 1965(I) to 1970(II), and seven quarters 1969(ii) to 1970(iv). (Throughout, a lower case Roman numeral following a date indicates a quarter; an upper case numeral denotes a half-year.) All the forecasts were quantified in issues of the quarterly *National Institute Economic Review*. For each series of quarterly or half-yearly data we examine two sets of forecasts. *P*1 denotes the set of forecasts published in the same quarter or half-year to which the forecasts refer, thus forecasts of the first, second, third and fourth quarters were extracted from the February, May, August and November numbers of the *Economic Review* respectively, and *P*1 forecasts for the first and second halves of each year were obtained from the May and November issues respectively. A second set of forecasts, *P*2, was obtained from the May *Economic Review* for successive years. *P*2 quarterly forecasts are for four quarters ahead, i.e. for the second, third and fourth quarter of the current year, and for the first quarter of the next year. *P*2 half-yearly forecasts are for the first and second six months of the current year. The May publication date is selected because it allows the forecasters to include the effects of recently revealed Budget policies on their projections. *P*1 and *P*2 predictions are evaluated on a rolling quarter to quarter or half-year to half-year basis: predicted percentage changes from one quarter or half-year to the next are compared with corresponding actual changes. This evaluation clearly favours the *P*1 forecast changes, which are based on estimates of outcomes in previous quarters or half-years and which are published one or five months into the forecast periods whereas the *P*2 series are chained or linked forecasts, the basis of each forecast change beyond the second quarter or first half-year being the preceding forecast level. The outcome data against which the forecasts are assessed are the latest published in the *Economic Review*. All forecasts and outcomes are seasonally adjusted. All the investment data are in constant prices, all the balance of payments data are in current prices, as are most of the income and expenditure data; real valued variables include consumers' expenditure, savings, and the savings ratio as well as real disposable personal income.

Forecasts of all but four of the variables are assessed by comparing predicted and actual percentage changes. A minor problem arises in the income and expenditure analysis when evaluating the accuracy of predicted changes in net contributions, net transfers abroad and the credit effect on account of these variables' levels being much smaller and more volatile than the others. Percentage changes tend to oscillate between very large positive and negative values. Also, if a_{t-1} is zero, which for quarterly observations is not unlikely, the implied actual or predicted percentage change is infinite and unquantifiable. Forecasts and outcomes of net contributions, net transfers abroad and the credit effect are therefore compared using absolute changes, $p_t - a_{t-1}$ and $a_t - a_{t-1}$, commensurable with the percentage changes, P_t, A_t, calculated for all other series. Although the relevant values are measured in current prices the time series are probably short enough to allow us to ignore the effects of trend or scale factors which might otherwise obscure the true degree of predictive accuracy. The savings ratio, another small, fluctuating number, is treated similarly; note that forecasts of its constituents, real savings and real disposable personal income, are evaluated in percentage change form, as usual.

Forecasts of personal income and expenditure are assessed by means of inequality, regression and observation-by-observation analysis in sections 2, 3 and 4 which follow. Similar analysis of gross fixed investment is reported in sections 5, 6 and 7, and our assessment of NIESR forecasts of the balance of payments on current account is presented in sections 8, 9, 10 and 11. The chapter ends with some conclusions, section 12.

2. Personal income and expenditure: time series analysis

With some exceptions, the NIESR forecasts of the variables comprising personal income and expenditure are examined over the twenty-four quarters of the sample period. The Institute no longer forecasts wage-rate changes so that our analysis of the hourly wage-rates index and also of disposable funds refers to the period 1965(i)-1968(iv) thus giving sixteen observations; forecasts of net transfers abroad were not published before the second quarter of 1967 so there are fifteen observations for this series.

Table 6.1 summarises the time series inequality coefficients for the current period, *P*1, and chained, *P*2, forecasts, together with corresponding *U* values for the naïve models. We first consider the *P*1 series. The wages and salaries variable is the most accurately predicted percentage

Table 6.1

Inequality coefficients for NIESR personal income and expenditure *P*1 and *P*2 forecasts and naïve models: time series 1965 (i)-1970 (iv)

	*P*1	*P*2	A_{t-1}	A_{t-4}	4-quarter moving average	$\bar{A}$
Hourly wage-rates index[a]	0.35	0.35	0.54	0.65	0.52	0.41
Average earnings	0.39	0.44	0.44	0.52	0.39	0.44
Employment	0.84	0.93	1.10	1.28	1.02	0.93
Wages and salaries	0.40	0.52	0.52	0.66	0.51	0.50
Forces' pay	0.81	0.87	1.38	1.29	1.10	0.95
Current grants	0.61	0.66	0.88	1.05	0.81	0.64
Other personal income	0.86	0.78	1.62	1.23	1.11	0.97
Net contributions[b]	0.95	1.04	1.15	1.46	1.18	1.00
Taxes	0.79	0.72	1.32	1.07	0.95	0.84
Net transfers abroad[bc]	1.05	1.00	1.59	1.62	1.11	0.98
Personal disposable income	0.67	0.61	1.12	0.97	0.80	0.70
Credit effect[b]	0.86	0.90	1.23	1.45	1.20	1.00
Disposable funds[a]	0.71	0.67	1.30	1.10	0.95	0.82
Consumers' price index	0.38	0.46	0.56	0.62	0.51	0.46
Real disposable personal income	0.88	0.81	1.48	1.26	1.13	0.97
Consumers' expenditure	0.83	0.90	1.53	1.53	1.17	0.96
Savings	1.08	1.05	1.59	1.42	1.17	0.99
Savings ratio[b]	1.09	1.08	1.63	1.51	1.17	1.00

a 1965(i)-1968(iv)

b Absolute changes are used throughout. i.e. $p_t - a_{t-1}$, $p_t - p_{t-1}$ and $a_t - a_{t-1}$.

c 1967(ii)-1970(iv).

change component of personal disposable income; its inequality coefficient, at 0.40, is less than half the coefficient of 0.86 obtained for other personal income (rent, income from self-employment and net interest receipts) which is more volatile and hence presumably more unpredictable. Current grants from authorities to persons and the forces' pay series are forecast (exogenously) better than other personal income and worse than wages and salaries. The inequality coefficient for taxes may be expected to resemble an average of the inequality coefficients of the different income groups weighted by their importance and their average tax rates; that the coefficient for taxes is closer to that for other personal income than to that for wages and salaries suggests that the high tax rates paid by this group is dominant. The inequality coefficient for personal disposable income is 0.67. Of the three variables for which forecast changes are examined in absolute terms the credit effect is most accurately predicted ($U = 0.86$) followed by net contributions (0.95) and net transfers abroad (1.05).

Average earnings and employment, both of which are forecast outside the National Institute's aggregate model and which are analysed here in the usual percentage change form have inequality coefficients of 0.39 and 0.84 respectively; the former in particular is not at all bad considering the Institute's concern with the forecasting implications of alleged recent structural shifts in labour market relations.[9] Moreover the hourly wage-rates index was well forecast in the period 1965(i) to 1968(iv), as was the consumers' price index over the whole sample period. Inequality coefficients as low as 0.35 and 0.38 for price change data are quite good but against this it must be recorded that including the credit-income transformation and deflation by the consumer price index results in less accurate forecasts of real disposable personal income, $U = 0.88$, than of nominal disposable income, $U = 0.67$. Consumers' expenditure, $U = 0.83$, is marginally better forecast than real disposable income, and appreciably better forecast than savings, which would be as accurately predicted by assuming no change. Inequality analysis of forecast absolute changes in the savings ratio yields a U statistic of 1.09, the highest of all the *P*1 time series results. If however one is more concerned with predicting the level of the savings ratio, than forecasting its changes, then the Institute's economists fare much better; the inquality coefficient for the savings ratio's level, which is not included in Table 6.1, is 0.18.

The mean inequality coefficient for the *P*1 series is 0.75, the mean for the *P*2 series is only marginally worse, 0.77, and the difference is insignificant. Indeed for half of the variables the *P*2 forecasts are more accurate than the *P*1 forecasts. As for the *P*1, so also the best *P*2 forecasts are of hourly wage rates and the worst are of the savings ratio. The $P2$ forecasts are more successful in predicting other personal income and less successful with wages and salaries. Also the $P2$ forecasts are superior in predicting the important aggregate, real disposable income, even though the consumers' price index is more accurately forecast by $P1$. Unlike savings, which are predicted marginally worse by $P1$ than $P2$, perhaps in response to inferior predictions of other personal income, the $P1$ forecasts of consumption are better than the $P2$ forecasts. Except for the imposition in July 1966 of a ten per cent surcharge on 1965-66 surtax liabilities there were no post-budget changes in the rates of direct taxation between 1965 and 1970, so there is no reason to suppose that the validity of our analysis of the Institute's $P2$ taxes' forecast is jeopardised by post-forecast adjustments. This is fortunate, since the May forecasts of taxes are rather more accurate than forecasts made in the current quarter. Three post-budget increases in National Insurance contribution rates may help to account for the inferiority of the $P2$ net contribution forecasts for six sample quarters. Some of the discrepancy between $P1$ and $P2$ accuracy in forecasting the consumers' price index may be due to the use of the fiscal regulator in the middle or late part of the year, but the Institute itself suggests that the effects of indirect tax changes on final prices are damped and lagged. [10] During our period of study there were frequent changes in credit and monetary policy which could not have been foreseen in May; even so, the $P1$ forecasts of the credit effect, which cannot have been invalidated by these measures, yield an inequality coefficient only marginally lower than does $P2$. Changes in interest rates, credit terms and availability may also prejudice forecasts of the consumption-saving decision, although there is no clear-cut evidence of the relevant $P2$ forecasts being impaired for this reason. May forecasts of net transfers abroad do not appear to be adversely affected by subsequent policies aimed at improving the balance of payments, as they, like taxes, are marginally less accurate when revised in the current quarter. Finally, forecasts made in May 1966 could not have anticipated the voluntary price and wage freeze introduced that July, but consideration of the potentially widespread implications for forecasting of this measure is more conveniently delayed until the cross-section, quarter by quarter, assessment of the Institute's predictive performance.

Naïve projections of income and expenditure are usually much less accurate than the genuine forecasts. The average inequality coefficients for the A_{t-1}, A_{t-4} four-quarter moving average and $\overline{A}$ models are 1.17, 1.15, 0.93 and 0.81 respectively. Both $P1$ and $P2$ yield significantly lower inequality coefficients than the no-change naïve assumption, $U = 1$, this at the 0.5 per cent level of significance. The $\overline{A}$ model presents more of a challenge to the Institute's accuracy: it is more accurate than both NIESR forecasts of net transfers abroad, savings and the savings ratio and also the *P*2 forecasts of wages and salaries, current grants and net contributions. The naïve no-change model generates at least as good forecasts as both *P*1 and *P*2 for net transfers, savings and the savings ratio and as *P*2 for net contributions. The four-quarter moving average is a little more accurate than the *P*2 forecasts of wages and salaries and average earnings. This variable is the one best forecast by three of the naïve models. $\bar{A}$'s most accurate prediction is of the hourly wage-rates index. When inequality coefficients are averaged across all time series for *P*1, *P*2 and the best naïve prediction of each variable, the National Institute forecasts emerge *en bloc* the more accurate, though the difference in the respective means is not statistically significant at the five per cent level.

Turning to the detailed inequality and regression results for *P*1 reported in Table 6.2, we see that in general there is very little bias in the forecasts. The most obvious exceptions are average earnings and wages and salaries, for which a third and a quarter of the respective mean-square prediction errors are attributable to underforecasting the mean actual percentage change. U^M, the bias proportion, is also relatively high for net contributions, where mean predicted and actual absolute changes have opposite sign. Otherwise U^M averages 0.05, varying between 0.11 for consumers' expenditure and real disposable personal income, where bias tends to accumulate, and 0.01 for the consumers' price index and the savings ratio. Just as average actual changes are typically underestimated ($\bar{P}<\bar{A}$), so the forecasters also underpredict the variation in outcomes as only for the hourly wage-rates index, current grants and the consumers' price index is s_P/s_A greater than unity. Underestimating the variance of outcomes is the main source of systematic error in twelve of the forecast series and on average it accounts for twenty-seven per cent of the total mean-square prediction error when the calculation is made over all variables for which s_P/s_A is less than one. U^S is 0.72 for other personal income, 0.67 for net transfers abroad, 0.50 for disposable funds, 0.36 for personal disposable income, 0.34 for the savings ratio, 0.28 for savings, 0.28 for employment and 0.26 for taxes. Some of these high U^S results are obviously interrelated; for example, other personal income, taxes, and personal disposable income, and savings as well if the savings propensity of the recipients of other personal income is significantly higher than that of wage and salary earners. The 'allocation' between consumption and savings of the variance proportion of forecasting error in real disposable personal income further supports this point. Surrey has shown the equilibrium marginal propensity to consume out of other disposable personal

Table 6.2

Accuracy analysis of NIESR personal income and expenditure *P*1 forecasts: time series 1965(i)-1970(iv)

	U	U^M	U^S	U^C	r	α	β	SE (α)	SE (β)	$\bar{P}$	$\bar{A}$	s_P/s_A
Hourly wage-rates index[a]	0.35	0.06	0.01	0.93	0.70	0.61	0.64	0.26	0.17	1.33	1.46	1.09
Average earnings	0.39	0.33	0.08	0.60	0.69	0.63	0.91	0.35	0.20	1.53	2.03	0.76
Employment	0.84	0.09	0.28	0.64	0.49	−0.10	0.95	0.07	0.36	−0.06	−0.16	0.52
Wages and salaries	0.40	0.25	0.12	0.64	0.72	0.45	0.99	0.34	0.21	1.48	1.92	0.73
Forces' pay	0.81	0.02	0.12	0.86	0.57	0.91	0.80	0.98	0.25	1.05	1.75	0.71
Current grants	0.61	0.06	0.08	0.86	0.69	1.49	0.55	0.43	0.12	2.15	2.66	1.25
Other personal income	0.86	0.02	0.72	0.26	0.59	−0.22	2.36	1.40	0.69	0.83	1.73	0.25
Net contributions[b]	0.95	0.17	0.00	0.83	0.60	2.37	0.64	1.56	0.18	−2.79	0.58	0.94
Taxes	0.79	0.03	0.26	0.71	0.40	1.37	0.77	1.37	0.37	2.52	3.31	0.52
Net transfers abroad[bc]	1.05	0.05	0.67	0.28	−0.32	0.72	−2.59	1.34	2.12	−0.13	1.07	0.12
Personal disposable income	0.67	0.10	0.36	0.54	0.43	0.52	0.99	0.62	0.45	1.18	1.69	0.43
Credit effect[b]	0.85	0.03	0.00	0.97	0.64	2.94	0.66	5.24	0.17	−5.46	−0.67	0.97
Disposable funds[a]	0.71	0.09	0.50	0.42	0.59	0.03	1.53	0.68	0.57	0.91	1.43	0.39
Consumers' price index	0.38	0.01	0.08	0.91	0.75	0.41	0.61	0.15	0.11	1.15	1.11	1.23
Real disposable personal income	0.88	0.11	0.17	0.71	0.53	0.58	0.85	0.35	0.29	−0.07	0.52	0.62
Consumers' expenditure	0.83	0.11	0.08	0.82	0.60	0.42	0.79	0.25	0.22	0.01	0.43	0.76
Savings	1.08	0.02	0.28	0.70	0.02	2.64	0.05	3.98	0.50	−0.38	2.62	0.40
Savings ratio[b]	1.09	0.01	0.34	0.65	−0.06	0.06	−0.17	0.30	0.59	−0.06	0.07	0.35

a 1965(i)-1968(iv).

b Absolute changes are used throughout, i.e. $p_t - a_{t-1}$ and $a_t - a_{t-1}$.

c 1967(ii)-1970(iv).

income to be approximately four-fifths that out of disposable wage and salary income, and three-quarters that out of current grants.[11] In this context it is somewhat disconcerting to learn that 'the theoretical background to these equations [for NIESR forecasts of income from rent and from self-employment, and income from dividends and net interest receipts] is clearly negligible; they serve merely as convenient guide lines pending further research.'[12]

There is almost no variance error in the forecasts of the hourly wage-rates index, net contributions and the credit effect, which is commendable. Deflation by the consumers' price index results in a halving of the variance proportion of error in forecasting real disposable personal income. This is rather surprising as in inflationary times one might expect nominal values to fluctuate less than their real equivalents and so prove easier to forecast. Random error, U^C, averages 0.69 across all $P1$ variables, which is close to the average non-systematic component of quarterly forecasting error for gross domestic product as a whole.

Two of the least accurately forecast series, net transfers abroad and the savings ratio, are subject to negative correlation between predictions and outcomes. Otherwise r is positive, and, except for these two variables and savings, the slope term, β, of the regression of A_t on P_t is significant at the five per cent level.

There is rather more systematic error in the $P2$ series (see Table 6.3), but once again this excess is not statistically significant. The $P2$ hourly wage rates forecast is notable for its total lack of systematic error, and bias is sufficiently reduced in the $P2$ wages and salaries forecast to raise the random U^C component from 0.64 to 0.79. A slight general reduction in $P2$ bias (mean changes are still underestimated) is offset by a more marked under-prediction of the variance of certain outcomes; see for example the increase from $P1$ to $P2$ in the U^S error proportion in forecasts of average earnings, forces' pay, taxes, net transfers abroad, credit effect (when the increase in U^S is from $P1 = 0.00$ to $P2 = 0.39$), nominal and real disposable personal income, savings and the savings ratio.

The earlier reported regression results are substantially unchanged for the analysis applied to the $P2$ forecasts. The degree of correlation between predictions and outcomes is now rather lower. For employment and wages and salaries the β coefficient in the regression of A_t on P_t is no longer significant at the five per cent level.

Table 6.3

Accuracy analysis of NIESR personal income and expenditure *P*2 forecasts: time series 1965(i)-1970(iv)

	U	U^M	U^S	U^C	r	α	β	SE (α)	SE (β)	$\bar{P}$	$\bar{A}$	s_P/s_A
Hourly wage-rates index[a]	0.35	0.00	0.00	1.00	0.63	0.51	0.65	0.35	0.22	1.46	1.46	0.97
Average earnings	0.44	0.24	0.24	0.52	0.50	0.53	0.97	0.59	0.36	1.55	2.03	0.52
Employment	0.93	0.14	0.36	0.51	0.37	–0.14	0.92	0.08	0.49	–0.02	–0.16	0.40
Wages and salaries	0.52	0.10	0.11	0.79	0.35	1.09	0.53	0.52	0.52	1.56	1.92	0.66
Forces' pay	0.87	0.05	0.34	0.61	0.46	1.12	0.98	1.05	0.40	0.64	1.75	0.47
Current grants	0.66	0.20	0.04	0.77	0.66	1.75	0.55	0.42	0.13	1.65	2.66	1.20
Other personal income	0.78	0.01	0.80	0.19	0.79	–1.08	2.76	1.07	0.46	1.02	1.73	0.29
Net contributions[b]	1.04	0.11	0.00	0.89	0.51	1.87	0.52	1.66	0.19	–2.46	0.58	0.98
Taxes	0.72	0.07	0.45	0.49	0.58	0.32	1.36	1.26	0.41	2.20	3.31	0.43
Net transfers abroad[b c]	1.00	0.02	0.79	0.19	–0.10	1.36	–1.11	1.61	3.12	0.27	1.07	0.09
Personal disposable income	0.61	0.08	0.48	0.45	0.58	–0.17	1.44	0.63	0.43	1.29	1.69	0.40
Credit effect[b]	0.90	0.01	0.39	0.60	0.44	–2.31	1.01	6.05	0.44	1.63	–0.67	0.44
Disposable funds[a]	0.67	0.03	0.50	0.47	0.61	–0.26	1.47	0.72	0.51	1.15	1.43	0.41
Consumers' price index	0.46	0.05	0.04	0.91	0.63	0.59	0.53	0.17	0.14	0.99	1.11	1.19
Real disposable personal income	0.81	0.02	0.30	0.68	0.56	0.23	1.04	0.35	0.33	0.28	0.52	0.54
Consumers' expenditure	0.90	0.06	0.10	0.85	0.48	0.36	0.68	0.28	0.26	0.10	0.43	0.71
Savings	1.05	0.00	0.40	0.60	–0.01	2.72	–0.03	4.49	0.64	3.25	2.62	0.33
Savings ratio[b]	1.08	0.01	0.44	0.56	–0.14	0.15	–0.48	0.32	0.74	0.18	0.07	0.29

a 1965(i)-1968(iv).

b Absolute changes are used throughout, i.e. $p_t - a_{t-1}$, $p_t - p_{t-1}$ and $a_t - a_{t-1}$.

c 1967(i)-1970(iv).

3. Personal income and expenditure: cross-section analysis

The forecasts are next examined in cross-section; that is, for each of the twenty-four sample quarters the inequality and regression techniques are applied across the income and expenditure variables. The variables included are wages and salaries, forces' pay, current grants, other personal income, taxes, personal disposable income, real disposable personal income, consumers' expenditure and savings. Omitted are all forecast absolute changes (as opposed to percentage changes), the wage, earnings and employment variables which are forecast outside the econometric model, the sub-total, disposable funds, and the consumers' price index which is hardly comparable to the included nominal and real components of income.

Cross-section inequality coefficients for the $P1$ forecasts are shown in Table 6.4, and the details of the inequality and regression results are presented in Table 6.5. The average value of the $P1$ inequality coefficient is 1.04, with a 0.42 standard deviation. This is not significantly different from the naïve no-change U value of unity. Twelve of the quarters have inequality coefficients greater than unity, one of which, for 1969(i), is as high as 2.34. Inspection of the partial coefficients, the regression analysis and the mean predicted and actual changes does not suggest any consistent cause of certain quarters being so badly forecast.

The endogenous income and expenditure variables are interrelated: other personal income (income from rent and self-employment, income from dividends and net interest receipts), the wage and salary bill and the consumer price index are all functions of forecast gross domestic product; taxes and consumers' expenditure are primarily determined by nominal and real income. Thus when an exogenous element of, say, gross domestic product is wrongly forecast for a given quarter, concurrent forecasts of a number of dependent income and expenditure components may be so erroneous that the resultant cross-section U for the quarter in question will be abnormally high. Likewise the simultaneity of the system may, on other occasions, yield low cross-section inequality coefficients.

All quarters in which $\bar{P}$ and $\bar{A}$ are of opposite sign have inequality coefficients greater than unity, but the partials indicate that these apparent instances of aggregate turning-point errors are as much due to wrongly forecasting the spread of the variables' outcomes (some positive, some negative) as they are caused by incorrectly predicting the mean sign of changes. In this respect the income and expenditure forecasts differ from those for gross domestic product as a whole. But the poor forecasts of 1970 cannot be so readily explained: although predictions and outcomes are negatively correlated, $\bar{P}$ and $\bar{A}$ are both positive, and except for the relatively well forecast second quarter, when bias and variance proportions are large, forecasting error is predominantly non-systematic. Paradoxically, the best forecast quarter, 1968(i), which is predicted with a U value of only 0.36, is subject to abnormally large bias: almost a third of mean-square error is attributable to this source. On average, bias accounts for twenty per cent while misforecast variance account for another twenty-seven per cent of total error. As with the time series results, mean actual changes are typically under-predicted, the freak value for $\bar{A}$ in 1966(i) is due to exceptional increases in other personal income and in savings. The variation in changes across variables is also underestimated, giving rise to very high U^S values in some quarters. In 1965(iii)

Table 6.4

Inequality coefficients for NIESR personal income and expenditure $P1$ and $P2$ forecasts and naïve models: cross-section 1965(i)-1970(iv)

		$P1$	$P2$	A_{t-1}	A_{t-4}	4-quarter moving average	$\bar{A}$
1965	(i)	0.65	0.65	1.27	1.23	0.61	0.68
	(ii)	0.87	0.87	1.10	1.18	1.07	1.01
	(iii)	0.77	1.47	1.09	1.25	0.77	1.04
	(iv)	0.79	1.00	2.22	2.02	1.57	0.61
1966	(i)	0.96	0.91	0.83	0.98	1.01	0.93
	(ii)	1.04	1.04	1.96	1.03	1.19	1.04
	(iii)	1.02	1.67	7.05	2.72	1.45	1.52
	(iv)	0.96	0.68	1.32	1.44	1.35	0.99
1967	(i)	0.77	0.55	1.12	1.13	0.97	0.89
	(ii)	0.39	0.39	0.84	3.75	1.35	0.85
	(iii)	0.79	1.04	1.71	1.45	0.97	0.61
	(iv)	1.04	1.50	1.19	0.98	1.57	1.14
1968	(i)	0.36	1.06	0.69	2.61	1.26	1.02
	(ii)	1.01	1.01	1.30	0.62	1.08	0.93
	(iii)	1.28	1.42	3.53	1.04	1.07	1.02
	(iv)	1.00	0.75	2.65	3.14	1.24	0.99
1969	(i)	2.34	0.94	0.78	1.74	0.63	0.79
	(ii)	1.56	1.56	1.90	3.38	1.73	1.17
	(iii)	1.30	1.22	2.40	1.86	0.43	0.94
	(iv)	0.81	0.87	1.05	0.55	0.88	0.58
1970	(i)	1.21	1.04	1.56	2.40	0.84	0.88
	(ii)	0.89	0.89	0.96	1.39	0.98	0,84
	(iii)	1.75	0.99	3.26	0.81	1.56	1.23
	(iv)	1.43	0.83	1.43	0.40	0.82	0.67

Table 6.5

Accuracy analysis of NIESR personal income and expenditure $P1$ forecasts: cross-section 1965(i)-1970(iv)

	U	U^M	U^S	U^C	r	α	β	SE (α)	SE (β)	$\bar{P}$	$\bar{A}$	s_P/s_A
1965 (i)	0.65	0.35	0.40	0.25	0.75	0.44	1.79	0.86	0.60	1.04	2.31	0.42
(ii)	0.87	0.61	0.02	0.37	0.88	−1.89	0.77	0.82	0.16	2.82	0.29	1.14
(iii)	0.77	0.01	0.96	0.03	0.96	−2.71	3.91	0.72	0.42	0.80	0.42	0.25
(iv)	0.79	0.25	0.44	0.31	0.06	2.40	0.26	2.35	1.69	1.28	2.73	0.23
1966 (i)	0.96	0.34	0.60	0.06	0.22	7.67	3.67	9.63	6.27	1.23	12.20	0.06
(ii)	1.04	0.03	0.44	0.53	0.04	−2.68	0.13	6.25	1.24	0.24	−2.64	0.31
(iii)	1.02	0.03	0.09	0.88	0.61	−0.22	0.46	0.69	0.23	−1.19	−0.77	1.33
(iv)	0.96	0.05	0.24	0.71	0.34	0.79	0.66	1.30	0.69	0.03	0.81	0.52
1967 (i)	0.77	0.21	0.66	0.13	0.80	0.45	2.96	2.20	0.83	1.48	4.83	0.27
(ii)	0.39	0.07	0.18	0.75	0.93	1.11	0.78	0.70	0.11	2.47	3.04	1.19
(iii)	0.79	0.53	0.20	0.26	0.44	1.94	1.07	0.94	0.83	0.76	2.74	0.41
(iv)	1.04	0.27	0.47	0.27	0.43	−4.46	1.62	3.08	1.27	1.79	−1.57	0.27
1968 (i)	0.36	0.31	0.04	0.66	0.95	1.01	1.03	0.58	0.13	0.18	1.19	0.92
(ii)	1.01	0.14	0.56	0.30	0.05	5.00	0.29	4.64	1.99	0.00	5.00	0.17
(iii)	1.28	0.08	0.01	0.92	0.13	0.69	0.15	2.09	0.41	2.81	1.10	0.87
(iv)	1.00	0.23	0.00	0.77	0.57	1.10	0.54	0.73	0.29	−0.22	0.98	1.06
1969 (i)	2.34	0.13	0.07	0.81	−0.78	2.12	−0.45	1.08	0.14	−1.57	2.82	1.73
(ii)	1.56	0.11	0.09	0.79	−0.98	2.00	−1.90	0.51	0.16	1.69	−1.20	0.52
(iii)	1.30	0.19	0.48	0.33	0.82	1.01	0.41	0.38	0.11	−0.18	0.93	2.00
(iv)	0.81	0.19	0.03	0.79	0.03	3.04	0.03	1.21	0.49	1.76	3.10	1.00
1970 (i)	1.21	0.09	0.03	0.88	−0.06	1.13	−0.08	1.14	0.49	1.77	0.98	0.75
(ii)	0.89	0.45	0.35	0.20	−0.06	7.37	−0.36	3.84	2.11	1.51	6.83	0.17
(iii)	1.75	0.08	0.01	0.91	−0.73	2.06	−0.90	0.95	0.32	1.86	0.39	0.81
(iv)	1.43	0.11	0.01	0.89	−0.48	3.46	−0.41	1.10	0.28	1.00	3.04	1.17

U^S is ninety-six per cent and the predicted variance is a quarter of the outcome. The mean values of U for each of the four quarters are 1.05 (first quarter), 0.96 (second), 1.15 (third) and 1.01 (fourth), and the mean values of U^C are, in the same quarterly order, 0.47, 0.49, 0.56 and 0.92. None of the inter-quarter differences in mean U or U^C are significant.

From Tables 6.4, 6.5 and 6.6 it can be seen that the cross-section performance of the May $P2$ forecasts is very similar to that of the $P1$ series. On average, the $P2$ forecasts are marginally more accurate with a mean U of 1.06 against 1.09 for $P1$, calculated for all quarters other than the second of each year (for the second quarter $P1 = P2$). It is interesting to observe that five of nine quarters for which the May forecasts are more accurate occur within the last two years of our sample period. Like $P1$, the $P2$ cross-section inequality coefficient averaged over all quarters is not significantly different from persistently forecast no-change: its mean and standard deviation are 1.02 and 0.42 respectively. Again like $P1$ there are twelve quarters for which the inequality coefficient is greater than unity, though the statistic for 1969(i) is now reduced to 0.94.

The bias and variance proportions average seventeen and thirty-one per cent respectively for $P2$ which are comparable with those for $P1$. The $P2$ average of 0.57 for U^C is not significantly larger than the $P1$ value of 0.55 when the comparison is made excluding the second quarter observations for which $P1$ and $P2$ are the same. As before both the general level of quarterly changes and the spread of changes between the different income and expenditure variables tend to be underestimated. A straightforward comparison of the accuracy of the two sets of forecasts over all quarters reveals no substantial difference in accuracy or the proportion of systematic error. This is confirmed by testing the differences in $P1$ and $P2$ mean U and U^C values for each quarter: $P2$ has the lower average inequality coefficient for all except the third quarter and the lower U^C value, that is more systematic error, in the first and fourth quarters, but none of these differences are significant at the five per cent level.

The $P2$ set of forecasts differ in accuracy between quarters: for quarters one to four through the year the mean inequality coefficients are 0.86, 0.96, 1.30 and 0.94 and the mean values of U^C are 0.32, 0.49, 0.78 and 0.50. The mean inequality coefficient for the third quarter is significantly higher at the five per cent level than the coefficients for each of the other quarters; it is also the quarter with least systematic error, and U^C is significantly lower in each of the other quarters at the five per cent level. None of the other interquarter differences for U or for U^C are significant at the five per cent level. Thus apart from the low U^C value for the first

Table 6.6

Accuracy analysis of NIESR personal income and expenditure $P2$ forecasts: cross-section 1965(i)-1970(iv)

	U	U^M	U^S	U^C	r	α	β	SE (α)	SE (β)	$\bar{P}$	$\bar{A}$	s_P/s_A
1965 (i)	0.65	0.35	0.40	0.25	0.75	0.44	1.79	0.86	0.60	1.04	2.31	0.42
(ii)	0.87	0.61	0.02	0.37	0.88	−1.89	0.77	0.82	0.16	2.82	0.29	1.14
(iii)	1.47	0.07	0.12	0.81	−0.77	4.81	−1.55	2.01	0.49	2.83	0.42	0.50
(iv)	1.00	0.55	0.46	0.00	–[a]	–[a]	–[a]	–[a]	–[a]	0.00	2.73	0.00
1966 (i)	0.91	0.30	0.61	0.09	0.33	3.57	3.58	10.83	3.86	2.41	12.20	0.09
(ii)	1.04	0.03	0.44	0.53	0.04	−2.68	0.13	6.25	1.24	0.24	−2.64	0.31
(iii)	1.67	0.05	0.40	0.55	0.59	−0.32	0.28	0.69	0.14	−1.59	−0.77	2.11
(iv)	0.68	0.06	0.62	0.32	0.83	−1.77	1.83	1.02	0.47	1.41	0.81	0.45
1967 (i)	0.55	0.15	0.81	0.05	0.98	−1.63	2.31	0.83	0.19	2.80	4.83	0.42
(ii)	0.39	0.07	0.18	0.75	0.93	1.11	0.78	0.70	0.11	2.47	3.04	1.19
(iii)	1.04	0.06	0.00	0.94	−0.25	3.16	−0.22	0.98	0.33	1.87	2.74	1.14
(iv)	1.50	0.15	0.12	0.73	−0.92	2.68	−2.03	1.11	0.32	2.09	−1.57	0.45
1968 (i)	1.06	0.00	0.67	0.33	−0.81	8.90	−7.54	2.35	2.04	1.02	1.19	0.11
(ii)	1.01	0.14	0.56	0.30	0.05	5.00	0.29	4.64	1.99	0.00	5.00	0.17
(iii)	1.42	0.00	0.10	0.90	−0.79	3.14	−1.50	1.23	0.44	1.37	1.10	0.53
(iv)	0.75	0.05	0.20	0.75	0.61	−0.38	0.96	0.97	0.47	1.42	0.98	0.64
1969 (i)	0.94	0.19	0.59	0.22	0.10	2.37	0.67	2.39	2.51	0.68	2.82	0.15
(ii)	1.56	0.11	0.09	0.79	−0.98	2.00	−1.90	0.51	0.16	1.69	−1.20	0.52
(iii)	1.22	0.00	0.12	0.88	−0.63	2.02	−1.21	0.72	0.56	0.90	0.93	0.52
(iv)	0.87	0.26	0.05	0.69	−0.14	3.41	−0.22	1.16	0.57	1.41	3.10	0.12
1970 (i)	1.04	0.00	0.01	0.99	0.23	0.72	0.26	0.83	0.42	0.99	0.98	0.88
(ii)	0.89	0.45	0.35	0.20	−0.06	7.37	−0.36	3.84	2.11	1.51	6.83	0.17
(iii)	0.99	0.09	0.32	0.60	0.33	−0.55	0.75	1.44	0.81	1.24	0.39	0.44
(iv)	0.83	0.22	0.28	0.49	0.19	2.41	0.48	1.72	0.94	1.32	3.04	0.40

a Regression impossible: $P_t = 0$ for all variables.

quarter forecasts, which in any case yielded the lowest random error component of the $P1$ predictions, it is clear that accuracy of the chained forecasts does not deteriorate with the length of the chain. As a further check on this surprising result the ratio of the quarterly mean inequality coefficients for $P2$ to $P1$ were calculated; they are 1.13, 0.93 and 0.82 in the third, fourth and first quarters respectively. Thus, the further ahead the period forecast by $P2$ the more accurate it is relative to the $P1$ forecast! The ratios for U^C in the same order are 1.39, 0.54 and 0.68 indicating that, relative to $P1$, $P2$ systematic error was most marked in the fourth quarter.

From Table 6.4 it appears that certainly the $\bar{A}$, no-change ($U = 1$ for all quarters) and four-quarter moving average generate predictions which in cross-section are of comparable accuracy to the Institute's forecasts. On the other hand the A_{t-1} extrapolation is very unreliable. Taking all five naïve models together, there are seventeen quarters in which at least one naïve forecast is more accurate than $P1$, and nineteen quarters in which at least one naïve forecast yields a lower inequality coefficient than $P2$. Given the extreme degree of naïveté of the models, this is hardly an encouraging result for genuine forecasting. However the very simplicity of the naïve prediction suggests that any marked difference in their accuracy between quarters may be due to the existence of various factors which regularly make the task of genuine forecasters that much more difficult when predicting economic changes in one quarter than in another. Thus we might expect that, other things being equal, the ratio of genuine to naïve accuracy would be fairly constant between quarters: when forecasting a 'difficult' quarter, both naïve and genuine forecasting accuracy should deteriorate; both should improve together when forecasting is easier. For each quarter U^* is defined as U/U_L, where U is the cross-section $P1$ or $P2$ inequality coefficient and U_L is the lowest naïve cross-section inequality coefficient, i.e. that model which, with the benefit of hindsight, we know predicts each quarter best. When U^* is averaged for each quarter, it appears that none of these differences in means is significant except for that between the $P1$ forecasts of the second and third quarters (their means of U^* are 1.10 and 1.63 respectively, a difference significant at the ten per cent level), while for $P2$ the third quarter mean U^*, 1.79, is significantly larger at the five per cent level than the corresponding values for the first and second quarters (1.18 and 1.10). To this extent then the NIESR third quarter forecasts are least accurate, even when their results are normalised for quarterly differences in the performance of the naïve models, and this conclusion holds for both current quarter and multi-period predictions.

The accuracy of the $P1$ forecasts has deteriorated absolutely and relatively to 'good' naïve forecasting over the sample period. The time correlation coefficients measured over all quarters are 0.51 for the inequality coefficient and 0.56 for U^*, both of which are significant at the one per cent level. This trend is particularly marked for current period third quarter forecasts, for which the time correlation coefficient is 0.90, again significant at the one per cent level; correlations for the other three quarters are all positive but not significant. Accuracy has declined little in spite of, or because of, increased non-systematic error: U^C and time are significantly correlated, also at the one per cent level, with a coefficient of 0.53. Of the individual quarters, the correlation with time is 0.88 for the first quarter, significant at the five per cent level, positive but insignificant for the third and fourth quarters, and negative and insignificant for the second quarter. If the observations are split into two equal sub-periods, 1965(i)-1967(iv) and 1968(i)-1970(iv), the mean values of U, U^* and U^C are 0.84, 1.01 and 0.38 respectively for the earlier period, and 1.25, 1.87 and 0.69 for the last three years. All relevant differences are significant at the five per cent level. None of the above criteria record any comparable deterioration or, for that matter, improvement in $P2$ accuracy, nor is there any significant inter-temporal change in the $P2$ proportion of total systematic error, although the cross-section correlation between P and A for both sets of forecasts tends to be negative more frequently in the last two years of the study. Neither has the accuracy of naïve forecasting significantly varied with time.

Fiscal and credit measures introduced after the spring Budget may be expected to impair the accuracy of other forecasts published in May, particularly forecasts of income and expenditure, for these are the aggregates against which policy changes are often most immediately directed. $P2$ forecasts for the more distant fourth and first quarters should be most vulnerable on this score. Despite this our results have indicated that the $P2$ forecasts do not deteriorate over the year (recall that the least accurately forecast quarter is the third). Post-budget policy measures, including the voluntary price and wage freeze of July 1966 to June 1967, may have contributed to artifically high values of U and low values of U^C for the following quarters: 1965(iii), (iv); 1966(i), (iii), (iv); 1967(i), (iii), (iv); 1968(i); 1969(i). Mean $P2$ U and mean $P2$ U^C for these quarters are 1.08 and 0.40, against corresponding values of 0.97 and 0.61 for the remaining sixteen quarters. The difference in U is not significant, but there does appear to be more systematic error, mainly due to misforecasting the variance of outcomes, in the quarters of post-forecast policy changes: the difference in mean U^C is significant at the five per cent level.

This may well reflect the differential impact of policy on the income and expenditure variables.

4. Personal income and expenditure: underestimation, overestimation and turning-point errors

The previous two sections have reported our quantitative analysis of the income and expenditure forecasts. We now offer a qualitative assessment: are the directions (signs) of actual changes correctly predicted and, if so, are actual changes underestimated or overestimated by the forecasters?

From Tables 6.7 and 6.8 we see that both sets of predictions, like the NIESR quarterly and annual gross domestic product forecasts, typically underestimate outcomes. This conservative propensity, which is rather more marked in the May series, is apparent for all positive or negative changes, except for *P*1 forecasts of the income effects of credit restrictions, reductions in forces' pay and disposable funds, and *P*2 forecast falls in net contributions. Recall also that the means and variances of actual changes are usually underpredicted. However, when $|(P_t - A_t)/A_t|$, the proportionate error, is correlated with $|A_t|$ for all pairs of observations (excluding the non-percentage change data) the result is a coefficient of -0.10 which is not significant at the five per cent level. When errors and outcomes are transformed into logarithms the correlation coefficient is -0.21 which is significant at the five per cent level. Thus we observe a diminishing marginal rate of error reduction as the value of the outcomes increases just as we did with the GDP and components forecasts. This overall nonlinear correlation between error and outcome comprises a negative linear correlation for small and relatively imperceptible changes together with a weaker positive linear correlation as the actual change increases and the forecasters revert to underestimating the size of outcomes. For *P*1, with $|A_t| \leqslant 1.5$, the correlation is -0.46 and with $|A_t| \geqslant 1.5$ the correlation is 0.22; both correlations are significant at the five per cent level. For *P*2 the correlation coefficients are -0.45 for $|A_t| \leq 1.0$ and 0.18 for larger outcomes; again both correlation coefficients are significant at the five per cent level. The forecasters are most successful at predicting outcomes in the range one to one and a half per cent; actual deviations beyond the threshold of this band are forecast with increasing error. This is a special case of the phenomena we have already observed, conservative underprediction of the variation in actual changes.

Between one-fifth and one-sixth of all forecasts miss the direction of the corresponding actual change and thus commit a turning-point error (column 9 of Tables 6.7 and 6.8). The proportion is higher, twenty-eight per cent on average for both sets of forecasts, for the more oscillatory real series: savings, the savings ratio, consumers' expenditure, real disposable personal income and employment. Overestimation of turning-points, misforecasting an actual downturn or predicting a false upturn, is much more marked in May than in the current period forecasts. The *P*1 series seem to overcorrect this bias, for fewer turning-points are overestimated at the cost of a virtual doubling in the number of unanticipated troughs or spuriously predicted peaks (columns 10 and 11 of the tables). Columns 14 and 16 respectively of Tables 6.7 and 6.8 give the number and the proportion (E_1) of actual turning-points misforecast; columns 13 and 17 give the number and proportion (E_2) of predicted turning-points that prove false. Thirty-five per cent of all actual turning-points were not predicted by both sets of NIESR forecasts; twenty-nine per cent of *P*1 predicted turning-points and thirty-two per cent of those predicted by *P*2 were spurious. For *P*1, at least half of the turning-points in employment, current grants, other personal income, taxes and personal disposable income are missed. E_1 is 0.73 for *P*1 savings forecasts. On the other hand all turning-points in disposable funds, the consumers' price index and, most notably, the credit effect are correctly predicted. The highest proportions of spurious *P*1 turning-points are recorded for average earnings, taxes and disposable funds, though the total number of type 2 errors in these series is small. $E2$ is zero for *P*1 forecasts of wage rates, wages and salaries, current grants, personal disposable income and the consumers' price index. $E_1 \geq E_2$ for all income and expenditure variables except average earnings, forces' pay, net contributions, taxes, the credit effect and disposable funds. No turning-point errors are made in *P*2 forecasts of average earnings; otherwise the position is the same for the May series. The chained forecasts are marginally more successful than the current period forecasts in predicting turning-points in forces' pay, other personal income, taxes, real disposable personal income and savings: worse forecast by *P*2 are turning-points in the consumers' price index, wages and salaries, net contributions, the credit effect, consumers' expenditure and the savings ratio. Forecasts of the latter four variables plus forces' pay are also subject to more spurious turning-points when predicted earlier in the year.

Our qualitative analysis of the income and expenditure forecasts concludes with an inspection of their success at timing fluctuations. Table 6.9 classifies forty-eight actual fluctuations, each of which comprises a downturn (peak) and an upturn (trough), according to the Institute's predictive performance in dating them. Peaks and troughs may be forecast to occur at the correct date, too early (lead), too late (lag) or

Table 6.7

Underestimation, overestimation and turning-point errors: NIESR personal income and expenditure $P1$ forecasts 1965(i)-1970(iv)

	Positive change			Negative change			Turning-point errors	Total no. of observations	E
	Under-estimation	Over-estimation	$P_t = A_t$	Under-estimation	Over-estimation	$P_t = A_t$			
	(1)	(2)	(3)	(4)	(5)	(6)	(7)	(8)	(9)
Hourly wage-rates index[a]	11	4	1	0	0	0	0	16	0.00
Average earnings	15	5	3	0	0	0	1	24	0.04
Employment	3	0	2	7	4	1	7	24	0.29
Wages and salaries	16	7	0	1	0	0	0	24	0.00
Forces' pay	10	2	3	2	2	0	5	24	0.21
Current grants	15	7	0	0	0	0	2	24	0.08
Other personal income	12	3	0	2	0	0	7	24	0.29
Net contributions[b]	10	0	1	3	2	1	7	24	0.29
Taxes	10	9	0	2	0	0	3	24	0.13
Net transfers abroad[bc]	5	0	1	6	0	0	3	15	0.20
Personal disposable income	16	5	2	0	0	0	1	24	0.04
Credit effect[b]	5	2	0	4	7	0	6	24	0.25
Disposable funds[a]	10	3	0	1	1	0	1	16	0.06
Consumers' price index	12	9	2	1	0	0	0	24	0.00
Real disposable personal income	8	5	1	4	1	0	5	24	0.21
Consumers' expenditure	8	3	1	5	1	0	6	24	0.25
Savings	5	2	0	5	2	0	10	24	0.42
Savings ratio[b]	7	1	1	6	3	0	6	24	0.25
Total	178	67	18	49	23	2	70	407	0.17

Table 6.7 (continued)

	Underestimation of turning-point errors	Overestimation of turning-point errors	A_t no turning-point		A_t turning-point		E_1	E_2
			P_t no turning-point	P_t turning-point	P_t no turning-point	P_t turning-point		
	(10)	(11)	(12)	(13)	(14)	(15)	(16)	(17)
Hourly wage-rates index [a]	0	0	16	0	0	0	0.00	0.00
Average earnings	1	0	23	1	0	0	0.00	1.00
Employment	2	5	13	2	5	4	0.56	0.33
Wages and salaries	0	0	22	0	0	2	0.00	0.00
Forces' pay	0	5	12	3	2	7	0.22	0.30
Current grants	0	2	20	0	2	2	0.50	0.00
Other personal income	2	5	11	1	6	6	0.50	0.14
Net contributions [b]	3	4	9	5	2	8	0.20	0.38
Taxes	3	0	20	2	1	1	0.50	0.67
Net transfers abroad [b,c]	2	1	3	1	2	9	0.18	0.10
Personal disposable income	0	1	22	0	1	1	0.50	0.00
Credit effect [b]	2	4	10	6	0	8	0.00	0.43
Disposable funds [a]	1	0	13	1	0	2	0.00	0.50
Consumers' price index	0	0	22	0	0	2	0.00	0.00
Real disposable personal income	4	1	13	2	3	6	0.33	0.25
Consumers' expenditure	5	1	11	3	3	7	0.30	0.30
Savings	5	5	11	2	8	3	0.73	0.40
Savings ratio [b]	3	3	13	2	4	5	0.44	0.40
Total	33	37	264	31	39	73	0.35	0.29

a 1965(i)-1968(iv).
b Absolute changes are used throughout, i.e. $p_t - a_{t-1}$ and $a_t - a_{t-1}$.
c 1967(ii)-1970(iv).

Table 6.8

Underestimation, overestimation and turning-point errors: NIESR personal income and expenditure *P*2 forecasts 1965(i)-1970(iv)

	Positive change			Negative change			Turning-point errors	Total no. of observations	E
	Under-estimation (1)	Over-estimation (2)	$P_t = A_t$ (3)	Under-estimation (4)	Over-estimation (5)	$P_t = A_t$ (6)	(7)	(8)	(9)
Hourly wage-rates index[a]	9	6	1	0	0	0	0	16	0.00
Average earnings	14	7	3	0	0	0	0	24	0.00
Employment	3	1	2	8	4	1	5	24	0.21
Wages and salaries	16	7	0	0	0	0	1	24	0.04
Forces' pay	9	1	2	4	1	0	7	24	0.29
Current grants	18	4	0	0	0	0	2	24	0.08
Other personal income	14	3	0	2	0	0	5	24	0.21
Net contributions[b]	11	0	1	2	2	1	7	24	0.29
Taxes	14	7	0	2	0	0	1	24	0.04
Net transfers abroad[b c]	7	1	0	5	0	0	2	15	0.13
Personal disposable income	16	7	0	0	0	0	1	24	0.04
Credit effect[b]	8	0	0	3	2	0	11	24	0.46
Disposable funds[a]	9	4	0	1	0	0	2	16	0.13
Consumers' price index	16	6	1	0	0	0	1	24	0.04
Real disposable personal income	12	4	1	3	1	0	3	24	0.13
Consumers' expenditure	11	3	0	2	1	0	7	24	0.29
Savings	7	3	0	4	1	0	9	24	0.38
Savings ratio[b]	8	1	1	2	1	1	10	24	0.42
Total	202	65	12	38	13	3	74	407	0.18

Table 6.8 (continued)

	Underestimation of turning-point errors	Overestimation of turning-point errors	A_t no turning-point		A_t turning-point		E_1	E_2
			P_t no turning-point	P_t turning-point	P_t no turning-point	P_t turning-point		
	(10)	(11)	(12)	(13)	(14)	(15)	(16)	(17)
Hourly wage-rates index[a]	0	0	16	0	0	0	0.00	0.00
Average earnings	0	0	24	0	0	0	0.00	0.00
Employment	1	4	15	0	5	4	0.56	0.00
Wages and salaries	0	1	22	0	1	1	0.50	0.00
Forces' pay	3	4	9	6	1	8	0.11	0.43
Current grants	0	2	20	0	2	2	0.50	0.00
Other personal income	0	5	12	0	5	7	0.42	0.00
Net contributions[b]	2	5	10	5	2	7	0.22	0.42
Taxes	1	0	21	1	0	2	0.00	0.33
Net transfers abroad[bc]	0	2	4	0	2	9	0.18	0.00
Personal disposable inccme	0	1	22	0	1	1	0.50	0.00
Credit effect[b]	1	10	8	8	3	5	0.38	0.62
Disposable funds[a]	1	1	12	2	0	2	0.00	0.50
Consumers' price index	0	1	22	0	1	1	0.50	0.00
Real disposable personal income	1	2	14	1	2	7	0.22	0.13
Consumers' expenditure	3	4	11	3	4	6	0.40	0.33
Savings	2	7	9	4	5	6	0.46	0.40
Savings ratio[b]	2	8	9	5	5	5	0.50	0.50
Total	17	57	260	35	39	73	0.35	0.32

a 1965(i)-1968(iv).

b Absolute changes are used throughout, i.e. $p_t - a_{t-1}$, $p_t - p_{t-1}$ and $a_t - a_{t-1}$.

c 1967(ii)-1970(iv).

Table 6.9

Dating of fluctuations: NIESR *P*1 and *P*2 forecasts of personal income and expenditure 1965(i)-1970(iv)

	*P*1							
	Downturns				Upturns			
	Not forecast	Date correct	Lead	Lag	Not forecast	Date correct	Lead	Lag
Hourly wage-rates index [a]								
Average earnings								
Employment	2	1	0	1	2	0	1	1
Wages and salaries	0	1	0	0	0	1	0	0
Forces' pay	1	3	0	0	0	2	2	0
Current grants	1	0	0	0	0	0	0	1
Other personal income	4	1	0	0	2	0	0	3
Net contributions [b]	0	2	2	1	0	1	3	1
Taxes	0	1	0	0	0	0	0	1
Net transfers abroad [bc]	1	2	0	1	1	3	0	0
Personal disposable income	1	0	0	0	0	1	0	0
Credit effect [b]	0	1	2	0	0	1	2	0
Disposable funds [a]	0	1	0	0	0	1	0	0
Consumers' price index	0	1	0	0	0	1	0	0
Real disposable personal income	1	2	1	0	1	2	0	1
Consumers' expenditure	2	2	1	0	2	1	1	1
Savings	0	0	3	1	0	1	3	0
Savings ratio [b]	0	1	0	3	0	3	0	1
Quarter (i)	5	3	1	1	3	4	2	0
(ii)	5	9	4	3	3	4	3	2
(iii)	0	2	2	3	1	7	3	4
(iv)	3	5	2	0	1	3	4	4
Column totals	13	19	9	7	8	18	12	10
Column total as a proportion of total fluctuations	0.27	0.40	0.19	0.15	0.17	0.38	0.25	0.21
Column totals for 23 cycles	1	13	4	5	1	11	8	3

a 1965(i)-1968(iv).

b Absolute changes are used throughout, i.e. $p_t - a_{t-1}$, $p_t - p_{t-1}$ and $a_t - a_{t-1}$.

c 1967(ii)-1970(iv).

Table 6.9 (continued)

P2								Total number of downturns	Total number of upturns
Downturns				Upturns					
Not forecast	Date correct	Lead	Lag	Not forecast	Date correct	Lead	Lag		
								0	0
								0	0
2	0	0	2	3	1	0	0	4	4
1	0	0	0	1	0	0	0	1	1
1	3	0	0	0	2	2	0	4	4
1	0	0	0	1	0	0	0	1	1
4	1	0	0	4	1	0	0	5	5
1	2	1	1	1	1	2	1	5	5
0	1	0	0	0	1	0	0	1	1
1	2	0	1	1	3	0	0	4	4
1	0	0	0	1	0	0	0	1	1
1	0	1	1	1	1	1	0	3	3
0	1	0	0	0	0	1	0	1	1
1	0	0	0	0	1	0	0	1	1
1	3	0	0	1	1	1	1	4	4
1	3	0	1	1	1	1	2	5	5
1	0	0	3	1	1	0	2	4	4
3	0	0	1	2	2	0	0	4	4
6	0	0	4	5	2	2	0	10	9
5	12	1	3	5	4	1	2	21	12
4	0	1	2	4	7	2	2	7	15
5	4	0	1	4	3	3	2	10	12
20	16	2	10	18	16	8	6	48	48
0.42	0.33	0.04	0.21	0.38	0.33	0.17	0.13		
5	10	1	7	4	9	9	1	23	23

not at all. In our classification, we pay particular attention to the sequence of the signs of corresponding predictions and outcomes. This approach is stricter than the observation-by-observation analysis reported in Tables 6.7 and 6.8, inasmuch as a prediction and outcome with the same sign, which formerly did not constitute a turning-point error, might now do so if it was clear that the forecasters were unaware that the actual timepath had changed direction from the previous quarter. In another respect it is more lenient than our earlier turning-point evaluation: it admits that some of the turning-point errors may be mistimed rather than ignored altogether.

Of a total of forty-eight downturns, *P*1 forecasts nineteen correctly, nine at least one quarter early (lead), seven at least one quarter late (lag), and thirteen downturns are missed altogether. The *P*2 chained forecasts are rather less successful: twenty downturns are not forecast at all, one-third are correctly dated, there are fewer leads and more lags. *P*2 also correctly dates a third of the forty-eight upturns; rather fewer upturns are not forecast or forecast with a lag; rather more are forecast to occur too early. Current period forecasts of upturns are similar, except that over half the upturns not forecast at all in May are now predicted but misdated; leads and lags occur with approximately equal frequency. It does appear that the earlier E_1 values are rather too lenient for most *P*2 income components and for *P*1 forecasts of forces' pay, other personal income, net transfers abroad and consumers' expenditure and too harsh for *P*2 forecasts of consumption and savings, *P*1 forecasts of employment, current grants, taxes, real disposable personal income, savings and the savings ratio and both *P*1 and *P*2 forecasts of net contributions. *P*1 never completely ignores fluctuations in net contributions, the credit effect, savings and the savings ratio; on the other hand no peaks in savings and no troughs in employment and other personal income are correctly dated in the current period. The May forecasts never miss upturns in forces' pay, yet nor do they ever correctly date downturns in employment, the credit effect and the two savings variables.

The cross-sectional analysis reveals that downturns in income and expenditure are markedly bunched in the second quarter of each year, with upturns consequently tending to follow one quarter later, although the distribution of troughs throughout the year is more even. Turning-points presumably being more difficult to forecast than continued growth or decline, this bunching of fluctuations in the second and third quarters suggests one reason why the accuracy of the chained *P*2 forecasts is at least as good for the distant fourth and first quarters as it is for the six months following publication. Those fluctuations that do occur in the first quarter are poorly timed from May. $P2$ and $P1$ dating of upturns are remarkably similar; when they differ, the $P1$ series detect, but typically do not correctly date, a trough which the earlier forecasts had ignored. Downturns in the first and fourth quarters respectively are worst and best timed by $P1$. No current period third quarter peaks are misforecast altogether although few are accurately dated.

In the final row of Table 6.9 we enumerate the Institute's timing of the twenty-three most substantial fluctuations, all of which persisted for at least two quarters. Dating them from peak to trough, they are employment 1966(iii)-1968(iii), 1969(i)-1970(i); forces' pay 1966(iv)-1967(iii), 1968(iv)-1969(iii); other personal income 1966(ii)-(iv); net contributions 1965(ii)-(iv), 1967(iv)-1968(ii), 1969(iv)-1970(iv); taxes 1966(ii)-(iv); net transfers abroad 1969(i)-(iii), 1969(iv)-1970(ii); credit effect 1966(ii)-1967(i), 1968(i)-(iii), 1968(iv)-1970(i); disposable funds 1966(ii)-(iv); real disposable personal income 1966(ii)-1967(i); consumers' expenditure 1966(ii)-1967(i); savings 1966(ii)-1967(i), 1967(iv)-1968(ii), 1969(ii)-(iv); savings ratio 1966(ii)-1967(i), 1967(iii)-1968(ii), 1969(ii)-(iv). Both sets of forecasts predict these cycles much better than the short fluctuations; only one peak and one trough are missed altogether by $P1$. When errors of timing are committed the tendency, most marked in the chained forecasts, is for the onset of recessions to be postdated and their duration to be underestimated.

5. Gross fixed investment: time series analysis

We turn to an examination of the National Institute's forecasts of gross fixed investment. The time series inequality coefficients for the current period ($P1$), May ($P2$) forecasts and the naïve models are presented in Table 6.10. The picture is depressing: all the coefficients for the $P1$ and $P2$ forecasts are high. The only investment series that are better forecast by the National Institute than by a no-change assumption are manufacturing for both $P1$ and $P2$ (with inequality coefficients of 0.97 and 0.94 respectively) and mainly public industries and services for $P2$ ($U = 0.93$). The series worst forecast are, by $P1$, total investment in dwellings ($U = 1.14$) and, by $P2$, private dwellings investment ($U = 1.10$). Private industrial investment is forecast better than dwellings but only marginally so. Fees are forecast as a constant between quarters, thus $U = 1$. Errors in the components accumulate for $P1$ which is not the case for $P2$. Only for industrial investment other than manufacturing are the May forecasts inferior to the current period forecasts. The mean inequality

Table 6.10

Inequality coefficients for NIESR gross fixed investment $P1$ and $P2$ forecasts and naïve models: time series 1965(i)-1970(iv)

	$P1$	$P2$	A_{t-1}	A_{t-4}	4-quarter moving average	$\bar{A}$
Dwellings:						
Public	1.03	1.03	1.50	1.26	1.06	0.99
Private	1.13	1.10	1.32	1.51	1.12	0.96
Total	1.14	1.08	1.47	1.35	1.09	1.00
Mainly private industries:						
Manufacturing	0.97	0.94	1.55	1.36	1.08	0.96
Other	1.00	1.04	1.67	1.54	1.13	0.99
Total	1.02	1.01	1.58	1.44	1.10	0.97
Mainly public industries and services	1.07	0.93	1.20	1.34	1.01	0.97
Fees	1.00	1.00	1.66	1.54	1.10	0.98
Total	1.09	1.03	1.63	1.40	1.11	0.97

coefficient for $P2$ is 1.02; that for $P1$ is 1.08 and this difference is significant at the five per cent level.

Both the $P1$ and $P2$ forecasts are outperformed by the no-change model and by the $\bar{A}$ model (which has mean U of 0.98) to an extent that is significant at the five per cent level. The A_{t-1} and A_{t-4} naïve models do not perform well but the four-quarter moving average model returns lower inequality coefficients than $P1$ for private and total dwellings and for public sector non-dwelling investment.

Tables 6.11 and 6.12 show the results of inequality and regression analysis in more detail. Less systematic error is evident in the $P1$ forecasts than in the $P2$ forecasts: the random U^C proportion of mean-square error is twenty per cent higher on average for current period investment forecasts, which is significant at the five per cent level. This is mainly due to improved forecasting of the variance of changes in the current period ($P1$ and $P2$ means for U^S are twenty-seven per cent and forty-five per cent respectively), in particular with respect to the forecasts of non-manufacturing private industrial investment and investment by public industries and services. The frequent sharp fluctuations of most investment series are markedly underestimated. All in all the only forecasts which emerge with any credit are those for private manufacturing investment which at least are superior to no-change predictions and for which error is almost entirely non-systematic.

Table 6.11

Accuracy analysis of NIESR gross fixed investment $P1$ forecasts: time series 1965(i)-1970(iv)

	U	U^M	U^S	U^C	r	α	β	SE (α)	SE (β)	$\bar{P}$	$\bar{A}$	s_P/s_A
Dwellings:												
Public	1.03	0.01	0.39	0.60	0.08	0.38	0.23	1.28	0.60	1.09	0.63	0.35
Private	1.13	0.28	0.18	0.54	0.24	−1.79	0.49	0.98	0.42	1.29	−1.17	0.49
Total	1.14	0.12	0.35	0.53	−0.05	−0.21	−0.15	1.07	0.65	1.12	−0.37	0.33
Mainly private industries												
Manufacturing	0.97	0.01	0.05	0.95	0.38	0.58	0.40	0.78	0.26	0.95	1.05	0.95
Other	1.00	0.05	0.33	0.62	0.24	1.22	0.58	1.24	0.50	−0.32	1.03	0.41
Total	1.02	0.05	0.15	0.80	0.25	0.96	0.43	0.80	0.35	0.08	1.00	0.58
Mainly public industries and services	1.07	0.08	0.17	0.75	0.16	0.25	0.30	0.87	0.39	1.65	0.75	0.53
Fees	1.00	0.04	0.50	0.46	0.13	1.47	0.47	1.56	0.76	0.00	1.47	0.28
Total	1.09	0.01	0.29	0.70	−0.12	0.90	−0.32	0.73	0.54	0.90	0.62	0.38

Table 6.12

Accuracy analysis of NIESR gross fixed investment *P*2 forecasts: time series 1965(i)-1970(iv)

	U	U^M	U^S	U^C	r	α	β	SE (α)	SE (β)	$\bar{P}$	$\bar{A}$	s_P/s_A
Dwellings:												
Public	1.03	0.00	0.44	0.56	0.02	0.57	0.07	1.26	0.69	0.88	0.63	0.29
Private	1.10	0.36	0.27	0.37	0.38	−2.66	0.96	1.09	0.49	1.55	−1.17	0.40
Total	1.08	0.15	0.45	0.40	0.14	−0.96	0.51	1.20	0.78	1.16	−0.37	0.27
Mainly private industries:												
Manufacturing	0.94	0.00	0.07	0.93	0.41	0.54	0.55	0.77	0.26	0.92	1.05	0.75
Other	1.04	0.04	0.53	0.43	0.00	1.03	−0.02	1.28	0.91	−0.25	1.03	0.25
Total	1.01	0.03	0.22	0.76	0.20	0.85	0.40	0.82	0.41	0.37	1.00	0.50
Mainly public industries and services	0.93	0.12	0.61	0.27	0.49	−2.64	2.00	1.38	0.75	1.69	0.75	0.26
Fees	1.00	0.04	0.96	0.00	– [a]	– [a]	– [a]	– [a]	– [a]	0.00	1.47	0.00
Total	1.03	0.02	0.52	0.46	−0.09	1.01	−0.40	1.04	0.90	0.98	0.62	0.23

a Regression impossible: $P_t = 0$ for all t.

Except for the high U^M statistics for both forecasts of private dwellings and, to a lesser extent for the forecasts of investment by public industries and services, bias is notably absent from the forecasts and, furthermore, tends to be self-cancelling in aggregation. It is interesting here that the tendency observed so far in the book, that mean actual changes are under-predicted, holds only for manufacturing and total industrial investment and for the rather trivial case of the fees forecasts. For the rest $|\bar{P}|$ is usually greater than $|\bar{A}|$ "even when $\bar{A}$ is negative" as it is with private dwellings and consequently with total dwellings. The upshot for these latter series is the relatively high bias proportion on which we have already remarked. Forecasts of other private industrial investment are unusual in that $\bar{P}$ is negative, $\bar{A}$ is positive and $|\bar{P}| < |\bar{A}|$. This is a consequence not so much of bias but rather of markedly underpredicting the variance of changes: one third of $P1$ error and one half of $P2$ error can be ascribed to this source. In this respect the results of time series investment analysis are similar to those of our cross-section analysis of personal income and expenditure. Several quite steep upturns were underestimated and three short fluctuations which occurred between the beginning of 1966 and the end of the following year were forecast as one prolonged recession.

Predictions and outcomes of total gross fixed investment and total dwellings are negatively correlated. Elsewhere the correlation coefficient is positive, if small, and while the constant term, α, in the regression of A_t on P_t is never significantly different from zero (at the five per cent level), which is encouraging, the same is usually true of the slope term, β, which is not.

6. Gross fixed investment: cross-section analysis

Table 6.13 summarises the cross-section analysis of the NIESR and naïve investment forecasts. The small volatile fees series is excluded from the calculations as are the sub-totals of dwellings and private industrial investment. With mean cross-section inequality values of 1.09 ($P1$) and 1.05 ($P2$) the Institute's forecasts are clearly superior to three of the naïve models, but comparisons with $\bar{A}$ and the no-change prediction are less favourable. $P1$ is less accurate at the ten per cent significance level than no change and both genuine forecasts are worse, at the one per cent significance level, than the most accurate naive forecast of each quarter. $P1$ is beaten by at least one naïve model on nineteen occasions, three more times than is $P2$. The variances of the cross-section inequality coeffi-

Table 6.13

Inequality coefficients for NIESR gross fixed investment $P1$ and $P2$ forecasts and naïve models: cross-section 1965(i)-1970(iv)

		$P1$	$P2$	A_{t-1}	A_{t-4}	4-quarter moving average	$\bar{A}$
1965	(i)	0.91	0.83	0.47	1.70	1.06	0.92
	(ii)	1.20	1.20	1.88	1.70	1.53	1.04
	(iii)	1.08	1.02	1.81	2.00	1.07	0.98
	(iv)	0.87	0.70	1.65	1.43	1.13	0.81
1966	(i)	1.07	1.16	1.61	1.00	0.99	1.03
	(ii)	0.46	0.46	2.08	1.70	1.12	1.04
	(iii)	1.18	1.07	1.06	1.39	0.72	0.79
	(iv)	0.79	0.76	1.08	1.20	0.85	0.97
1967	(i)	1.12	0.83	1.14	2.18	0.98	0.93
	(ii)	1.34	1.34	0.82	0.92	0.89	0.90
	(iii)	0.61	0.62	1.65	1.49	1.23	1.17
	(iv)	1.03	1.46	1.50	1.64	1.51	1.15
1968	(i)	0.87	1.02	1.34	0.86	1.00	0.95
	(ii)	1.69	1.69	4.68	2.93	1.93	1.30
	(iii)	1.01	1.06	1.17	2.07	1.14	0.86
	(iv)	0.96	0.68	1.02	1.48	0.78	0.90
1969	(i)	1.16	1.04	1.67	2.54	1.46	1.00
	(ii)	1.07	1.07	1.39	0.75	0.60	1.00
	(iii)	1.18	1.16	1.38	0.66	1.02	0.87
	(iv)	1.97	1.27	2.43	2.73	1.08	0.95
1970	(i)	1.02	1.02	0.83	0.75	0.94	1.05
	(ii)	0.95	0.95	1.92	1.16	1.22	0.93
	(iii)	0.96	0.99	2.84	2.22	1.53	1.25
	(iv)	1.59	1.78	2.56	1.44	1.20	0.97

cients, 0.32 and 0.31, are low in comparison with the statistics for personal income and expenditure, presumably reflecting the relative independence of these exogenous forecasts.

Current period forecasting yields cross-section inequality values greater than unity for fifteen quarters, in twelve of which the mean predicted and actual changes had opposite signs. The detailed results of Table 6.14 show the high bias associated with misforecasting the general direction of investment in these quarters: U^M is over seventy per cent in the second quarters of 1967 and 1968, and in the first quarter of 1970. In 1967(ii) the forecasters incorrectly predicted recession for all but investment by public

Table 6.14

Accuracy analysis of NIESR gross fixed investment $P1$ forecasts: cross-section 1965(i)-1970(iv)

	U	U^M	U^S	U^C	r	α	β	SE (α)	SE (β)	$\bar{P}$	$\bar{A}$	s_P/s_A
1965 (i)	0.91	0.03	0.82	0.15	0.49	−5.33	3.68	5.93	3.24	1.77	1.17	0.13
(ii)	1.20	0.37	0.37	0.26	0.06	−1.76	0.27	3.71	2.24	1.45	−1.37	0.22
(iii)	1.08	0.01	0.39	0.61	−0.08	0.26	−0.24	1.98	1.53	0.45	0.15	0.33
(iv)	0.87	0.06	0.41	0.54	−0.11	2.61	−0.35	2.69	1.68	1.38	2.12	0.31
1966 (i)	1.07	0.60	0.17	0.23	0.50	−3.26	1.14	1.49	0.98	0.78	−2.37	0.44
(ii)	0.46	0.39	0.31	0.31	0.93	0.53	1.34	0.44	0.26	0.70	1.47	0.69
(iii)	1.18	0.25	0.09	0.66	0.10	1.47	0.17	1.64	0.81	−0.65	1.37	0.59
(iv)	0.79	0.45	0.10	0.46	0.80	1.84	1.07	1.06	0.40	−1.02	0.75	0.75
1967 (i)	1.12	0.67	0.03	0.30	0.59	2.31	0.77	0.94	0.52	−0.77	1.72	0.77
(ii)	1.34	0.79	0.04	0.17	−0.78	4.34	−0.33	0.31	0.13	−1.00	4.67	2.36
(iii)	0.61	0.07	0.11	0.82	0.80	−0.72	1.02	1.30	0.38	0.25	−0.47	0.78
(iv)	1.03	0.32	0.05	0.63	0.56	−1.83	0.43	0.93	0.32	−0.20	−1.92	1.30
1968 (i)	0.87	0.50	0.36	0.15	0.56	4.10	2.17	2.81	1.60	0.88	6.02	0.26
(ii)	1.69	0.78	0.01	0.22	0.51	−2.23	0.58	1.24	0.50	1.98	−1.07	0.88
(iii)	1.01	0.39	0.47	0.14	0.76	−5.52	2.50	2.55	1.08	2.05	−0.40	0.30
(iv)	0.96	0.02	0.03	0.95	−0.08	3.78	−0.10	3.19	0.66	4.02	3.37	0.80
1969 (i)	1.16	0.42	0.18	0.40	−0.27	−2.68	−0.76	1.96	1.36	0.55	−3.10	**0.36**
(ii)	1.07	0.21	0.26	0.54	0.27	−1.44	0.61	2.10	1.09	1.02	−0.82	**0.44**
(iii)	1.18	0.01	0.33	0.66	−0.50	2.34	−1.60	2.44	1.37	1.07	0.63	**0.31**
(iv)	1.97	0.65	0.02	0.33	−0.17	−0.41	−0.24	1.71	0.69	2.17	−0.93	0.71
1970 (i)	1.02	0.73	0.25	0.02	0.92	−9.00	3.05	1.33	0.65	1.28	−5.08	0.30
(ii)	0.95	0.71	0.00	0.29	−0.04	6.25	−0.04	1.27	0.50	0.88	6.22	1.00
(iii)	0.96	0.58	0.07	0.35	0.74	−2.26	1.02	1.06	0.47	1.03	−1.20	0.73
(iv)	1.59	0.13	0.00	0.86	−0.12	0.70	−0.11	1.04	0.46	1.50	0.53	1.09

industries and services, and in the other two quarters the turning-point errors were in the opposite direction, missing downturns. Bias is also seventy-one per cent in the second quarter of 1970, although $\bar{P}$ and $\bar{A}$ are both positive: here the forecasters massively underestimated growth, especially in the non-manufacturing, industrial sectors. Turning-point errors are primarily responsible for the thirty-eight per cent bias proportion of total mean-square error averaged across all investment series, much larger than the corresponding figure for personal income and expenditure. Forecasts of those quarters for which $\bar{P}$ and $\bar{A}$ have the same sign are evenly divided between those which under- and over-predict the mean outcome. The variance of changes is underestimated in cross-sections in the usual way. At twenty per cent on average, the cross-section variance proportion, U^S, is lower than for personal income and expenditure forecasts. Although over time the forecasters' skills are tested by frequent fluctuations in investment, for any one quarter the different series tend to move together, thus making the lower, cross-sectional spread of changes rather easier to predict. *In toto*, over half the cross-section error is systematic, and while accuracy does not vary significantly between quarters, either absolutely or relatively to naïve prediction, the systematic proportion of mean-square error does. Systematic error, measured by $U^M + U^S$, averages seventy-nine per cent in the first quarter of each year, seventy per cent in the second, forty-six in the third and thirty-seven per cent in the fourth. At the five per cent level there is significantly more bias and variance error in the first half-year than in the last six months' forecasts.

Averaged over the *P*2 cross-section results, given in Table 6.15, bias error accounts for thirty-three per cent and variance error accounts for twenty-seven per cent of the mean-square error. Turning-point errors, and their associated high bias, are primarily responsible for the majority of the fifteen inequality coefficients which are greater than unity, though in some of these instances the forecasters also substantially underpredict the spread of the positive and negative outcomes. There are no significant inter-quarter differences in the accuracy of the May forecasts: the mean U values for quarters one to four are 0.98, 1.12, 0.99 and 1.11. This conclusion also holds when the *P*2 results are compared with the best naïve predictions (U^* = 1.24, 1.30, 1.19, 1.21 for the four quarters in calendar order). Systematic error however is not invariant with the quarter-year, but neither does it increase with the forecasting span. U^C is lowest in the first quarter and the (current period) second quarter with average U^C values of 0.33 and 0.30 respectively. The second quarter figure is significantly lower, at the five per cent significance level, than that for the fourth quarter (0.55) and at the ten per cent level than that for the third

Table 6.15

Accuracy analysis of NIESR gross fixed investment $P2$ forecasts: cross-section 1965(i)-1970(iv)

	U	U^M	U^S	U^C	r	α	β	SE (α)	SE (β)	$\bar{P}$	$\bar{A}$	s_P/s_A
1965 (i)	0.83	0.01	0.43	0.56	0.49	–0.46	1.16	2.13	1.02	1.40	1.17	0.42
(ii)	1.20	0.37	0.37	0.26	0.06	–1.76	0.27	3.71	2.24	1.45	–1.37	0.22
(iii)	1.02	0.12	0.64	0.24	0.34	–2.54	1.81	4.13	2.52	1.48	0.15	0.19
(iv)	0.70	0.19	0.70	0.11	0.84	–1.32	3.22	1.34	1.05	1.07	2.12	0.26
1966 (i)	1.16	0.56	0.27	0.17	0.21	–3.16	0.87	2.38	2.06	0.92	–2.37	0.24
(ii)	0.46	0.39	0.31	0.31	0.93	0.53	1.34	0.44	0.26	0.70	1.47	0.69
(iii)	1.07	0.04	0.17	0.78	–0.04	1.42	–0.08	1.67	0.97	0.62	1.37	0.50
(iv)	0.76	0.01	0.50	0.50	0.67	–0.06	1.48	1.29	0.82	0.55	0.75	0.45
1967 (i)	0.83	0.28	0.08	0.64	0.47	1.37	0.67	0.98	0.63	0.52	1.72	0.70
(ii)	1.34	0.79	0.04	0.17	–0.78	4.34	–0.33	0.31	0.13	–1.00	4.67	2.36
(iii)	0.62	0.11	0.48	0.41	0.86	–1.13	1.52	1.12	0.45	0.43	–0.47	0.57
(iv)	1.46	0.38	0.02	0.60	0.12	–1.99	0.10	1.14	0.39	0.72	–1.92	1.20
1968 (i)	1.02	0.37	0.25	0.39	–0.49	7.50	–1.74	2.89	1.57	0.85	6.02	0.28
(ii)	1.69	0.78	0.01	0.22	0.51	–2.23	0.58	1.24	0.50	1.98	–1.07	0.88
(iii)	1.06	0.38	0.36	0.26	0.58	–3.88	1.63	2.88	1.13	2.13	–0.40	0.36
(iv)	0.68	0.09	0.27	0.65	0.47	1.23	0.89	2.58	0.85	2.40	3.37	0.53
1969 (i)	1.04	0.59	0.25	0.16	0.56	–4.41	1.68	1.85	1.26	0.78	–3.10	0.33
(ii)	1.07	0.21	0.26	0.54	0.27	–1.44	0.61	2.10	1.09	1.02	–0.82	0.44
(iii)	1.16	0.00	0.37	0.63	–0.50	1.80	–1.75	2.20	1.51	0.67	0.63	0.29
(iv)	1.27	0.37	0.11	0.52	–0.05	–0.88	–0.10	1.01	0.96	0.57	–0.93	0.50
1970 (i)	1.02	0.58	0.39	0.04	0.71	–8.33	5.73	2.49	2.88	0.57	–5.08	0.12
(ii)	0.95	0.71	0.00	0.29	–0.04	6.25	–0.04	1.27	0.50	0.88	6.22	1.00
(iii)	0.99	0.60	0.08	0.32	0.73	–2.40	1.06	1.11	0.50	1.13	–1.20	0.69
(iv)	1.78	0.06	0.00	0.94	–0.61	1.28	–0.59	0.79	0.39	1.27	0.53	1.03

quarter (0.44). Also first quarter forecasts are more subject to systematic error than fourth quarter forecasts at the ten per cent significance level.

The effects of post-forecast policy changes on May predictive accuracy is slight and not particularly detrimental. The average value of the inequality coefficient falls (from 1.10 to 0.95) as does the random U^C proportion (from 0.42 to 0.37) when the results for those quarters 'clean' of unexpected policy influences are compared with those potentially affected, but neither the reduction in total error nor the increase in systematic error are statistically significant.[13] Nor is there any evidence that policy changes worsen the May forecasts relative to the accuracy obtained from current period forecasting: again, relative accuracy and relative systematic error are both very marginally higher for the policy quarters.

It only remains to inspect the NIESR investment forecasts to see how, if at all, their accuracy has changed with time. On the whole the results are negative. Correlations of the $P1$ and $P2$ cross-section inequality and U^C statistic with time are positive but non-significant over all observations. Similar analysis for the naïve forecasts shows no change in the intrinsic difficulty of forecasting over our period, nor has the accuracy of the NIESR forecasts improved or worsened in comparison with the naïve performance. For the individual quarters only the time correlation for fourth quarter values produce results of any interest. $P1$ forecasting accuracy for the fourth quarter has deteriorated: the correlation between U and time is 0.80, significant at the five per cent level. $P2$ systematic error in fourth quarter forecasts has been reduced: the correlation between random U^C and time is 0.85, significant at two-and-a-half per cent. Although there has been no trend as such, the investment forecasts made in the last half of the sample period are less accurate than the earlier predictions: for 1965(i)-1967(iv) the inequality coefficient averages 0.97 for $P1$ and 0.95 for $P2$; the corresponding means for 1968(i)-1970(iv) are 1.20 and 1.14 and the differences are significant at the five and ten per cent levels respectively. Similar calculations using mean values of U^*, the ratio of the actual $P1$ or $P2$ inequality coefficient to that of the best naïve forecast of each quarter, confirm this result.

7. Gross fixed investment: underestimation, overestimation and turning-point errors

Tables 6.16 and 6.17 report the results of observation-by-observation analysis of the investment forecasts. The fees variable, usually predicted as no change, is omitted from this classification. Even though mean actual changes are not consistently underestimated, the tables show a clear majority of positive and negative outcomes to be under-predicted by both sets of forecasts. Moreover the correlation of proportionate error, $|(P_t - A_t)/A_t|$ with magnitude of outcome, $|A_t|$, for all pairs of observations excluding fees and excluding turning-point errors confirms the forecasters' conservatism. Error and outcome are negatively correlated over all $|A_t|$: the $P1$ correlation coefficients are -0.22 for linear correlation, and -0.25 for the logarithmic transformation, both of which are significant at the five per cent level, while the $P2$ coefficients are negative but insignificant. For subsamples selected according to outcome size, the percentage prediction error increases around a threshold for smaller and larger outcomes. With $|A_t| \leq 2.0$ the linear correlations between error and outcome are -0.56 ($P1$) and -0.47 ($P2$); for $|A_t| \geq 2.0$ the $P1$ and $P2$ correlation coefficients are 0.42 and 0.34 respectively. These results are significant at at least the one per cent level.

Almost half the forecasts wrongly predict the sign of the outcome, on which count the chained forecasts are only marginally worse. The frequency of these turning-point errors is lowest for forecast private manufacturing investment (no more than a quarter), and worst for $P1$ forecasts of private dwellings, $P2$ forecasts of other private investment, and both forecasts of total dwellings and total gross fixed investment, for all of which at least fifty per cent of the forecast changes are in the wrong direction. Turning-point errors tend to accumulate in the sub-totals, particularly for dwellings. Three-quarters of the turning-point errors are overestimated, and sixty per cent of them represent wrongly forecast actual fluctuations (rather than spurious, predicted fluctuations), so the typical investment turning-point error occurs when the forecasters fail to predict a downturn. Failure to predict actual turning-points is not too surprising when over half the outcome data describe fluctuations, and indeed this is the most common type of turning-point error. E_1, the proportion of actual turning-points not correctly forecast, averages just under fifty per cent; sixty-four per cent of the turning-points in public dwelling are not forecast by $P1$. There are rather fewer Type 2 turning-point errors, i.e. predictions of spurious turning-points. None at all are committed by either forecast of private manufacturing investment, and other private manufacturing investment is also relatively trouble-free on this score.

The Institute's success in dating forty-six fluctuations in investment is recorded in Table 6.18. Downturns are badly timed both from May and in the current period: approximately three quarters ($P2$) and two thirds ($P1$) are not forecast at all. Very few of the remainder are correctly dated: they are just as likely to be forecast with a lead or lag. Current period forecasts of peaks in private dwellings investment are rather better than most, in as much as only one of the five downturns is missed altogether. On the other hand, no downturn in total gross fixed investment is ever correctly predicted. Upturns are more accurately dated, at least in the current period. Seventeen are not forecast at all, fourteen correctly dated and the remaining fifteen are fairly evenly split between the lead and lag dating errors.

Table 6.16

Underestimation, overestimation and turning-point errors: NIESR gross fixed investment $P1$ forecasts 1965(i)-1970(iv)

	Positive change		
	Under-estimation (1)	Over-estimation (2)	$P_t = A_t$ (3)
Dwellings:			
Public	6	3	1
Private	5	2	0
Total	5	3	1
Mainly private industries:			
Manufacturing	6	7	1
Other	8	1	0
Total	6	3	0
Mainly public industries and services	11	3	0
Total	5	3	0
Total	52	25	3

	Underestimation of turning-point errors (10)	Overestimation of turning-point errors (11)
Dwellings:		
Public	3	8
Private	3	9
Total	2	12
Mainly private industries		
Manufacturing	2	2
Other	4	5
Total	4	6
Mainly public industries and services	0	8
Total	3	10
Total	21	60

Half the eight troughs in total investment are correctly dated and another two are mistimed. *P*2 forecasts only sixteen upturns, of which six are correctly dated; least successfully timed from May are upturns in public dwellings and total private industrial investment. Apart from a rather higher number of peaks in the first quarter and troughs in the second, the distribution of investment fluctuations over the year is very even. Success in predicting downturns however is confined to those occurring in the first

Table 6.16 (continued)

Negative change			Turning-point errors	Total no. of observations	E
Under-estimation	Over-estimation	$P_t = A_t$			
(4)	(5)	(6)	(7)	(8)	(9)
2	1	0	11	24	0.45
4	0	1	12	24	0.50
1	0	0	14	24	0.58
4	2	0	4	24	0.17
3	3	0	9	24	0.38
2	1	2	10	24	0.42
2	0	0	8	24	0.33
2	1	0	13	24	0.54
20	8	3	81	192	0.42

A_t no turning-point		A_t turning-point			
P_t no turning-point	P_t turning-point	P_t no turning-point	P_t turning-point	E_1	E_2
(12)	(13)	(14)	(15)	(16)	(17)
9	4	7	4	0.64	0.50
7	7	5	5	0.50	0.58
4	5	9	6	0.60	0.46
13	0	4	7	0.36	0.00
5	2	7	10	0.41	0.17
5	3	7	9	0.44	0.25
11	5	3	5	0.38	0.50
2	6	7	9	0.44	0.40
56	32	49	57	0.47	0.35

six months. Both forecasts are least successful in dating third quarter fluctuations, and although neither forecast correctly dates fourth quarter peaks the *P*1 series pre-empts one more and recognises three more than *P*2. Far from more timing errors being committed by *P*2 in the distant first quarter as one might expect, fluctuations occurring then are relatively well predicted: downturns are most successfully dated in that quarter and the proportion of peaks and troughs which are not forecast at all is lowest.

Table 6.17

Underestimation, overestimation and turning-point errors: NIESR gross fixed investment *P*2 forecasts 1965(i)-1970(iv)

	Positive change		
	Under-estimation (1)	Over-estimation (2)	$P_t = A_t$ (3)
Dwellings:			
Public	6	2	1
Private	5	4	0
Total	7	2	1
Mainly private industries:			
Manufacturing	7	6	0
Other	5	0	0
Total	6	2	0
Mainly public industries and services	8	6	0
Total	7	1	2
Total	51	23	4

	Underestimation of turning-point errors (10)	Overestimation of turning-point errors (11)
Dwellings:		
Public	4	6
Private	1	9
Total	1	11
Mainly private industries:		
Manufacturing	3	3
Other	8	4
Total	5	6
Mainly public industries and services	0	10
Total	1	13
Total	23	62

Upturns are best dated by $P2$ in the second quarter, the current forecasting period. Twenty-two complete cycles persisted six months or longer. Dating them from peak to trough they are: public dwellings 1967(iii)-1968(i), 1968(iv)-1969(iii), 1969(iv)-1970(ii); private dwellings 1966(iii)-1967(i), 1969(i)-1970(ii); total dwellings 1965(iv)-1966(ii), 1968(ii)-(iv), 1969(i)-(iii), 1969(iv)-1970(ii); manufacturing private industries 1966(iv)-1967(ii), 1967(iii)-1968(i); other private industries 1966(i)-(iii), 1967(iii)-

Table 6.17 (continued)

Negative change			Turning-point errors	Total no. of observations	E
Under-estimation (4)	Over-estimation (5)	$P_t = A_t$ (6)	(7)	(8)	(9)
5	0	0	10	24	0.42
5	0	0	10	24	0.42
1	0	1	12	24	0.50
4	1	0	6	24	0.25
5	2	0	12	24	0.50
3	1	1	11	24	0.46
0	0	0	10	24	0.42
0	0	0	14	24	0.58
23	4	2	85	192	0.44

A_t no turning-point		A_t turning-point		E_1	E_2
P_t no turning-point (12)	P_t turning-point (13)	P_t no turning-point (14)	P_t turning-point (15)	(16)	(17)
9	4	6	5	0.55	0.44
8	6	4	6	0.40	0.50
3	6	6	9	0.40	0.40
13	0	6	5	0.55	0.00
3	4	8	9	0.47	0.31
6	2	9	7	0.56	0.22
10	6	4	4	0.50	0.60
2	6	8	8	0.50	0.43
54	34	51	53	0.49	0.39

1968(i); total private industries 1965(ii)-1966(iv), 1966(i)-(iii), 1967(iii)-1968(i); public industries and services 1968(i)-1969(iv); total gross fixed investment 1965(ii)-(iv), 1967(iii)-1968(i), 1968(ii)-(iv), 1969(i)-(iii), 1969(iv)-1970(ii). Current period forecasts of these major fluctuations improve to the extent that rather more downturns are correctly dated than mistimed, while twice as many upturns are mistimed as are wholly ignored. There is no improvement in the proportion of peaks which are misforecast nor in the number of troughs which are correctly dated, and very little improvement in the accuracy with which the cycles are dated by the May forecasts. The proportion of correctly dated downturns is

Table 6.18

Dating of fluctuations: NIESR *P*1 and *P*2 forecasts of gross fixed investment 1965(i)-1970(iv)

	*P*1							
	Downturns				Upturns			
	Not forecast	Date correct	Lead	Lag	Not forecast	Date correct	Lead	Lag
Dwellings:								
Public	2	0	1	2	2	0	1	2
Private	1	2	0	2	1	0	2	2
Total	3	0	2	1	2	2	2	0
Mainly private industries:								
Manufacturing	4	1	0	0	3	2	0	0
Other	5	1	0	1	4	2	0	1
Total	5	1	1	0	2	2	1	2
Mainly public industries and services	2	1	0	0	1	2	0	0
Total	6	0	2	0	2	4	1	1
Quarter (i)	8	4	1	2	3	4	2	2
(ii)	7	2	1	0	4	4	4	3
(iii)	9	0	1	0	6	2	0	2
(iv)	4	0	3	4	4	4	1	1
Column totals	28	6	6	6	17	14	7	8
Column total as a proportion of total fluctuations	0.61	0.13	0.13	0.13	0.37	0.30	0.15	0.17
Column totals for 23 cycles	14	5	1	2	5	7	5	5

reduced, but fewer fluctuations are not forecast at all as the chain forecasts tend rather more frequently to delay in their dating of investment cycles.

8. Balance of payments on current account: time series analysis

Unlike the forecasts of personal income and expenditure and gross fixed investment, the subject matter of the earlier sections of this chapter, the majority of balance of payments forecasts which we next examine are for

P2								Total number of downturns	Total number of upturns
Downturns				Upturns					
Not forecast	Date correct	Lead	Lag	Not forecast	Date correct	Lead	Lag		
3	0	1	1	3	0	1	1	5	5
3	1	1	0	2	1	2	0	5	5
4	1	1	0	3	1	2	0	6	6
4	1	0	0	3	1	0	1	5	5
5	1	1	0	5	1	0	1	7	7
6	0	0	1	6	0	0	1	7	7
3	0	0	0	2	1	0	0	3	3
7	0	1	0	6	1	1	0	8	8
10	3	1	1	4	0	4	3	15	11
9	1	0	0	9	5	0	1	10	15
8	0	2	0	8	0	2	0	10	10
8	0	2	1	9	1	0	0	11	10
35	4	5	2	30	6	6	4	46	46
0.76	0.09	0.11	0.04	0.65	0.13	0.13	0.09		
16	1	2	3	11	3	4	4	22	22

half-yearly changes, valued exclusively at current prices. (Detailed quarterly forecasts of the balance of payments were not published by the National Institute until 1969). The time period covered is the same, 1965-1970, but each forecast and actual series now comprises twelve half-yearly, rather than the usual twenty-four quarterly observations. *P*1 and *P*2 half-yearly forecasts are compared with each other, and, when data availability permits, with an A_{t-1} naïve model (the subscript referring to the half-year), with one-year and three-year moving averages and with $\bar{A}$, the average actual half-yearly change over the sample period. The comparison for the quarterly forecasts is exactly comparable with that of our earlier analysis, except that the sample period is shorter, 1969(ii)-1970(iv), and data limitations restrict the application of all our naïve models.

Table 6.19 summarises our time-series inequality analysis. Consider first the results for the half-yearly *P*1 forecasts. The *U* coefficients range from a low of 0.29 for exports of goods to a high of 1.27 for net transfers. Visible exports are forecast more accurately than visible imports, an order which is reversed for exports and imports of services. Although the individual components of visible trade are better forecast than the invisible items, errors accumulate in the predicted balance of visible trade whereas they offset each other in the summation of invisibles, so that the invisible balance is more accurately forecast than the balance of trade in goods. The current balance (visibles and invisibles) is forecast marginally worse than if no change were assumed. All the *P*2 forecasts are less accurate, though the difference is slight for imports of goods, exports of services and the balance of invisibles. Forecast from May, imports of goods are now more accurate than exports of goods, and exports of services are better than imports of services. Again the visible components have lower *U* values than the individual invisibles, and the balance of invisibles is forecast better than the balance of visible trade. The inequality coefficient for *P*2 forecasts of the visible balance is unity.

One or more of the naïve models predicts more accurately than *P*1 and *P*2 forecasts of the visible balance, exports and imports of services, net transfers and the current balance. Usually $\bar{A}$ provides the best naïve forecasts, but both the one-year and three-year moving averages are more accurate than the genuine forecasts on occasions: for example, both moving averages are more accurate than both NIESR forecasts of exports of services. Over all time series forecasts, the naïve no-change assumption is statistically inferior to *P*1 (at the five per cent level of significance) and to *P*2 (but only at the ten per cent level). On the basis of the naïve models' inequality coefficients it appears that the balance of payments series easi-

Table 6.19

Inequality coefficients for NIESR balance of payments on current account $P1$ and $P2$ forecasts and naïve models: time series 1965(I)-1970(II) and 1969(ii)-1970(iv)

	$P1$	$P2$	A_{t-1} [a]	1-year moving average [b]	3-year moving average [c]	$\bar{A}$
Half-yearly forecasts 1965(I)-1970(II)						
Exports of goods	0.29	0.47	1.28	1.10	0.90	0.82
Imports of goods	0.37	0.41	1.34	0.98	0.86	0.80
Balance of visible trade	0.87	1.00	1.37	1.25	0.75	0.96
Exports of services	0.77	0.79	1.23	0.70	0.62	0.70
Imports of services	0.74	0.84	0.97	0.67	1.03	0.66
Net property income	0.72	0.84	1.63	1.17	1.04	0.97
Net transfers	1.27	1.33	1.60	1.35	1.28	0.98
Balance of invisibles	0.62	0.67	1.48	1.09	1.04	0.93
Current balance	1.07	1.27	1.32	1.47	1.29	1.00
Quarterly forecasts 1969(ii)-1970(iv)						
Exports of goods	0.53	0.88	1.25			0.80
Imports of goods	0.54	0.88	1.53			0.84
Balance of visible trade	1.43	1.12	1.24			0.93
Exports of services	0.96	0.95	1.60			0.91
Imports of services	0.97	0.92	1.41			0.81
Net property income	1.03	1.00	1.51			0.95
Net transfers	0.89	0.98	1.72			1.00
Balance of invisibles	1.33	1.24	1.46			0.98
Current balance	1.15	1.12	1.41			0.83

a Quarterly data for 1969(iii)-1970(iv).
b Half-yearly data for 1965(II)-1970(II).
c Half-yearly data for 1967(II)-1970(II).

est to predict is imports of services, and the hardest is the current balance itself.

Two points of interest emerge from the analysis of quarterly balance of payments also summarised in Table 6.19. First, the quarterly forecasts are less accurate than predictions of half-yearly changes; the exceptions are for both forecasts of net transfers and $P2$ forecasts of the current balance. This one would expect: problems of correctly anticipating turning-points are more acute for quarterly data. Forty-four per cent of the half-yearly actual observations refer to turning-points against sixty-four per cent of the quarterly actual data. Thus the second conclusion is all the more surprising: that for quarterly forecasts and outcomes the inferior accuracy of the $P2$ series, relative to $P1$, is much less marked indeed the May forecasts of the visible balance, three of the invisible components, the invisible balance and the current balance are the more accurate.

The $P1$ quarterly inequality coefficients range from 0.53, for exports of goods, to 1.43 for the balance of visible trade. The range for the $P2$ forecasts is from 0.88, indicating that exports and imports of goods are forecast with equal accuracy, to 1.24 for the balance of invisibles. All three balances, together with net property income, would be at least as accurately predicted by assuming no quarterly change. Goods are forecast better than invisibles, as was the case for the half-yearly forecasts, and also the accumulation of errors is such that for $P1$ and $P2$ the balance of invisibles is better predicted than the balance of visible trade. Unlike the half-yearly results, the inequality coefficients for quarterly forecasting do not reveal any marked difference in forecasting accuracy between exports and imports, whether the comparison is made for goods or for services. Data limitations preclude any naive quarterly predictions other than for the A_{t-1} and $\bar{A}$ models. $\bar{A}$ is more accurate than A_{t-1} throughout, and is comparable to the performance of many of the genuine forecasts. It is inferior only to the $P1$ forecasts of exports and imports of goods, and both NIESR forecasts of net transfers.

The partial inequality coefficients suggest that much of the $P1$ forecasting error was inevitable, in the sense that the U^C random term predominates especially for those variables that are worst forecast (see Table 6.20). For the half-yearly forecasts the mean value for U^M is 0.07 and for U^C 0.12, and the corresponding figures for the quarterly forecasts are 0.06 and 0.36 for the bias and variance proportions respectively. Least accurately forecast over the half-year are net transfers and the current balance, for both of which the non-systematic proportion of mean-square error is over ninety per cent. Bias is marked only for the forecasts of the visible and invisible balances, and for exports of services. For the visible balance the sign of $\bar{A}$ is incorrectly predicted, and for the other two the mean actual change is underestimated. The visible balance forecasts also under-predict the variance of outcomes, and this is a substantial source of error ($U^S = 0.34$). Systematic, as well as total error, accumulates as imports of goods are subtracted from exports. Under-prediction of the variance of outcomes accounts for thirty-six per cent of the error in net property income, and a more modest fourteen per cent for exports of services. However, as the results in the lower half of Table 6.20 show, the variance error is rather higher in the quarterly balance of payments forecasts. U^S averages thirty-six per cent over all variables, and over seventy per cent of

Table 6.20

Accuracy analysis of NIESR balance of payments on current account $P1$ forecasts: time series (1965(I)-1970(II) and 1969(ii)-1970(iv)

	U	U^M	U^S	U^C	r	α	β	SE (α)	SE (β)	$\bar{P}$	$\bar{A}$	s_P/s_A
Half-yearly forecasts 1965(I)-1970(II)												
Exports of goods	0.29	0.01	0.11	0.88	0.94	−0.06	1.06	1.01	0.13	4.89	5.15	0.89
Imports of goods	0.37	0.08	0.01	0.92	0.91	1.12	0.88	0.85	0.13	3.34	4.04	1.03
Balance of visible trade	0.87	0.14	0.34	0.52	0.55	−62.90	1.16	47.60	0.56	7.89	−53.77	0.47
Exports of services	0.77	0.23	0.14	0.64	0.35	3.71	0.59	1.98	0.50	2.58	5.24	0.59
Imports of services	0.74	0.01	0.05	0.94	0.52	2.62	0.41	1.28	0.22	3.78	4.18	1.27
Net property income	0.72	0.01	0.36	0.64	0.69	0.99	1.23	7.95	0.41	5.72	8.04	0.56
Net transfers	1.27	0.01	0.01	0.98	0.25	−1.47	0.23	2.42	0.28	−0.45	−1.58	1.07
Balance of invisibles	0.62	0.15	0.03	0.82	0.80	21.43	0.90	15.28	0.21	10.41	30.74	0.89
Current balance	1.07	0.02	0.07	0.92	0.28	10.91	0.38	58.43	0.42	−27.13	0.58	0.74
Quarterly forecasts 1969(ii)-1970(iv)												
Exports of goods	0.53	0.02	0.23	0.75	0.76	0.10	1.12	2.15	0.43	3.49	3.99	0.68
Imports of goods	0.54	0.13	0.36	0.51	0.83	0.30	1.35	1.10	0.41	1.51	2.34	0.61
Balance of visible trade	1.43	0.04	0.01	0.95	−0.37	86.09	−0.44	81.08	0.50	19.91	77.27	0.84
Exports of services	0.96	0.05	0.73	0.22	−0.24	10.15	−2.43	10.97	4.44	2.26	4.66	0.10
Imports of services	0.97	0.10	0.36	0.54	−0.38	6.32	−1.37	3.48	1.48	1.83	3.81	0.28
Net property income	1.03	0.08	0.80	0.12	−0.81	82.47	−21.03	41.10	6.81	1.64	47.91	0.04
Net transfers	0.89	0.06	0.77	0.18	0.68	9.94	3.14	6.60	1.53	−3.47	−0.94	0.22
Balance of invisibles	1.33	0.00	0.09	0.91	−0.41	6.04	−0.69	6.71	0.69	3.96	3.31	0.59
Current balance	1.15	0.04	0.00	0.96	0.17	67.68	0.16	76.00	0.41	121.91	86.59	1.06

the total error in forecasts of exports of services, net property income and net transfers is attributable to this source. Always the actual variance is under-predicted. Bias in the quarterly forecasts is larger than ten per cent only for imports of goods and services: again the mean outcome is under-predicted. Both sources of systematic error in the quarterly components are offset as the forecasts are aggregated.

Comparison of the foregoing *P*1 results with those for *P*2, which are presented in Table 6.21, shows the May half-yearly and quarterly forecasts to have the higher systematic error. On average, the bias proportion in the half-yearly forecasts is doubled in the May series, accounting for over twenty per cent of the forecasting error for imports of goods, the balance of visible trade, and exports and imports of services. U^S is virtually unchanged. The opposite is the case for the May quarterly forecasts: average bias is little above its *P*1 value, but the variance proportion averages fifty-two per cent. Nevertheless, bias and variance error are partially offset in the visible and invisible balances and are zero in the *P*2 quarterly forecast of the total current balance.

Further evidence of the deterioration in accuracy from *P*1 to *P*2 is provided by the regression analysis. Recall that perfect forecasting requires $\alpha = 0$ and $\beta = 1$. Thus significantly non-zero values of α and values of β not significantly different from zero are indicative of bad forecasting. Of the half-yearly *P*1 forecasts, none have significantly non-zero α's, and four of the forecast series have insignificant β terms: for *P*2, α is non-zero for three series, and β is insignificant for six series. Turning to the quarterly forecasts, α is significant for one *P*1 series but no *P*2 series, and β is not significant for six *P*1 series and all nine *P*2 series.

9. Balance of payments on current account: cross-section analysis

Table 6.22 displays the cross-section inequality coefficients for NIESR *P*1 and *P*2 balance of payments forecasts, and for the naive models.[14] For the 1965-1970 period the most accurately forecast half-year is 1968(I), when the *U* value is 0.26, and the least accurately forecast half-year is the first of our sample, 1965(I), when the inequality coefficient is 1.77. Two other half-years, 1966(II) and 1969(I), forecast by *P*1 have inequality coefficients equal to or greater than unity, and five other half-years, 1965(II), 1966(II), 1967(II), 1969(I) and 1969(II) would be more accurately predicted by the no-change assumption than by *P*2. These results might suggest, first, that *P*2 is significantly less accurate than *P*1, and second, that the second and more distant half-year is less accurately forecast by *P*2

Table 6.21

Accuracy analysis of NIESR balance of payments on current account $P2$ forecasts: time series 1965(I)-1970(II) and 1969(ii)-1970(iv)

	U	U^M	U^S	U^C	r	α	β	SE (α)	SE (β)	$\bar{P}$	$\bar{A}$	s_P/s_A
Half-yearly forecasts 1965(I)-1970(II)												
Exports of goods	0.47	0.03	0.11	0.86	0.82	0.64	1.02	1.63	0.22	4.42	5.15	0.80
Imports of goods	0.41	0.50	0.03	0.46	0.95	2.26	0.86	0.60	0.10	2.07	4.04	1.10
Balance of visible trade	1.00	0.24	0.22	0.54	0.42	−84.38	0.83	55.23	0.56	36.96	−53.77	0.51
Exports of services	0.79	0.30	0.17	0.53	0.34	3.87	0.65	1.92	0.57	2.10	5.24	0.52
Imports of services	0.84	0.20	0.10	0.70	0.04	4.05	0.06	1.61	0.53	2.13	4.18	0.67
Net property income	0.84	0.00	0.27	0.73	0.51	2.00	0.93	9.58	0.49	6.48	8.04	0.55
Net transfers	1.33	0.04	0.00	0.96	0.12	−1.65	0.12	2.48	0.32	0.61	−1.58	1.00
Balance of invisibles	0.67	0.02	0.09	0.89	0.71	10.64	0.90	18.92	0.29	22.35	30.74	0.79
Current balance	1.27	0.02	0.05	0.94	−0.04	2.37	−0.06	60.98	0.43	30.03	0.58	0.67
Quarterly forecasts 1969(ii)-1970(iv)												
Exports of goods	0.88	0.13	0.61	0.26	−0.11	5.38	−0.74	6.35	3.14	1.87	3.99	0.15
Imports of goods	0.88	0.13	0.41	0.46	0.21	1.69	0.66	2.06	1.36	0.99	2.34	0.32
Balance of visible trade	1.12	0.02	0.15	0.83	−0.15	90.31	−0.28	93.79	0.84	46.11	77.27	0.54
Exports of services	0.95	0.09	0.89	0.02	0.36	−22.95	17.73	32.62	20.77	1.56	4.66	0.02
Imports of services	0.92	0.22	0.64	0.14	0.01	3.75	0.07	5.30	4.80	0.99	3.81	0.14
Net property income	1.00	0.08	0.90	0.02	−0.06	62.43	−4.73	100.00	36.17	3.07	47.91	0.01
Net transfers	0.98	0.01	0.86	0.13	0.31	7.11	3.44	12.18	4.73	−2.34	−0.94	0.09
Balance of invisibles	1.24	0.03	0.26	0.71	−0.66	15.65	−1.90	8.10	0.97	6.50	3.31	0.35
Current balance	1.12	0.00	0.00	1.00	0.11	77.28	0.11	68.73	0.44	83.86	86.59	1.00

Table 6.22

Inequality coefficients for NIESR balance of payments on current account $P1$ and $P2$ forecasts and naïve models: cross-section 1965(I)-1970(II) and 1969(ii)-1970(iv)

	$P1$	$P2$	A_{t-1}	A_{t-4}	1-year moving average	3-year moving average	$\bar{A}$
Half-yearly forecasts							
1965 (I)	1.77	1.77	1.92				0.77
(II)	0.96	1.48	2.17		0.71		0.96
1966 (I)	0.93	0.93	0.92		0.93		0.83
(II)	1.00	1.04	1.83		1.04		1.30
1967 (I)	0.55	0.55	2.74		2.19		0.83
(II)	0.74	1.09	1.17		0.86	0.90	1.20
1968 (I)	0.26	0.26	1.43		1.16	1.08	0.86
(II)	0.66	0.79	2.21		0.55	0.84	0.57
1969 (I)	1.35	1.35	0.71		0.72	0.88	0.74
(II)	0.84	1.15	1.48		1.35	1.15	1.10
1970 (I)	0.71	0.71	1.73		1.15	0.91	0.88
(II)	0.34	0.66	2.67		0.92	0.73	0.64
Quarterly forecasts							
1969 (ii)	1.12	1.12					3.80
(iii)	0.83	1.41	1.39				4.96
(iv)	1.13	1.02	0.95				1.49
1970 (i)	1.02	0.99	1.21				0.88
(ii)	0.91	0.91	13.06	1.41	1.79		0.91
(iii)	0.87	0.98	2.40	0.68	5.36		3.19
(iv)	0.52	0.84	1.16	4.21	3.30		1.70

than the current, first half-year. The comparison between $P1$ and $P2$ involves only the results of second half-year forecasts (for the first half-year $P1$ and $P2$ are identical). Mean U for $P1$ forecasts of the second half-year is 0.76, the corresponding figure for $P2$ is 1.04, and the difference in means is significant at the five per cent level. However the $P2$ average for the second half-year is not significantly larger than the average inequality coefficient, 0.93, for forecasts of the first six months of the year.

As usual, $\bar{A}$ provides the best naïve prediction, but there are four half-years when the one-year moving average is more accurate. No one half-year emerges as being clearly easier or more difficult to forecast than any other, however $\bar{A}$ and the one-year moving average return their lowest inequality values in 1968(II), and the highest U values for the one-year moving average and the A_{t-1} model are recorded in 1967(I). The $P1$ forecasts are less accurate than at least one naïve model in 1965(I), $\bar{A}$,

1965(II), one-year moving average and $\bar{A}$, 1966(I), A_{t-1}, and $\bar{A}$, 1968(II), one-year moving average and $\bar{A}$, and 1969(I), all naïve models. $P2$ is similarly inferior to naïve forecasting in the following additional half-years: 1967(II), one-year and three-year moving averages, 1969(II) and 1970(II), $\bar{A}$. The genuine forecasts are better in cross-section than the no-change assumption, but their superiority is not statistically significant.

Much the same conclusions hold for the smaller number of quarterly, cross-section inequality coefficients, which for $P1$ average 0.91 and range from 1.13 in 1969(iv) to 0.52 in 1970(iv), and which for $P2$ average 1.04 and range from 1.41 in 1969(iii) to 0.84 in 1970(iv). $P2$ is less accurate than the A_{t-1} extrapolation in 1969(iii), which also beats both genuine forecasts in the following quarter. NIESR accuracy is inferior to that of $\bar{A}$ in 1970(i) and A_{t-4} in 1970(iii). There is no significant difference between the performance of $P1$ and $P2$, or between the two genuine forecasts and the no-change model.

The partial cross-section inequality coefficients for $P1$ are presented in Table 6.23. They show that, although over-prediction of the variance of outcomes accounts for twelve per cent of the large error in the 1965(I) balance of payments forecasts, non-systematic factors dominate the deviations between forecast and actual changes. In 1966(II), when the U value is unity, the variance proportion is very high, sixty-nine per cent. The variance of the predictions was less than a fifth that of the outcomes. The forecasters simultaneously underestimated the rate of growth of most balance of payments variables, while falsely predicting increases in imports of goods and net property income: the downturns in these two latter series, in particular in net property income, are responsible for the small, negative $\bar{A}$ for that half-year. Although $\bar{P}$ is positive, we re-iterate that it is the poor forecast of the variance of actual changes, not of their mean, which is primarily responsible for the overall error. Contrast this with the forecasters' performance in 1969(I). Again the inequality coefficient is high, and $\bar{P}$ and $\bar{A}$ have opposite signs. Approximately a quarter of the error is now due to misforecasting the mean outcome, and another thirteen per cent results from under-predicting the variance. Here the forecasters underestimated the growth in visible trade, over-predicted a fall in exports of services and an increase in imports of services, and erroneously predicted a downturn in net property income. Underestimating the variance of outcomes is the main reason for the non-systematic proportion of error, U^C, averaging thirty-five per cent, which is rather low. Note however that there is no simple relationship between the degree of overall inaccuracy and the proportion of error which is systematic: in 1970 bias and misforecast variance account for all but four per cent of the total error, but the

Table 6.23

Accuracy analysis of balance of payments on current account $P1$ forecasts: cross-section 1965(I)-1970(II) and 1969(ii)-1970(iv)

	U	U^M	U^S	U^C	r	α	β	SE (α)	SE (β)	$\bar{P}$	$\bar{A}$	s_P/s_A
Half-yearly forecasts												
1965 (I)	1.77	0.03	0.12	0.85	−0.20	4.57	−0.11	2.84	0.28	2.05	4.33	1.82
(II)	0.96	0.20	0.49	0.31	0.88	1.84	0.48	0.69	0.13	0.62	2.13	1.83
1966 (I)	0.93	0.35	0.57	0.09	0.79	−7.78	3.57	2.92	1.37	1.02	−4.15	0.22
(II)	1.00	0.06	0.69	0.25	0.28	−3.61	1.60	7.50	2.79	2.10	−0.25	0.18
1967 (I)	0.55	0.10	0.02	0.88	0.79	1.06	0.87	1.35	0.34	1.85	2.67	0.91
(II)	0.74	0.27	0.26	0.47	0.76	−5.67	1.27	4.36	0.54	0.87	−4.57	0.60
1968 (I)	0.26	0.27	0.44	0.29	0.98	−9.46	1.25	3.60	0.13	22.12	18.27	0.78
(II)	0.66	0.43	0.01	0.56	0.61	5.46	0.69	2.90	0.45	3.73	8.05	0.88
1969 (I)	1.35	0.24	0.13	0.63	−0.78	2.85	−1.77	3.40	0.71	−1.78	6.00	0.44
(II)	0.84	0.01	0.83	0.16	0.76	−0.93	3.19	7.17	1.38	−0.20	−1.57	0.24
1970 (I)	0.71	0.29	0.67	0.04	0.95	0.91	3.06	4.24	0.49	4.68	15.25	0.31
(II)	0.34	0.17	0.78	0.04	1.00	−0.01	1.50	0.46	0.07	2.68	4.02	0.67
Quarterly forecasts												
1969 (ii)	1.12	0.02	0.41	0.57	−0.26	0.46	−0.91	3.55	1.71	0.80	−0.27	0.29
(iii)	0.83	0.32	0.46	0.22	0.79	−2.70	1.97	1.38	0.77	0.57	−1.58	0.40
(iv)	1.13	0.02	0.60	0.38	−0.98	24.07	−7.95	4.57	0.82	3.28	−2.02	0.12
1970 (i)	1.02	0.14	0.77	0.09	−0.72	57.29	−22.80	53.72	11.02	−0.30	64.13	0.03
(ii)	0.91	0.53	0.33	0.14	0.22	7.62	1.21	5.22	2.69	1.35	9.25	0.18
(iii)	0.87	0.32	0.44	0.24	0.65	−3.56	1.92	2.37	1.13	0.03	−3.50	0.34
(iv)	0.52	0.44	0.08	0.48	0.87	3.16	1.07	2.03	0.30	2.72	6.05	0.81

inequality coefficients for the two half-years are 0.71 and 0.34, while when U^C is at its maximum, 0.88 in 1967(I), the inequality value is 0.55.

The $P1$ quarterly forecasts are less accurate and rather more subject to systematic error. Bias is greater than ten per cent in all but two quarters. But it is the marked under-prediction of the variance of changes which is most noticeable. For example, the high U values of 1969(iv) and 1970(i) are associated with U^S terms of 0.60 and 0.77 respectively. U^S averages 0.44 across the seven quarters. In 1970(iv), when the variance error is reduced to 0.08, the inequality coefficient is also relatively low in spite of a substantial bias proportion.

$P2$ cross-section results are given in Table 6.24. As a result of reductions in bias, systematic error is marginally lower in the chained half-yearly forecasts. For the quarterly $P2$ forecasts the increase in both sources of systematic error is slight. The spread of the quarterly predictions are once again too bunched: less than a quarter of the actual variation in changes is typically forecast.

Taken together, the result of our cross-section inequality analysis is encouraging inasmuch as it affords some evidence that United Kingdom balance of payments forecasting has improved over time. We have correlated the half-yearly $P1$ inequality coefficients with a time trend for the complete period 1965(I) to 1970(II). Also, time correlation coefficients have been calculated for the $P1$ and $P2$ cross-section U values for the two half-years, (I) and (II). All the correlations are negative, but, in view of the limited number of observations, most are not significant. However the negative value of the correlation between time and the $P1$ inequality coefficient for the second half-year is large, –0.81, and significant at the five per cent level. Similar calculations involving U^C and the cross-section inequality coefficients of the naïve models are also usually negative, but always non-significant. Forecasting the balance of payments may have become easier as well as more accurate.

10. Balance of payments on current account: underestimation, overestimation and turning-point errors

The paucity of quarterly data precludes any detailed analysis of the forecasters' success of predicting and dating fluctuations. Tables 6.25 and 6.26, which classify the forecasts on a qualitative, observation-by-observation basis, show a marked tendency on the part of both $P1$ and $P2$ to underestimate actual changes, particularly in the quarterly series. Percentage error $|(P_t - A_t)/A_t|$ is inversely associated with $|A_t|$: for half-yearly

Table 6.24

Accuracy analysis of balance of payments on current account *P*2 forecasts: cross-section 1965(I)-1970(II) and 1969(ii)-1970(iv)

	U	U^M	U^S	U^C	r	α	β	SE (α)	SE (β)	$\bar{P}$	$\bar{A}$	s_P/s_A
Half-yearly forecasts												
1965 (I)	1.77	0.03	0.12	0.85	0.20	4.57	−0.11	2.84	0.28	2.05	4.33	1.82
(II)	1.48	0.22	0.14	0.64	0.35	2.21	0.21	1.35	0.28	−0.35	2.13	1.67
1966 (I)	0.93	0.35	0.57	0.09	0.79	−7.78	3.57	2.92	1.37	1.02	−4.15	0.22
(II)	1.04	0.00	0.50	0.50	0.00	−0.25	−0.01	4.91	1.87	0.28	−0.25	0.27
1967 (I)	0.55	0.10	0.02	0.88	0.79	1.06	0.87	1.35	0.34	1.85	2.67	0.91
(II)	1.09	0.10	0.51	0.39	−0.39	−3.86	−2.13	6.23	2.48	0.33	−4.57	0.18
1968 (I)	0.26	0.27	0.44	0.29	0.98	−9.46	1.25	3.60	0.13	22.12	18.27	0.78
(II)	0.79	0.84	0.07	0.09	0.88	6.95	1.37	1.47	0.38	0.80	8.05	0.64
1969 (I)	1.35	0.24	0.13	0.63	−0.78	2.85	−1.76	3.40	0.71	−1.78	6.00	0.44
(II)	1.15	0.03	0.51	0.47	−0.66	8.33	−3.60	9.92	2.03	2.75	−1.57	0.18
1970 (I)	0.71	0.29	0.67	0.04	0.95	0.91	3.06	4.24	0.49	4.68	15.25	0.31
(II)	0.66	0.12	0.81	0.07	0.95	−1.15	2.79	1.63	0.48	1.85	4.02	0.34
Quarterly forecasts												
1969 (ii)	1.12	0.02	0.41	0.57	−0.25	0.46	−0.91	3.55	1.71	0.80	−0.27	0.27
(iii)	1.41	0.32	0.05	0.63	−0.08	−1.33	−0.12	2.63	0.76	2.03	−1.58	0.67
(iv)	1.02	0.01	0.91	0.09	−0.49	7.31	−16.37	18.07	14.65	0.57	−2.02	0.03
1970 (i)	0.99	0.15	0.84	0.02	0.32	45.70	41.86	77.95	29.61	0.92	64.13	0.01
(ii)	0.91	0.53	0.33	0.14	0.22	7.62	1.21	5.22	2.69	1.35	9.25	0.18
(iii)	0.98	0.39	0.45	0.16	0.57	−5.50	2.35	2.92	1.68	0.85	−3.50	0.24
(iv)	0.84	0.45	0.53	0.03	0.93	3.34	4.28	1.45	0.82	0.63	6.05	0.22

data the correlation coefficients are –0.60 (*P*1) and –0.62 (*P*2), and for quarterly data the correlations are –0.58 (*P*1) and –0.50 (*P*2). These correlations are between the logarithms of the percentage error and outcome, and all are significant at the five per cent level. We have tested the correlations with subsamples of data, and it appears that, unlike other NIESR quarterly forecasts, the balance of payments forecasts are not constrained within an upper threshold. Error simply reduces asymptotically at a diminishing rate as the outcome increases.

The *P*2 forecasts commit a higher proportion of turning-point errors than *P*1, and for both current and chained forecasts the proportion of turning-point errors is higher for the quarterly data, the volatile net property income and transfers series, and the three trade balances. The type of *P*1 turning-point error differs between half-yearly and quarterly forecasts. For the former, turning-point errors are typically underestimates and spurious, that is the forecasters predict downturns which do not subsequently take place. For the latter, the errors are typically overestimates of actual turning-points, i.e. missed downturns. Errors are similar for *P*2 except that there is little difference in the E_1 and E_2 values for the half-yearly forecasts. No actual turning-point in the visible balance is missed by *P*1, nor are half-yearly turning-points in exports and imports of services and quarterly turning-points in the current balance. *P*1 predicts no false turning-points in exports of goods, exports and imports of services, and in quarterly changes in imports of goods and net transfers. The chained forecasts do not miss turning-points in the visible balance, nor in half-yearly changes in imports of goods, imports and exports of services, and the quarterly current balance. No spurious *P*2 turning-points are recorded for exports and imports of services, nor in quarterly changes in exports and imports of goods, and net transfers.

11. Balance of payments on current account: annual forecasts

We end our evaluation of NIESR balance of payments forecasts by briefly comparing our results with those of R. L. Major and M. J. C. Surrey. [15] Major and Surrey concentrate on annual forecast changes, evaluated against the first official estimates of the outcomes. The forecasts are adjusted for subsequent policy changes and for dock strikes and other irregular disturbances. Of the years common to both their study and ours, Major and Surrey adjust May forecasts of visible and invisible trade in 1965 for hire purchase restrictions, a change in bank rate and a deferment of loan interest, in 1966 for a change in bank rate and the imposition of a

Table 6.25

Underestimation, overestimation and turning-point errors: NIESR balance of payments on current account $P1$ forecasts 1965(I)-1970(II) and 1969(ii)-1970(iv)

		Positive change			Negative change					
		Under-estimation (1)	Over-estimation (2)	$P_t = A_t$ (3)	Under-estimation (4)	Over-estimation (5)	$P_t = A_t$ (6)	Turning-point errors (7)	Total no. of observations (8)	E (9)
Exports of goods	A	6	4	0	1	0	0	1	12	0.08
	B	5	1	0	0	0	0	1	7	0.14
Imports of goods	A	6	3	0	0	1	0	2	12	0.17
	B	4	1	0	0	1	0	1	7	0.14
Balance of visible trade	A	3	1	0	4	1	0	3	12	0.25
	B	2	1	0	2	0	0	2	7	0.29
Exports of services	A	7	3	0	0	2	0	0	12	0.00
	B	5	1	0	0	0	0	1	7	0.14
Imports of services	A	7	4	0	1	0	0	0	12	0.00
	B	5	0	0	0	0	0	2	7	0.29
Net property income	A	4	1	0	3	0	0	4	12	0.33
	B	2	0	0	0	0	0	5	7	0.71
Net transfers	A	1	1	0	3	3	0	4	12	0.33
	B	1	0	0	4	0	0	2	7	0.29
Balance of invisibles	A	3	1	0	2	2	0	4	12	0.33
	B	2	1	0	1	0	0	3	7	0.43
Current balance	A	3	3	0	3	0	0	3	12	0.25
	B	2	1	0	1	0	0	3	7	0.43
Total	A	40	21	0	17	9	0	21	108	0.19
	B	28	6	0	8	1	0	20	63	0.32

Table 6.25 (continued)

				A_t no turning-point		A_t turning-point			
		Underestimation of turning-point errors (10)	Overestimation of turning-point errors (11)	P_t no turning-point (12)	P_t turning-point (13)	P_t no turning-point (14)	P_t turning-point (15)	E_1 (16)	E_2 (17)
Exports of goods	A	0	1	10	0	1	1	0.50	0.00
	B	0	1	5	0	1	1	0.50	0.00
Imports of goods	A	1	1	7	1	1	3	0.25	0.25
	B	0	1	3	0	1	3	0.25	0.00
Balance of visible trade	A	2	1	3	3	0	6	0.00	0.33
	B	1	1	3	2	0	2	0.00	0.50
Exports of services	A	0	0	8	0	0	4	0.00	0.00
	B	0	1	5	0	1	1	0.50	0.00
Imports of services	A	0	0	10	0	0	2	0.00	0.00
	B	0	2	3	0	2	2	0.50	0.00
Net property income	A	3	1	2	3	1	6	0.14	0.33
	B	1	4	1	2	3	1	0.75	0.67
Net transfers	A	3	1	2	2	2	6	0.25	0.25
	B	2	0	1	0	2	4	0.33	0.00
Balance of invisibles	A	3	1	2	3	1	6	0.14	0.33
	B	1	2	2	1	2	2	0.50	0.33
Current balance	A	2	1	4	2	1	5	0.17	0.29
	B	2	1	2	3	0	2	0.00	0.60
Total	A	14	7	48	14	7	39	0.15	0.26
	B	7	13	25	8	12	18	0.40	0.31

A—half-yearly forecasts; B—quarterly forecasts.

Table 6.26

Underestimation, overestimation and turning-point errors: NIESR balance of payments on current account *P2* forecasts 1965(I)-1970(II) and 1969(ii)-1970(iv)

		Positive change			Negative change					
		Under-estimation	Over-estimation	$P_t = A_t$	Under-estimation	Over-estimation	$P_t = A_t$	Turning-point errors	Total no. of observations	*E*
		(1)	(2)	(3)	(4)	(5)	(6)	(7)	(8)	(9)
Exports of goods	A	7	3	0	0	0	0	2	12	0.17
	B	5	1	0	0	0	0	1	7	0.14
Imports of goods	A	7	1	0	1	1	0	2	12	0.17
	B	4	1	0	1	0	0	1	7	0.14
Balance of visible trade	A	3	2	0	3	1	0	3	12	0.25
	B	4	0	0	1	1	0	1	7	0.14
Exports of services	A	7	3	0	0	2	0	0	12	0.00
	B	5	1	0	0	0	0	1	7	0.14
Imports of services	A	7	4	0	1	0	0	0	12	0.00
	B	5	0	0	0	0	0	2	7	0.29
Net property income	A	4	1	0	2	0	0	5	12	0.42
	B	3	0	0	0	0	0	4	7	0.57
Net transfers	A	0	1	0	4	2	0	5	12	0.42
	B	0	0	0	4	0	0	3	7	0.43
Balance of invisibles	A	3	2	0	2	1	0	4	12	0.33
	B	3	1	0	0	0	0	3	7	0.43
Current balance	A	4	3	0	2	0	0	3	12	0.25
	B	2	2	0	1	0	0	2	7	0.29
Total	A	42	20	0	15	7	0	24	108	0.22
	B	31	6	0	7	1	0	18	63	0.29

Table 6.26 (continued)

		Underestimation of turning-point errors	Overestimation of turning-point errors	A_t no turning-point		A_t turning-point		E_1	E_2
				P_t no turning-point	P_t turning-point	P_t no turning-point	P_t turning-point		
		(10)	(11)	(12)	(13)	(14)	(15)	(16)	(17)
Exports of goods	A	0	2	9	1	1	1	0.50	0.50
	B	0	1	5	0	1	1	0.50	0.00
Imports of goods	A	2	0	6	2	0	4	0.00	0.33
	B	0	1	3	0	1	3	0.25	0.00
Balance of visible trade	A	1	2	3	3	0	6	0.00	0.33
	B	0	1	4	1	0	2	0.00	0.33
Exports of services	A	0	0	8	0	0	4	0.00	0.00
	B	0	1	5	0	1	1	0.50	0.00
Imports of services	A	0	0	10	0	0	2	0.00	0.00
	B	0	2	3	0	2	2	0.50	0.00
Net property income	A	3	2	3	2	3	4	0.43	0.33
	B	0	4	1	2	2	2	0.50	0.50
Net transfers	A	4	1	2	2	3	5	0.38	0.29
	B	3	0	1	0	3	3	0.50	0.00
Balance of invisibles	A	2	2	4	1	3	4	0.43	0.20
	B	0	3	2	1	2	2	0.50	0.33
Current balance	A	1	2	4	2	1	5	0.17	0.29
	B	1	1	3	2	0	2	0.00	0.50
Total	A	13	11	49	13	11	35	0.24	0.27
	B	4	14	27	6	12	18	0.40	0.25

A–half-yearly forecasts; B–quarterly forecasts.

travel allowance, in 1967 for changes in hire purchase terms and bank rate, closure of the Suez Canal, dock strikes and devaluation, in 1968 for the U.S. dock strike, the introduction of the import deposit scheme and further deferment of loan interest, and in 1969 for the reduction and renewal of the import deposit scheme. Their conclusion, based on the average annual error in the adjusted forecast changes, is that the Institute's forecast of the current balance has been over-optimistic, mainly as a result of persistently underpredicting the value of imports. This over-optimism is reduced as forecasts are revised during the year. There is no comparable bias in exports. Errors cancel so that the forecasts of invisibles are comparatively accurate. But when forecast from February the overall current balance tends to be predicted with errors commensurate with no-change forecasting.

In general our study supports these findings. Half the $P2$ error in forecasting half-yearly changes in imports of goods is due to under-predicting the mean actual change, but this bias is substantially reduced in current period forecasts. Export forecasts do not appear to be subject to comparable over-optimism; rather the opposite, as a third of the $P2$ error in predicting export of services is due to underestimating the average change. Errors, including underestimating the variance of changes, are larger for the invisible items but cancel in the balance which is forecast more accurately than that for visible trade. As for the current balance itself, we agree that it is predicted rather less accurately than it would be by assuming no-change, on the other hand most of the forecasting error is due to non-systematic factors. We find no evidence of undue optimism in forecasting the current balance. Systematic error, including the aforementioned bias in forecasting imports, cancels out. For our sample period, $\bar{P}$ is larger than $\bar{A}$ for $P2$, and smaller than $\bar{A}$ (negative, in fact) for $P1$, but the result of eliminating this discrepancy would be to reduce the mean-square prediction error by only two per cent.

The National Institute's own evaluation adjusts the forecasts using early official outcome data. Our forecasts are unadjusted and the data are the most recently available. Also, the studies are for different periods, and theirs is of annual (absolute) changes while ours refers to half-yearly and quarterly percentage changes. And the analytical techniques are different. To make the comparison more valid, we have calculated inequality coefficients from the Major and Surrey data for the May forecasts,[16] and for our own unadjusted $P2$ data over the same period, converted to an annual basis. The results are presented in Table 6.27. The cross-section analysis excludes the three trade balances. Given the anomalies that undoubtedly still exist in the underlying data on forecasts and outcomes, we find the

Table 6.27

Balance of payments on current account: inequality coefficients for annual forecasts 1965-1969

Time series	Adjusted change data	Unadjusted change data	Unadjusted percentage change data
Exports of goods	0.24	0.36	0.32
Imports of goods	0.27	0.32	0.33
Balance of visible trade	0.69	0.75	1.04
Exports of services	0.17	0.57	0.49
Imports of services	0.24	0.43	0.41
Net property income	1.25	1.17	1.03
Net transfers	1.76	2.50	1.82
Balance of invisibles	0.77	0.75	0.36
Current balance	0.37	0.81	1.14
Cross-section			
1965	0.68	0.68	2.59
1966	0.11	0.41	1.02
1967	0.79	0.92	1.26
1968	0.16	0.10	0.60
1969	0.36	0.52	0.87

inequality coefficients obtained remarkably similar. Inequality coefficients for change data diverge most for exports of services, forecasts of which have only been slightly adjusted by Major and Surrey for later disruption, the current balance and, of the cross-section results, for 1966, when there was one post-forecast change in bank rate, and the late year imposition of the travel allowance. Inequality coefficients for unadjusted changes in net property income, the balance of invisibles and for cross-section 1968 are lower than those for the comparable adjusted changes. Converting the unadjusted changes into percentage change form results in the inequality coefficients given in the last column of Table 6.27. The time series results seem eminently fair: they emphasise the accuracy, due to offsetting errors, of the forecasts of the invisible balance, and the fact that the current balance would be marginally more accurately predicted by a no-change forecast, which the National Institute itself concludes, but which is not obvious from calculations using the adjusted change data. The final cross-section inequality results are probably less satisfactory, not because the raw data are inadequate but rather because cross-sectional calculations using percentage changes are on occasion dominated by large percentage errors in relatively small fluctuating series. Thus the high inequality value for 1965 primarily reflects very large turning-point errors in the forecasts of net property income and net transfers.

Most annual inequality coefficients for time series analysis are lower than our $P2$ half-yearly and quarterly results. This is as one would expect; forecast annual changes do not have to account for all short, quarterly fluctuations. For some net items and for some cross-sections the annual coefficients are larger as errors for the shorter time periods accumulate. $P2$ accuracy is lower for the second half-year. Given that most of the post-forecast policies were introduced late in the year this inferior accuracy is more likely to be caused by the same unexpected deviations which compelled the policy-makers to act rather than the actual implementation of policy adjustments. In this context we note the relatively large forecasting errors prior to devaluation at the end of 1967, and the low U values for the following year as the effects of devaluation worked through the economy. Moreover, chain forecasting is at a disadvantage in view of the speedy availability of official balance of payments statistics.

12. Conclusions

Our conclusions to the present chapter are reported as follows: (1) to (11) personal income and expenditure; (12) to (18) gross fixed investment; (19) to (30) balance of payments on current account.

(1) NIESR forecasts of personal disposable income and expenditure are predominantly directed towards predicting different types of money income, rather than the disposal of real income between alternative patterns of consumption and savings. Thus total income is disaggregated to its sources, some of which are taken to be endogenous to the Institute's small econometric model, while others are predicted using single-equation methods, and yet others are treated wholly exogenously. Variations in predictive accuracy, however, do not neatly correspond to this simple taxonomy. Of the current period forecasts, evaluated here as percentage changes, the wage and salary bill is forecast more than twice as accurately, in terms of the numerical value of the Theil inequality coefficient, as is other personal income. These forecasts' accuracy is superior to that of naïve, no-change predictions by factors of approximately two and a half and one and a fifth respectively. But both wages and salaries and other personal income are predicted endogenously. The wage bill usually grew steadily from quarter to quarter, tending to accelerate towards the end of the sample period, so that a quarter of the error was due to a downwards bias in the forecast average growth rate, whereas there were frequent

fluctuations in other personal income: downturns were often not forecast at all, and upturns only recognised with a lag. Three quarters of the large forecasting error can be attributed to underestimating the variance of actual changes. All other (percentage change) sources, as well as aggregate disposable money income, are forecast with intermediate success, while the few income variables examined as absolute changes are on average predicted marginally worse.

(2) The accuracy of forecast wage-rates and consumers' price indices is impressive; the relevant inequality values are approximately one third that of predicted no change. Over ninety per cent of forecasting error is non-systematic. Persistent inflation may have helped the forecasters, although the Institute has ceased publication of the wage-rates forecast in the face of alleged recent labour market abnormalities. However, good as the price forecasts are, the real values and quantities are forecast less accurately and with a greater frequency of turning-point errors than those series predicted in current prices, whether the comparison is made across all variables, or just those which are endogenous.

(3) Average earnings and employment are forecast outside the NIESR model. The earnings forecast is much the more accurate. Systematic error accounts for a third of total mean-square prediction error in both cases, and the remainder is primarily attributable to underpredicting the mean outcome of earnings, and the variance of changes in employment. Over half the turning-points in employment are either not forecast at all or incorrectly dated.

(4) Consumption is forecast more accurately than savings; indeed, naïve no-change predictions of savings and the savings ratio are more accurate than the NIESR forecasts. Again with savings, a high proportion of turning-point errors are committed and the variance error proportion is large.

(5) The simultaneity of the NIESR income and expenditure forecasts contributes to their differing accuracy between quarters. Some of the worst cross-section results in the period 1965-68 occur when turning-point errors are committed and the forecasters underestimate the range of positive and negative values taken by the outcomes. But in the last two sample years, current period forecasting errors are large and predominantly random.

(6) Most time-series and cross-section prediction error is non-systematic. Bias is slight in time series, accounting for ten per cent or more of the total error only in forecasts of average earnings, wages and salaries, net contributions, disposable income and consumers' expenditure, but, at an average twenty per cent, U^M is rather higher in cross-section. The variance proportion, averaging twenty-seven per cent in time series and cross-sec-

tion, with a maximum of seventy-two per cent for other personal income, is the major source of systematic error. The forecasters are conservative. Actual changes and their means and variances are consistently underpredicted. Proportionate forecasting error increases as changes occur in either direction outside the range one to one-and-a-half per cent.

(7) The May chained forecasts of income and expenditure are not significantly less accurate or more subject to systematic error in time series analysis than current period predictions. Half the variables, including other personal income and savings, have lower inequality values. *P*2 is notably worse in forecasting wages and salaries. In cross-section, and especially in the last two years of the study the May forecasts are marginally more accurate. Accuracy does not deteriorate with the length of the chain. The third quarter is least accurately forecast, and with least systematic error; otherwise there is no difference in accuracy between quarters.

(8) Naïve extrapolation and averaging of past changes in the income and expenditure variables is generally inferior to genuine forecasting in time series. *P*1 and *P*2 are significantly better than the no-change prediction over all variables, but not significantly better than the best naïve forecast of each series, which in a majority of cases is $\bar{A}$, as here defined an inoperable forecasting device. The naïve predictions are more competitive in cross-section: *P*1 and *P*2 are now not significantly superior to no-change, and for seventy-five per cent of the quarters at least one of the naïve models generates predictions of comparable or superior accuracy to the NIESR forecasts. Compared to the inequality results of naïve forecasting the third quarter of each year is significantly worst forecast by *P*1 and *P*2; there is no similar differential accuracy between the other quarters, nor is there evidence that the third quarter is in any sense intrinsically more difficult to forecast, for example, rather more troughs occur in this quarter than on average in the other three, but this is offset by fewer economic downturns.

(9) The accuracy of the current period income and expenditure forecasts has worsened during the six years studied, and the proportion of non-systematic error has increased. Of the individual quarters, the third and the first exhibit the largest reductions in, respectively, overall predictive accuracy and the systematic component of mean-square prediction error. Forecasting accuracy in May shows no similar decline, but then neither have the chained forecasts improved. Structural shifts in the relevant equations would be reflected in higher systematic error, adversely affecting the accuracy of both sets of forecasts, so it seems more reasonable to hypothesise that the disconcerting deterioration in *P*1 accuracy, occurring at a time when increasingly sophisticated econometric techni-

ques were being used by the forecasters, may be due to larger errors in current period, unrevised data. Errors of observation fall into the U^C category.

(10) Time series results do not suggest that the May forecasts are much impaired by subsequent policy changes. On the other hand, compared to the accuracy of current period predictions, the May forecasts are less accurate in the quarters potentially affected by post-forecast policy adjustments, and systematic error, usually variance error, is significantly higher in those quarters than it is in the remaining quarters forecast by $P2$.

(11) Between a fifth and a sixth of all pairs of observations are turning-point errors, a low proportion in comparison to the aggregate expenditure constituents of gross domestic product. There is a little difference in the turning-point performance of the two sets of forecasts other than that the May forecasts tend to misforecast downturns and predict spurious upturns more frequently. Approximately a third of all actual turning-points are missed, and another third of the predicted turning-points are spurious. Peaks and troughs are dated with virtually equal success by $P1$, though fewer upturns are ignored altogether, while those fluctuations which are wrongly dated are evenly divided between leads and lags. As expected, the May forecasts time fluctuations less accurately, tending to omit those which are forecast but wrongly dated in the current period. It is fortunate that downturns are bunched in the second quarter of the year, for it is clearly more difficult in May to date the onset of fluctuations six or nine months ahead. Longer cycles are better timed: when the NIESR forecasters err, they tend to do so on the side of optimism by post-dating the onset of a recession and/or pre-dating its end.

(12) Although the inaccuracy of naïve prediction shows that investment expenditures are difficult to predict, the NIESR forecasts of the different components of total gross fixed investment are uniformly disappointing. Time series accuracy is comparable to that of simply assuming no-change from quarter to quarter. Best forecast is investment by private manufacturing industries: the inequality coefficient is less than unity, error is predominantly non-systematic and none of the forecast turning-points are spurious. Dwellings on the other hand are forecast badly. Forecasting errors accumulate as investment is aggregated: one reason for this is that aggregated investment series tend to fluctuate with each of their components, thus in total fluctuating more and being more difficult to predict than any individual component.

(13) In cross-section the current period forecasts are less accurate than no-change predictions. Those quarters in which the general direction of

change is incorrectly predicted (i.e. those in which turning-point errors are committed) are particularly badly forecast.

(14) Most time series error is non-systematic, but the propotion of error due to under-predicting the variance of changes is also high. Bias is virtually absent from the forecasts. Outcomes tend to be underestimated, even though mean actual changes are not markedly underestimated. Over all pairs of observations other than turning-point errors the proportionate forecasting error is inversely correlated with the size of outcome. Error increases however as outcomes deviate above and below the (approximate) two per cent threshold. Over half the *P*1 cross-section error is systematic: the variance proportion is lower than for personal income and expenditure but bias is very high in those quarters where turning-points are misforecast. Rather more fluctuations occur in the first six months of the year, which explains the larger systematic error proportions observed for the first and second quarters.

(15) The May, chained forecasts yield superior predictions for eight of the investment series. Overall, *P*2 is more accurate though subject to larger systematic error, mainly variance error, stemming from its inferior dating of fluctuations. In cross-section analysis there is no significant difference in the accuracy of the two sets of forecasts.

(16) Accuracy in May does not deteriorate with the length of the forecasting span. Fourth quarter turning-points are not well dated, but *P*2 predicts peaks most successfully in the first quarter. Systematic error is high in both the distant first quarter and the current second quarter. Nor, in view of the four quarter lag required to stimulate investment, are the May forecasts impaired by subsequent policy changes.

(17) The forecasts are less accurate in the last half of the sample period. This is not reflected in any trend-like deterioration except for *P*1 forecasts of the fourth quarter. *P*2 systematic error has been reduced over time.

(18) Over half the actual percentage changes indicate fluctuations; over forty per cent of the predictions and outcomes constitute turning-point errors. Typically, the forecasters fail to predict or incorrectly time a downturn in investment expenditure. Troughs are better dated than peaks, *P*2 is markedly inferior to *P*1 in dating both, and longer recessions in investment are dated only marginally better than minor fluctuations.

(19) The best forecast balance of payments variables are exports and imports of goods. This is true of half-yearly and quarterly forecasts, whether made by *P*1 or *P*2. *P*1 half-yearly forecasts are the most accurate and show visible exports more accurately forecast than imports, with respective errors rather lower and rather higher than a third of that which

would result from a no-change forecast. For the quarterly forecasts there is no difference in accuracy between imports and exports of goods: both are forecast by *P*1 with fifty per cent of the no-change error, and ninety per cent of the no-change error by *P*2.

(20) Worst forecast of the components are half-yearly changes in net transfers, and quarterly changes in net property income. None of the quarterly invisibles are much better forecast than they would be by no-change.

(21) Errors accumulate in the visible balance and are mutually offsetting in the invisible balance. Thus, apart from *P*2 quarterly forecasts, the invisible balance is forecast more accurately.

(22) The current balance of payments (visibles and invisibles) is uniformly forecast with rather more than the no-change error. By way of amelioration, it should be noted that, judged by the relatively high inequality coefficients for naïve forecasting, this is not an easy series to predict. Also, the error is highly non-systematic.

(23) Systematic error is not particularly marked in the forecasts of the individual variables which comprise the balance. In the half-yearly *P*2 forecasts, imports of goods are conspicuously underestimated, as, to a lesser extent, are changes in exports and imports of services. Except for exports of services, this bias is successfully suppressed in current period predictions. The variance of half-yearly changes in net property income is also substantially underestimated. Under-prediction of the variance is much more substantial in all the quarterly forecasts; for example, it accounts for over seventy per cent of the prediction error of exports of services, net property income and net transfers.

(24) The cross-section inequality coefficients vary between 1.77 for 1965(I) to 0.26 for the post-devaluation 1968(I). Systematic error is higher than in time series, mainly because in many quarters and half-years the forecasters underestimate the range of actual changes in the different balance of payments variables.

(25) There is evidence that the accuracy of balance of payments forecasting has improved since 1965.

(26) In cross-section the *P*2 forecasts are less accurate than forecasts made in the current period. But in time series the comparison is more ambiguous. Half-yearly results confirm the superiority of *P*1; quarterly changes in six of the balance of payments variables are better forecast by *P*2.

(27) At least one of the naïve models is more accurate than genuine forecasts of half-yearly changes in the balance of payments series, including the current balance itself. At least one of the naïve models is more

accurate than $P1$ forecasts of five half-years and $P2$ forecasts of eight half-years. $\bar{A}$ is usually the best naïve predictor. Both sets of genuine forecasts are significantly superior to naïve no-change predictions over all the half-yearly time series inequality coefficients, but this is not the case for the other results.

(28) Actual changes are underestimated by the forecasts. Forecasting error, measured as a percentage of the actual value, falls at a diminishing rate as the size of the outcome increases. Small changes are difficult to perceive and so are forecast comparatively badly, but unlike the forecasts of income and expenditure and gross fixed investment, there is no evidence that these forecast values are restricted by a conservative upper threshold.

(29) Between twenty and thirty per cent of all the balance of payments forecasts commit turning-point errors. Half-yearly forecasts tend to predict spurious downturns. Quarterly forecasts miss actual downturns.

(30) A brief evaluation of forecasts of annual changes in the balance of payments supports our earlier conclusions, and those of the National Institute's own researchers. There appears to be no grounds for supposing that our results would be much altered had our forecast data been adjusted for subsequent policy changes, or had our outcome data been taken from earlier official estimates.

Notes

[1] The principal source for the National Institute's methods of forecasting personal income and expenditure is M. J. C. Surrey, *The Analysis and Forecasting of the British Economy* National Institute of Economic and Social Research, Occasional Paper 25, Cambridge University Press, London, (1971) Chs. 5, 6, 7. For additional references on specific areas of the forecasts, see the following. Consumers' price index: W. A. H. Godley and D. A. Rowe, 'Retail and consumer prices, 1955-63,' *National Institute Economic Review* (November 1964) pp. 44-57; W. A. B. Hopkin and W. A. H. Godley, 'An analysis of tax changes,' *National Institute Economic Review* (May 1965) pp. 33-42; *National Institute Economic Review* (May 1970) pp. 17-18; R. R. Nield, *Pricing and Employment in the Trade Cycle* National Institute of Economic and Social Research, Occasional Paper 21, Cambridge University Press, London, 1963. Consumers' expenditure: M. J. C. Surrey, 'Personal incomes and consumers' expenditure,' in Kenneth Hilton and David F. Heathfield, eds., *The Econometric Study of the United Kingdom* Macmillan, London, (1970) pp. 99-109. Employ-

ment: W. A. H. Godley and J. R. Shepherd, 'Long-term growth and short-term policy,' *National Institute Economic Review* (August 1964) pp. 26-38; J. R. Shepherd, 'Productive potential and the demand for labour,' *Economic Trends* (August 1968) pp. xxv-xxvii. Wage rates and average earnings: C. Gillion, 'Wage-rates, earnings and wage-drift,' *National Institute Economic Review* (November 1968) pp. 52-67.

[2] M. J. C. Surrey, *The Analysis and Forecasting of the British Economy, op. cit.* p. 54.

[3] The credit effect is the transformation of a change in credit into equivalent income. It is defined as 0.9 times the change in credit, when credit is a weighted sum equal to 100 per cent of hire purchase credit and fifty per cent of personal and professional bank advances (*ibid.* p. 63). For empirical justification of this treatment, see M. J. C. Surrey, 'Personal incomes and consumers' expenditure,' *op. cit.* (1970). pp. 103-108.

[4] M. J. C. Surrey, *op. cit.* (1971) pp. 29-35 describes the fixed investment forecasts. Relevant NIESR studies of investment behaviour include J. A. Bispham, 'The use of engineering orders for forecasting,' *National Institute Economic Review* (August 1970) pp. 38-53; A. R. Nobay, 'Short-term forecasting of housing investment: a note,' *National Institute Economic Review* (August 1967) pp. 41-49; A. R. Nobay, 'Forecasting manufacturing investment—some preliminary results,' *National Institute Economic Review* (May 1970) pp. 58-66; E. A. Shirley, 'Engineering orders: their use in forecasting,' *National Institute Economic Review* (August 1962) pp. 37-48.

[5] M. J. C. Surrey, *op. cit.* (1971) p. 5.

[6] The global reference for NIESR balance of payments forecasting is again M. J. C. Surrey, *op. cit.* (1971) Ch. 4 for visible foreign trade, and pp. 92-95 for invisibles and a synthesis of the forecasts. See also R. L. Major, 'Forecasting exports and imports: introduction,' *National Institute Economic Review* (November 1967) pp. 32-34.

[7] Quantitative experiments in forecasting exports of goods are reported in A. H. C. Broadbent, E. A. Anyanwu and N. Garganas, 'Forecasting trade between OECD countries and primary producers,' *National Institute Economic Review* (May 1970) pp. 46-51; G. A. Renton, 'Forecasting British exports of manufactures to industrial countries,' *National Institute Economic Review* (November 1967) pp. 35-41.

[8] The import relationship involving disaggregated final demand was formulated by W. A. H. Godley and J. R. Shepherd, 'Forecasting imports,' *National Institute Economic Review* (August 1965) pp. 35-42, and reappraised by I. G. Black, J. E. Kidgell and G. F. Ray, 'Forecasting im-

ports: a re-examination,' *National Institute Economic Review* (November 1967) pp. 52-57.

[9] J. A. Bispham, 'The current inflation and short-term forecasting,' in M. Parkin and M. T. Sumner, eds., *Incomes Policy and Inflation* Manchester University Press, Manchester, (1972) Ch. 13; *National Institute Economic Review* (February 1971) Ch. 3.

[10] W. A. B. Hopkin and W. A. H. Godley, 'An analysis of tax changes,' *op. cit.*

[11] M. J. C. Surrey, 'Personal incomes and consumers' expenditure,' *op. cit.* (1970).

[12] M. J. C. Surrey, *op. cit.* (1971) p. 53.

[13] The quarters in which investment may have been influenced by post-forecast policies are those listed in section 3 of the present chapter, with the exception of the third and fourth quarters of 1967.

[14] Excluded from the cross-sections are data on the visible, invisible and current balances. These variables take relatively small absolute values as levels, and hence large, oscillatory values as percentage changes, which consequently would tend to dominate the results. Also, to include the balances as well as their constituents would in a sense be double-counting.

[15] R. L. Major and M. J. C. Surrey, 'Errors in National Institute forecasts of the balance of payments,' *National Institute Economic Review* (May 1970) pp. 35-45.

[16] R. L. Major and M. J. C. Surrey, *ibid.* Table 4, p. 39.

7 Half-Yearly Forecasts

1. The half-yearly forecasts

In recent years the business and financial community has increasingly appreciated the value of macroeconomic forecasts for its own operations. As a result, not only have forecasts by official bodies, particularly the Treasury and OECD, and the independent NIESR received more attention in the press, but also *The Sunday Times* and *The Sunday Telegraph* have begun publishing regular forecasts. *The Sunday Times* forecasts appear three times a year and are made by R. J. Ball and T. Burns using the model developed at the London Business School; *The Sunday Telegraph* forecasts appear monthly and are prepared by a team of business economists led by James Morrell. As the Treasury, OECD, LBS and *Sunday Telegraph* predict economic activity over consecutive six-monthly intervals, this chapter concerns the accuracy of half-yearly forecasts.

The period covered by the OECD and *The Sunday Telegraph* forecasts is 1967(I)-1971(II). (The January-June and July-December halves of years are denoted by capital Roman numerals I and II respectively). The National Institute does not make specific half-yearly forecasts but half-yearly forecasts may be inferred from their quarterly series. For comparability we examine the NIESR forecasts for the period 1967(I)-1971(II) also. The data periods for the Treasury and *The Sunday Times* are one year shorter, 1968(I)-1971(II). The Treasury only began publishing half-yearly forecasts at the time of the 1968 Budget and while forecasts did appear in *The Sunday Times* as early as 1966 they were not put on to a consistent constant price and seasonally adjusted basis until 1968. The techniques of model building, estimation and forecasting used by the five teams have been described in Chapter I.

The Treasury makes only one set of forecasts each year, the OECD publishes forecasts in July and December, the London Business School makes three forecasts a year, NIESR forecasts appear quarterly and *The Sunday Telegraph* forecasts are revised every month. As a result of this diversity, it has been necessary to restrict our analysis to just one comparable set of predictions, a *P*2 series, published annually by each team.

The Treasury forecasts that we analyse are those made at the time of the Budget and published in the annual *Financial Statement and Budget*

Report; the National Institute forecasts are those published in the May issues of the *Economic Review*; the London Business School and *The Sunday Telegraph* forecasts are the first published after the Budget in *The Sunday Times* and *The Sunday Telegraph*; the OECD forecasts are those published in the July issues of the *OECD Economic Outlook*. Thus all these forecasts incorporate the effects of Budget changes but not the effect of post-budget policy measures. However, *The Sunday Telegraph* does base its forecasts on predictions of government policy; these predictions are not fully specified and we have made no attempt to adjust the forecasts to a 'no policy change' basis or to correct for any misforecasts of policy changes.

To generate a *P*2 series we adopt the following procedure. For the January-June half-years we take the percentage predicted change over the estimate available to the forecaster of the last half of the previous year. For the July-December half-years we take the percentage predicted change over the forecast level for the January-June half year. The values of P_t obtained for the January-June and July-December periods are then pooled. There are no problems with this pooling procedure for when we used the cross-section results to test if there were any significant difference between the accuracy with which the first and second halves of years were predicted, we found that there was not. It is unlikely that second half-year forecasts would have been invalidated by post-budget policy changes for the only such measures of any consequence were the devaluation package of November 1967 and the fiscal and credit squeeze a year later, both of which surely occurred too late in the year to have any appreciable effect on the economy before the end of the year. The A_t series are constructed using the most recently available actual data.[1]

Except for *The Sunday Telegraph* forecasts and the OECD exports and imports series, half-yearly predictions are seasonally adjusted and at constant prices. *The Sunday Telegraph* forecasts are in current prices and not seasonally adjusted; and they are published as index numbers rather than in aggregate values. However, a constant price, seasonally adjusted forecast of gross domestic product is also presented. The OECD forecasts of exports and imports are in current prices and are seasonally adjusted. All the OECD forecasts are given as percentage changes at annual rates, which have been converted to half-yearly rates.

Gross domestic product is not measured in the same way by all forecasters. The Treasury and National Institute use compromise measures of gross domestic product, a simple average of GDP calculated from the expenditure, output and income estimates. The burden of reconciliation between the individual expenditure variables and compromise GDP seems to fall almost entirely on the stockbuilding series. Until the end of 1970 the London Business School forecasts in *The Sunday Times* simply summed the expenditure components, but starting with the forecast for 1971(I) the London Business School team also adopted a compromise measure, a simple average of the expenditure and output estimates. The forecasts in *The Sunday Telegraph* use the expenditure measure. The OECD forecasts are of a compromise measure of gross domestic product at market prices whereas all the other forecasts are of GDP at factor cost. Throughout we endeavour to evaluate forecasts against strictly comparable actual data.

In our analysis of stockbuilding we have excluded pairs of observations for which either the predicted change or the actual change or both are one thousand per cent or more. Typically such large percentage changes are based on very small values of a_{t-1} so that the percentage changes are subject to a very large margin of error. For each set of forecasts only one pair of observations is involved; failure to exclude such pairs of observations yields high inequality coefficients that do not do the forecasters justice. We do not have a stockbuilding series for the OECD on a comparable basis to the other forecasters.

Because the forecasts cover different periods, are of different variables or measure the same variable in different ways, and because, in order to be compatible with the forecasts, the outcome data are taken from different sources, it follows that the inequality coefficients for the four naïve models, A_{t-1}, a one-year moving average, a three-year moving average and $\bar{A}$, will vary with whichever genuine forecasts they are compared. Accordingly we present separate naïve models with the accuracy analysis for each set of forecasts.

As usual the cross-section analysis of each set of forecasts excludes the stockbuilding series because of scale effects. We do not include both disaggregated components of consumption and fixed investment and their totals. For the London Business School we include durable and non-durable consumption expenditure and not total consumption, private dwelling and non-dwelling gross private fixed investment but not total gross private fixed investment. The Treasury cross-sections include total gross fixed investment but exclude the individual components, public and private investment, forecasts of which were not published until 1969. Also excluded are *The Sunday Telegraph*'s constant price seasonally adjusted GDP observations as all its other forecasts are in nominal terms and are not seasonally adjusted. We have included exports and imports in the OECD calculations even though they are in current prices; to prevent the scale of the current price changes dominating the constant price changes of the other variables we have divided the values of P_t and A_t for exports and imports by two, which approximately removes the average rate of inflation. With the exceptions and modifications noted above all the variables examined in time series calculations are included in the cross-section analysis. Because the variables included in the cross-sections for the different forecasters do not coincide exactly some care should be exercised in comparing their cross-section inequality coefficients.

To avoid repetition we report some negative findings common to all sets of forecasts in this chapter. Using the cross-section inequality coefficients we tested the differences in the mean values of U and U^C between the January-June and July-December half years. None were significant at the five per cent level. We also correlated U and U^C with time to see if forecasting accuracy had improved and if systematic error had been reduced. Again the results for all forecasters were not significant at the five per cent level. Finally, the inequality coefficients for the naïve models do not have time trends significant at the five per cent level.

2. The Treasury forecasts 1968(I)-1971(II)

Table 7.1 presents the time series accuracy analysis for the Treasury forecasts together with the inequality coefficients for the naïve models.

The forecasts do not fare too well in comparison with the naïve models. The $\bar{A}$ model is superior to the forecasts for six variables (consumers' expenditure, public authorities' current spending, the three investment series and imports of goods and services) and as good as the forecasts for two (adjustment to factor cost and gross domestic product) so that for only three variables (exports of goods and services, total final expenditure and stockbuilding) are the forecasts better than the $\bar{A}$ model. The no-change and three-year moving average models outperform the forecasts of three series (public authorities' current spending and private investment by both models, public investment by the no-change, and imports by the three-year moving average model), the one-year moving average is superior to the forecast of two variables (public authorities' current spending and imports) and the A_{t-1} to forecasts of public authorities' current spending. Only exports, total final expenditure and stockbuilding are superior to all the naïve models.

Public authorities' current spending is forecast worst with an inequality coefficient of 1.42! It is surely surprising that Government expenditure should be forecast better by all five naïve models than by the Treasury. The next highest inequality coefficient is for gross fixed investment, 1.23, followed by public investment, 1.10, total investment, 0.93, consumers' expenditure, 0.83, imports, 0.76, stockbuilding, 0.74, gross domestic product, 0.71, adjustment to factor cost, 0.67, total final expenditure (including stockbuilding), 0.47, and exports, 0.39.

Looking at the partial coefficients we see that bias is high for adjustment to factor cost (sixty-eight per cent) and exports (forty-eight per cent); it is ten per cent or greater also for imports (twenty per cent), private and total gross fixed investment (seventeen and sixteen per cent respectively), public authorities' current spending (thirteen per cent) and stockbuilding (ten per cent). Total gross fixed investment, private investment, stockbuilding, total final expenditure and consumers' expenditure all have variance proportions of ten per cent or greater (the respective U^S coefficients being 0.23, 0.17, 0.14, 0.13 and 0.10). Systematic error is most marked for adjustment to factor cost (U^C = 0.31), exports (0.51), total and private investment (0.61 and 0.66 respectively), stockbuilding (0.76), public authorities' current expenditure and imports (both 0.80) and total final expenditure (0.86). There is no systematic tendency for $\bar{P}$ to be less than $\bar{A}$ or for s_P to be less than s_A

The cross-section accuracy analysis is presented in Table 7.2 together with the inequality coefficients for the naïve models.

It is apparent that the half-years fall into two groups, the badly forecast 1968(II) and 1969(I), with inequality coefficients 1.18 and 1.50 respectively, and the remaining half-years for which the inequality coefficients range between 0.37 in 1968(I) and 0.56 in 1969(II). In the two badly forecast half-years the forecasts are bettered by all the naïve models, except the A_{t-1} model in 1968(II). In the six half-years with the relatively low inequality coefficients the forecasts are superior to all the naïve models in all the half-years except 1969(II) when $\bar{A}$ and the one-year and three-year moving averages perform better than the Treasury forecasters.

It is interesting to note that the period without markedly bad forecasts followed the greater econometric formalisation of the Treasury methods, for 'in the second half of 1969 the Treasury short-term forecasting team began to build up its own stock of programming expertise',[2] and that 1970 was the year with smallest recorded annual inequality coefficient, 0.25. However, this was apparently a fairly easy year to forecast, the inequality coefficients for the naïve models being low as well. Clearly no strong implications can be drawn from so few observations, and testing the hypothesis that the increased use of econometric analysis by the

Table 7.1

Accuracy analysis of Treasury half-yearly forecasts: time series 1968(I)-1971(II)

A_{t-1}	*U* for naïve models: 1-year moving average	3-year moving average	$\bar{A}$	
1.03	0.94	0.79	0.71	Consumers' expenditure
0.79	1.06	1.39	0.90	Public authorities' current spending
1.69	1.30	1.43	0.98	Gross fixed investment: Public[a]
1.61	1.40	1.19	0.97	Private[a]
1.38	1.07	1.06	0.91	Total
1.36	1.08	0.81	0.67	Exports of goods and services
1.62	1.27	1.08	0.94	Stockbuilding
0.98	0.69	0.65	0.55	Total final expenditure
1.02	0.58	0.67	0.61	Imports of goods and services
0.99	0.85	0.69	0.67	Adjustment to factor cost
0.92	0.74	0.68	0.56	Gross domestic product: compromise estimate at factor cost

a 1969(I)-1971(II)

Table 7.2

Accuracy analysis of Treasury half-yearly forecasts: cross-section 1968(I)-1971(II)

A_{t-1}	*U* for naïve models: 1-year moving average	3-year moving average	$\bar{A}$	
1.41	1.07	0.70	0.57	1968 (I)
1.61	0.66	0.62	0.52	1968 (II)
0.73	0.97	0.73	1.02	1969 (I)
0.76	0.55	0.49	0.35	1969 (II)
1.06	0.90	0.52	0.80	1970 (I)
0.63	0.70	0.56	1.08	1970 (II)
1.10	1.11	0.88	1.09	1971 (I)
1.05	0.78	0.62	0.70	1971 (II)

Table 7.1 (continued)

U	U^M	U^S	U^C	r	α	β	SE (α)	SE (β)	$\bar{P}$	$\bar{A}$	s_P/s_A
0.83	0.01	0.10	0.89	0.55	0.69	0.41	0.44	0.25	0.95	1.08	1.34
1.42	0.13	0.06	0.80	−0.66	1.69	−1.09	0.64	0.51	1.09	0.50	0.61
1.10	0.00	0.06	0.94	0.19	−0.40	0.26	1.39	0.67	−0.45	−0.52	0.73
1.23	0.17	0.17	0.66	−0.13	1.58	−0.27	3.18	1.04	2.62	0.88	0.48
0.93	0.16	0.23	0.61	0.38	−0.33	0.74	1.37	0.75	1.58	0.84	0.51
0.39	0.48	0.02	0.51	0.89	1.72	0.97	0.93	0.20	3.05	4.68	0.92
0.74	0.10	0.14	0.76	0.63	−21.61	0.90	83.31	0.25	−18.28	−38.14	0.70
0.47	0.01	0.13	0.86	0.55	0.38	0.80	0.78	0.49	1.43	1.51	0.69
0.76	0.20	0.00	0.80	0.40	1.88	0.39	0.87	0.37	1.36	2.41	1.03
0.67	0.68	0.01	0.31	0.86	1.66	0.79	0.41	0.19	0.53	2.08	1.09
0.56	0.07	0.01	0.93	0.58	0.48	0.54	0.56	0.31	1.53	1.30	1.07

Table 7.2 (continued)

U	U^M	U^S	U^C	r	α	β	SE (α)	SE (β)	$\bar{P}$	$\bar{A}$	s_P/s_A
0.37	0.62	0.01	0.37	0.94	1.72	0.99	0.67	0.15	2.59	4.29	0.95
1.18	0.15	0.01	0.85	−0.02	1.27	−0.02	0.71	0.46	0.30	1.26	1.00
1.50	0.01	0.05	0.94	0.10	0.55	0.07	0.67	0.30	0.88	0.61	1.43
0.56	0.03	0.48	0.49	0.73	−0.40	1.48	0.93	0.57	1.35	1.60	0.49
0.39	0.20	0.44	0.36	0.74	−0.52	1.61	0.89	0.59	1.44	1.80	0.46
0.40	0.30	0.03	0.67	0.63	0.60	0.53	0.60	0.27	2.13	1.73	1.19
0.44	0.00	0.15	0.85	0.85	−0.04	1.07	0.40	0.27	0.94	0.96	0.79
0.49	0.12	0.22	0.67	0.60	0.50	0.99	1.16	0.54	1.89	2.38	0.61

Treasury forecasting team has led to improved accuracy must await the analysis of further forecasts.

The bias and variance proportions vary greatly from year to year. U^M is zero in 1971(I) and is as high as 0.62 in 1968(I). U^S varies from 0.01 in 1968(I) and 1968(II) to 0.48 in 1969(II). Unsystematic error varies from thirty-six per cent of total forecasting error in 1970(I) to ninety-four

Table 7.3

Underestimation, overestimation and turning-point errors: Treasury half-yearly forecasts 1968(I)-1971(II)

	Positive change		
	Under-estimation (1)	Over-estimation (2)	$P_t = A_t$ (3)
Consumers' expenditure	2	4	0
Public authorities' current spending	3	3	0
Gross fixed investment: Public	0	1	0
Private	1	2	0
Total	3	2	0
Exports of goods and services	7	1	0
Stockbuilding	1	1	0
Total final expenditure (including stockbuilding)	4	3	0
Imports of goods and services	3	3	0
Adjustment to factor cost	3	0	1
Gross domestic product at factor cost	5	2	0
Total	32	22	1

	Underestimation of turning-point errors (10)	Overestimation of turning-point errors (11)
Consumers' expenditure	1	0
Public authorities' current expenditure	0	2
Gross fixed investment: Public	1	2
Private	1	2
Total	0	3
Exports of goods and services	0	0
Stockbuilding	1	1
Total final expenditure (including stockbuilding)	0	1
Imports of goods and services	2	0
Adjustment to factor cost	2	0
Gross domestic product at factor cost	0	0
Total	8	11

per cent in 1969(I). There are no significant patterns between $\bar{P}$ and $\bar{A}$ or between s_P and s_A.

Table 7.3 classifies the forecasts by whether they are underestimates or overestimates of actual changes and analyses turning-point errors.

In Chapter 3 we found that the Treasury tended to underestimate changes rather than overestimate them and that this tendency to under-

Table 7.3 (continued)

Negative change					
Under-estimation (4)	Over-estimation (5)	$P_t = A_t$ (6)	Turning-point errors (7)	Total no. of observations (8)	E (9)
0	1	0	1	8	0.12
0	0	0	2	8	0.25
1	1	0	3	6	0.50
0	0	0	3	6	0.50
0	0	0	3	8	0.37
0	0	0	0	8	0.00
3	1	0	2	8	0.25
0	0	0	1	8	0.12
0	0	0	2	8	0.25
0	2	0	2	8	0.25
1	0	0	0	8	0.00
5	5	0	19	84	0.23

A_t no turning-point		A_t turning-point			
P_t no turning-point (12)	P_t turning-point (13)	P_t no turning-point (14)	P_t turning-point (15)	E_1 (16)	E_2 (17)
5	1	0	2	0.00	0.33
5	1	1	1	0.50	0.50
1	1	2	2	0.50	0.33
2	0	3	1	0.75	0.00
4	1	2	1	0.67	0.50
7	0	0	1	0.00	0.00
1	2	0	5	0.00	0.29
6	0	1	1	0.50	0.00
6	2	0	0	—	1.00
2	2	0	4	0.00	0.33
5	0	0	3	0.00	0.00
44	10	9	21	0.30	0.32

estimation was highly significant. Again there is a tendency for underestimation but it does not occur for all series and is only marked for exports, adjustment to factor cost when the actual change is positive, and gross domestic product. Overall, for forecasts that are not turning-point errors, the number of observations that are underestimates exceed those that are overestimates by ten but, making use of the normal approximation to the binomial distribution, this difference is not significant at the five per cent level. Eight turning-points are underestimated and eleven are overestimated.

Forecasting error, measured as a proportion of the size of the outcome, is reduced as outcomes increase. The correlation coefficient between $|(P_t - A_t)/A_t|$ and $|A_t|$ for all pairs of predicted and actual observations of the same sign, excluding the data for stockbuilding, is -0.38, and for the logarithmic transformation of the errors and outcomes -0.81. Both coefficients are significant at the five per cent level. The very high logarithmic correlation suggests that there is no upper threshold to the Treasury's forecasts. Proportionate forecasting errors diminish sharply as outcome values become increasingly perceptible, and then tend to stabilise.

Twenty-three per cent of the forecasts are turning-point errors. Turning-point errors are found most frequently in the investment series (fifty per cent of the forecasts for public and private investment are turning-point errors and thirty-seven per cent for total investment), public authorities' current spending, stockbuilding, total final expenditure and imports (for all of which twenty-five per cent of forecasts represent turning-point errors).

Overall the E_1 statistic, the proportion of actual turning-points missed by forecasters, is 0.30. The incidence of such turning-point errors is unevenly distributed: E_1 is 0.75 for private investment, 0.67 for total investment, 0.50 for public authorities' current expenditure, public investment and total final expenditure and zero for all other series. For all observations the E_2 statistic which measures the proportion of turning-point forecasts that eventually prove spurious, is 0.32: it is 1.00 for imports, 0.50 for public authorities' current expenditure and total investment, 0.33 for consumers' expenditure, public investment and adjustment to factor cost, 0.29 for stockbuilding; for other series there are no errors of this type.

3. NIESR forecasts 1967(I)-1971(II)

Table 7.4 presents detailed results for the NIESR time series analysis including the inequality coefficients for the naïve models.

Clearly the best forecast variables are gross domestic product and total final expenditure (excluding stockbuilding) with inequality coefficients of 0.32 and 0.34 respectively. Errors in the individual GDP components, forecast less successfully, offset each other when the variables are aggregated. The balance of payments variables are the next best forecast series, the inequality coefficient for exports, 0.54, being smaller than that for imports, 0.68; then follow consumers' expenditure ($U = 0.72$), adjustment to factor cost (0.74), public authorities' current spending (0.88), stockbuilding (0.98) and gross fixed investment (1.15).

The general order of accuracy of the forecasts is borne out by comparison with the naïve models, none of which can predict the relatively well forecast GDP, total final expenditure and exports series better than the National Institute. At the other extreme all the naïve models except A_{t-1} are more accurate than the NIESR forecasts of gross fixed investment, and public authorities' current spending is more accurately predicted by the one-year moving average and $\bar{A}$ models. The best predicting naïve model is $\bar{A}$ which is more accurate than the NIESR forecasts of six GDP components. Total final expenditure, not gross domestic product, appears to be the easiest to forecast in that all the naïve models predict it the most accurately.

Bias, misforecasting the mean actual change, accounts for sixty-six per cent of forecasting error for total final expenditure, fifty-two per cent for the factor cost adjustment, forty-two per cent for consumers' expenditure, twenty-five per cent for GDP and ten per cent for stockbuilding and imports; except for stockbuilding the average outcome is under predicted. It is noteworthy that bias tends to accumulate in total final expenditure forecasts and yet is reduced in aggregation to GDP.

Variance error, measured by U^S, is less marked. The highest variance proportion is for stockbuilding, 0.52, followed by public authorities' current spending, 0.30, exports, 0.16, and gross domestic product, 0.15; the remaining values are less than 0.10. Unlike bias, wrongly forecast variances are offset in estimating total final expenditure yet accumulate in GDP. The variance of actual changes are underestimated for five series and overestimated for the remaining four.

In general, error is non-systematic and is lowest for those forecasts which are among the most accurate, e.g. imports and exports, and the worst, the investment series.

The foregoing inequality results are supported by correlation and regression analysis. Predictions and outcomes are fairly highly correlated for the better forecast series, for example the correlation coefficient is 0.92

for both total final expenditure and GDP, and the β coefficient is usually significant and close to, albeit less than, the desired value of unity. The α term however, which should be zero if forecasts were perfect, is only statistically indifferent from zero for exports, which are relatively well forecast, and public authorities' current spending, fixed and inventory investment which are least accurately predicted. With α positive, and low, positive values of β, the forecasters are likely to be predicting no-change and presumably negative changes for some small positive outcomes, that is, forecasting spurious downturns. This is unusual, and will be checked later against the results of observation-by-observation analysis.

Cross-section results are presented in Table 7.5. From 1967(II) to 1969(I) the Institute's forecasts are at their most erratic. The second six months of 1967, which culminated in November with the devaluation of sterling, seems to have been particularly difficult to predict; the inequality coefficients for all the naïve models are large and inferior to the NIESR forecasts so the National Institute may have some excuse for their large inequality coefficients. From the partial coefficients we observe that the variance proportion, sixty-two per cent, was abnormally high for the 1967(II) forecasts and predictions and outcomes were, if anything, negatively correlated. The forecasts were too bunched: typically, modest

Table 7.4

Accuracy analysis of NIESR half-yearly forecasts: time series 1967(I)-1971(II)

	U for naïve models			
A_{t-1}	1-year moving average	3-year moving average	$\bar{A}$	
1.08	0.99	0.73	0.64	Consumers' expenditure
0.86	0.87	0.94	0.87	Public authorities' current spending
1.20	1.11	0.86	0.82	Gross fixed investment
1.33	1.10	0.92	0.83	Exports of goods and services
0.86	0.62	0.54	0.47	Total final expenditure excluding stockbuilding
1.62	1.27	1.08	0.96	Stockbuilding
1.25	0.83	0.75	0.63	Imports of goods and services
1.38	0.95	0.83	0.67	Adjustment to factor cost
0.92	0.74	0.68	0.58	Gross domestic product: compromise estimate at factor cost

growth of the order of a half or a third of one per cent was forecast and in the event this was justified for total final expenditure but not for most of the GDP components which either grew faster than expected (for example the actual change in consumption was over three per cent) or declined (exports fell by over seven per cent). The variance of the predicted changes was only a fifth of that of the outcomes. Then followed the good forecasts of 1968(I): the mean and variance of outcomes were almost perfectly predicted, so that whatever error there was can be attributed to random factors. The next two half years, 1968(II) and 1969(I) were also forecast with relatively low systematic error, but with much inferior accuracy. No-change predictions would have been more accurate, as would have been all our naïve models in 1969(I) and all but the A_{t-1} prediction in 1968(II). Nor do the inequality coefficients for the naïve models suggest that these half-years were particularly difficult to forecast; for example, the one-year moving average performs quite well in 1968(II) as does the sample A_{t-1} extrapolation in 1969(I). Rather it seems that in both cases a number of spurious downturns were predicted.

The later half-years are predicted more evenly with accuracy much superior to that of the naïve models, although systematic mistakes, in the form of consistently under-predicted means and variances of outcomes,

Table 7.4 (continued)

U	U^M	U^S	U^C	r	α	β	SE (α)	SE (β)	$\bar{P}$	$\bar{A}$	s_P/s_A
0.72	0.42	0.02	0.56	0.69	1.02	0.60	0.31	0.22	0.52	1.33	1.15
0.88	0.08	0.30	0.61	−0.24	1.75	−0.68	1.27	0.99	1.24	0.90	0.35
1.15	0.00	0.02	0.98	−0.20	1.52	−0.25	0.82	0.44	1.26	1.20	0.80
0.54	0.03	0.16	0.81	0.77	0.50	1.03	1.41	0.31	2.77	3.36	0.75
0.34	0.66	0.00	0.34	0.92	0.59	0.91	0.20	0.14	1.10	1.59	1.01
0.98	0.10	0.52	0.38	0.33	−105.61	1.18	161.32	1.57	36.58	−62.59	0.28
0.68	0.10	0.03	0.87	0.57	1.82	0.48	0.81	0.24	2.01	2.78	1.18
0.74	0.52	0.01	0.47	0.69	1.76	0.76	0.55	0.28	0.63	2.24	0.91
0.32	0.25	0.15	0.60	0.92	0.46	0.76	0.15	0.11	0.95	1.18	1.21

accounts for an average forty-one per cent of error from the second half of 1969 onwards. $\bar{A}$ is the best naïve predictor for all half-years except 1967(II), when the three-year moving average and the no-change assumption yield lower inequality values.

Table 7.6 presents an observation-by-observation analysis of the NIESR half-yearly forecasts. Two thirds of all actual changes are under-predicted. This tendency is most marked for increases in consumers' expenditure, exports and total final expenditure, but not at all for increases in public authorities' current spending and gross fixed investment, nor for negative changes for the series as a whole. Outcomes may be underestimated, but the error, measured as a percentage of the outcome, decreases with outcome size. For all pairs of predictions and outcomes with the same sign, excluding the observations for stockbuilding, the linear correlation between $|(P_t - A_t)/A_t|$ and $|A_t|$ is -0.27, and the correlation between the logarithms of the error and outcome magnitudes is -0.41, both of which are significant at the five per cent level. As the value of the outcome is reduced it becomes more difficult to perceive and predict.

Less than a fifth of the forecasts commit turning-point errors, and none at all of the GDP forecasts have the incorrect sign. There are four actual turning-points in fixed investment and seven in stockbuilding, and both series have four turning-point errors. However the sign of changes in factor

Table 7.5

Accuracy analysis of NIESR half-yearly forecasts: cross-section 1967(I)-1971(II)

A_{t-1}	*U* for naïve models 1-year moving average	3-year moving averege	$\bar{A}$	
1.36	0.96	0.69	0.55	1967 (I)
1.43	1.43	1.19	1.34	1967 (II)
1.41	1.07	0.90	0.70	1968 (I)
1.61	0.66	0.71	0.62	1968 (II)
0.73	0.97	0.78	0.73	1969 (I)
0.76	0.55	0.55	0.49	1969 (II)
1.06	0.90	0.56	0.52	1970 (I)
0.63	0.70	0.69	0.56	1970 (II)
1.10	1.11	1.06	0.88	1971 (I)
1.05	0.78	0.80	0.62	1971 (II)

cost adjustment are correctly predicted, even though this series is also fairly volatile; there are five actual turning-points out of a total of ten observations. Turning-point errors in fixed investment and stockbuilding are predominantly overestimates (either missed downturns or forecast upturns which did not occur when predicted), otherwise underestimation characterises the misforecasting of signs. Note also from columns 13 and 17 of Table 7.6 that there are no spurious turning-points, specifically, no spurious downturns, forecast for public authorities' current spending and exports. For the remaining series there are clearly the few spuriously predicted peaks required to give the significant α regression coefficients on which we have already commented. Altogether, twenty-eight per cent of the forecast turning-points were false, and a quarter of the total number of actual turns were not correctly predicted (see the E_2 and E_1 totals). There were no errors in forecasting actual turning-points in imports, factor cost adjustment and gross domestic product.

4. The OECD forecasts 1967(I)-1971(II)

Table 7.7 presents the time series accuracy analysis for the OECD forecasts together with the inequality coefficients for the naïve models.

Table 7.5 (continued)

U	U^M	U^S	U^C	r	α	β	SE (α)	SE (β)	$\bar{P}$	$\bar{A}$	s_P/s_A
0.67	0.40	0.02	0.58	0.43	2.08	0.51	0.88	0.44	1.41	2.80	0.84
1.03	0.01	0.62	0.36	−0.02	0.12	−0.10	1.59	2.17	0.45	0.08	0.20
0.14	0.01	0.01	0.98	0.98	0.22	0.96	0.46	0.08	4.00	4.06	1.02
1.27	0.15	0.03	0.83	0.18	1.35	0.14	0.76	0.32	0.26	1.39	1.29
1.11	0.06	0.10	0.84	−0.12	1.27	−0.20	0.90	0.67	0.51	1.16	0.60
0.48	0.11	0.45	0.44	0.79	−0.34	1.51	0.86	0.48	1.51	1.94	0.52
0.36	0.33	0.17	0.50	0.78	0.23	1.15	0.62	0.38	1.48	1.93	0.68
0.41	0.07	0.32	0.62	−0.15	2.30	−0.42	1.71	1.14	1.49	1.68	0.36
0.78	0.21	0.03	0.76	0.67	0.70	0.78	0.51	0.36	0.15	0.81	0.86
0.56	0.11	0.26	0.63	0.40	0.91	0.80	1.50	0.74	1.84	2.39	0.50

Except for its forecasts of fixed investment the OECD forecasts compare favourable with the naïve models. The inequality coefficients for private consumption, public consumption, final domestic demand and gross domestic product at market prices are lower than those for the corresponding naïve models; the inequality coefficients for exports and imports are lower than those of naïve models except the three-year moving average model which performs better than the OECD forecasts of exports and as well as the imports forecasts. However, the naïve models all predict fixed investment better than OECD and by a wide margin; the worst

Table 7.6

Underestimation, overestimation and turning-point errors: NIESR half-yearly forecasts 1967(I)-1971(II)

	Positive change		
	Under-estimation (1)	Over-estimation (2)	$P_t = A_t$ (3)
Consumers' expenditure	7	1	0
Public authorities' current spending	3	6	0
Gross fixed investment	3	3	0
Exports of goods and services	8	1	0
Total final expenditure excluding stockbuilding	8	0	1
Stockbuilding	3	0	0
Imports of goods and services	4	3	0
Adjustment to factor cost	5	1	1
Gross domestic product: compromise estimate at factor cost	5	3	1
Total	46	18	3

	Underestimation of turning-point errors (10)	Overestimation of turning-point errors (11)
Consumers' expenditure	1	0
Public authorities' current spending	0	1
Gross fixed investment	1	3
Exports of goods and services	0	1
Total final expenditure excluding stockbuilding	1	0
Stockbuilding	1	3
Imports of goods and services	2	0
Adjustment to factor cost	1	0
Gross domestic product: compromise estimate at factor cost	0	0
Total	7	8

fitting naïve model is A_{t-1} with an inequality coefficient of 1.08 whereas the forecasters' inequality coefficient is 1.33.

Gross domestic product at market prices and final domestic demand (excluding stockbuilding) with inequality coefficients of 0.37 and 0.48 respectively are forecast better than individual components of expenditure indicating some offsetting errors. Imports, with an inequality coefficient of 0.59 are better forecast than exports for which U equals 0.66; these two balance of payments variables are in current prices. In 1967(II) the OECD failed to predict the large fall in exports and in 1968(II) a fall in

Table 7.6 (continued)

Negative change						
Under-estimation (4)	Over-estimation (5)	$P_t = A_t$ (6)	Turning-point errors (7)	Total no. of observations (8)	E (9)
0	1	0	1	10	0.10
0	0	0	1	10	0.10
0	0	0	4	10	0.40
0	0	0	1	10	0.10
0	0	0	1	10	0.10
2	1	0	4	10	0.40
0	0	1	2	10	0.20
1	1	0	1	10	0.10
0	1	0	0	10	0.00
3	4	1	15	90	0.17

A_t no turning-point		A_t turning-point			
P_t no turning-point (12)	P_t turning-point (13)	P_t no turning-point (14)	P_t turning-point (15)	E_1 (16)	E_2 (17)
7	0	1	2	0.33	0.00
8	0	1	1	0.50	0.00
4	2	2	2	0.50	0.50
8	0	1	1	0.50	0.00
9	1	0	0	0.00	1.00
1	2	2	5	0.29	0.29
5	2	0	3	0.00	0.40
4	1	0	5	0.00	0.17
8	0	0	2	0.00	0.00
54	8	7	21	0.25	0.28

imports was predicted when instead they increased. Apart from these half-years, exports and imports were well forecast (omitting the badly forecast half-year in each case gave an inequality coefficient of 0.27 for imports and 0.35 for exports). Private consumption has an inequality coefficient of 0.60 and this coefficient would be much lower (0.46) but for a spurious decline that was predicted for the second half of 1968. Public consumption is forecast with an inequality coefficient of 0.75. Fixed investment is badly forecast with a U value of 1.33.

Bias error is greater than ten per cent for four variables, private consumption, final domestic demand, gross domestic product and imports, with U^M statistics of 0.42, 0.21, 0.18 and 0.12 respectively; $\bar{A}$ being overestimated on average for imports and underestimated on average for the others; bias is negligible for public consumption, investment and exports.

The magnitude of fluctuations in exports and public consumption are markedly underestimated, the respective values of U^S being 0.63 and 0.62. Final domestic demand (U^S = 0.16) and imports (0.10) are the only other series with variance error exceeding ten per cent of total mean-square error.

Overall there is a fair amount of systematic error, which is least evident in the badly forecast fixed investment series (U^C =0.95) and in the

Table 7.7

Accuracy analysis of OECD half-yearly forecasts: time series 1967(I)-1971(II)

	U for naïve models			
A_{t-1}	1-year moving average	3-year moving average	$\bar{A}$	
1.07	0.90	0.75	0.69	Private consumption
0.94	0.88	0.99	0.76	Public consumption
1.08	0.99	1.02	0.82	Fixed investment
0.95	0.85	0.74	0.96	Final domestic demand (excluding stockbuilding)
1.18	0.80	0.56	0.82	Exports [a]
1.06	0.71	0.59	0.65	Imports [a]
1.11	0.82	0.73	0.66	Gross domestic product at market prices

a Current prices

GDP and imports series (U^C = 0.70 and 0.78 respectively); systematic error is largest for exports and public consumption (U^C = 0.36 and 0.38 respectively) as a result of their high variance proportions.

The cross-section accuracy analysis and the inequality coefficients for the naïve models on a cross-section basis are given in Table 7.8.

In five half-years, 1967(II), 1968(I), 1969(I), 1971(I) and (II), the OECD forecasts are superior to all five naïve models; in 1970(I) the forecasts are inferior only to the $\bar{A}$ model, and in 1970(II) inferior only to the three-year moving average, in 1967(I) they are inferior to three naïve models, and in 1968(II) and 1969(II) to four naïve models. The worst forecast half-year is 1968(II), the only half-year for which the cross-section inequality coefficient is greater than one. In that half-year, turning-point errors were made for private and public consumption, total final expenditure and imports, investment was greatly overpredicted and exports underpredicted; however, some of these errors offset each other and growth in GDP was well forecast. The next highest inequality coefficient is in 1967(II) (U = 0.95) when the major errors were in underestimating consumption, investment and total final expenditure and in predicting an increase in exports which in fact fell sharply. In 1969(I) (U = 0.86) expansion was forecast whereas domestic variables declined, and in the second half of the same year there is a high inequality coefficient almost

Table 7.7 (continued)

U	U^M	U^S	U^C	r	α	β	SE (α)	SE (β)	$\bar{P}$	$\bar{A}$	s_P/s_A
0.60	0.42	0.02	0.57	0.75	0.84	0.85	0.05	0.07	0.64	1.33	0.88
0.75	0.00	0.62	0.38	0.19	0.10	0.85	4.56	2.33	0.99	0.94	0.34
1.33	0.01	0.04	0.95	0.06	1.01	0.05	0.27	0.07	1.37	1.07	1.33
0.48	0.21	0.16	0.63	0.77	0.30	1.08	0.14	0.10	0.84	1.20	0.71
0.66	0.01	0.63	0.36	0.67	–4.12	1.86	20.18	0.54	4.34	3.96	0.34
0.59	0.12	0.10	0.78	0.65	2.37	0.49	0.63	0.04	2.82	3.74	1.34
0.37	0.18	0.03	0.79	0.87	0.30	0.95	0.07	0.04	0.98	1.24	0.91

entirely as the result of the prediction of a big increase in investment instead of a small decline. By far the best forecast half-year is 1968(I) for which the inequality coefficient is 0.06 when the OECD forecasters were extremely accurate in predicting all variables. This is the lowest United Kingdom inequality coefficient that we find in the study.

The partial inequality coefficients vary greatly from year to year. The bias proportion ranges from zero in 1967(II) to 0.54 in 1970(I) and the variance proportion from zero in the January-June half of 1967 to 0.63 in the second half of the same year. Most and least systematic error are found in the first and second halves of 1969 respectively. There is no consistent pattern between predicted and actual means or between the variances of predictions and outcomes.

An analysis of under-prediction, over-prediction and turning-point errors is provided in Table 7.9.

Underestimation of changes is marked for private consumption, imports and gross domestic product and is present to a lesser extent in the public consumption, final domestic demand and exports series. Combining positive and negative changes that are not turning-points there are thirty-nine underestimates and seventeen overestimates and this difference is significant at the five per cent level. Forecasts that are turning-point errors are overestimates more often than underestimates.

Overall the OECD makes turning-point errors nineteen per cent of the time; thirty-three per cent of actual turning-points go unpredicted and

Table 7.8

Accuracy analysis of OECD half-yearly forecasts: cross-section 1967(I)-1971(II)

	U for naïve models			
A_{t-1}	1-year moving average	3-year moving average	$\bar{A}$	
1.09	0.74	0.62	0.64	1967 (I)
1.03	1.15	1.05	1.08	1967 (II)
1.76	0.48	0.79	0.50	1968 (I)
0.55	1.17	0.96	0.69	1968 (II)
1.56	1.74	1.73	1.49	1969 (I)
0.79	0.59	0.67	0.60	1969 (II)
0.65	0.61	0.57	0.39	1970 (I)
0.69	0.69	0.47	0.52	1970 (II)
1.18	0.81	0.86	0.93	1971 (I)
1.10	0.75	0.74	0.52	1971 (II)

thirty per cent of forecast turning-points are spurious. Half the forecasts of fixed investment represent turning-point errors; three out of four actual turning-points are missed and two of three predicted turning-points do not eventuate. The public consumption and final domestic demand series have two turning-point errors each, the remaining series each have one.

5. The London Business School forecasts in The Sunday Times 1968 (I)-1971(II)

The time series accuracy analysis for the predictions made by R. J. Ball and T. Burns using the London Business School econometric model are given in Table 7.10 together with the inequality coefficients for the naïve models.

Except for three series, consumers' expenditure on durables, gross fixed private investment in dwellings and imports, the London Business School forecasts perform well against the naïve models; the forecasts for the other seven variables are superior to all the naïve models except that stockbuilding is forecast marginally worse than by the $\bar{A}$ model. However, it should be noted that the forecasts in *The Sunday Times* do not include forecasts of public authorities' current and capital spending; other forecasters usually predict these badly relative to the naïve models, and poor predictions of public investment provide one reason for inaccurate total (public and

Table 7.8 (continued)

U	U^M	U^S	U^C	r	α	β	SE (α)	SE (β)	$\bar{P}$	$\bar{A}$	s_P/s_A
0.83	0.29	0.00	0.70	0.10	1.94	0.10	0.32	0.19	0.92	1.92	1.03
0.95	0.00	0.63	0.37	0.15	0.17	0.71	6.82	4.28	0.89	0.81	0.21
0.06	0.01	0.45	0.54	0.99	0.19	0.91	0.02	0.01	2.01	2.03	1.09
1.13	0.08	0.07	0.85	0.35	1.11	0.26	0.08	0.05	0.64	1.27	1.39
0.86	0.15	0.54	0.31	0.69	−0.65	1.87	0.18	0.77	0.34	−0.07	0.37
0.87	0.05	0.05	0.90	−0.08	1.58	−0.11	2.49	0.40	1.75	1.39	0.70
0.50	0.54	0.02	0.43	0.88	0.87	0.79	0.04	0.04	0.75	1.46	1.11
0.48	0.20	0.34	0.46	0.58	1.24	0.27	0.29	0.03	2.25	1.84	2.16
0.57	0.05	0.19	0.76	0.79	0.17	1.09	0.10	0.15	0.60	1.61	0.72
0.41	0.31	0.06	0.63	0.31	1.60	0.43	2.34	0.36	1.79	2.37	0.76

private) investment forecasts which total is not forecast by the London Business School.

The highest inequality coefficient is for gross fixed private investment in dwellings with an inequality coefficient of 1.35; the London Business School forecasts of this variable are inferior to those of all five naïve models. Other particularly high inequality coefficients are those for stockbuilding and consumers' expenditure on durables with inequality coefficients of 0.94 and 0.93 respectively. The forecasts of consumers' durables are inferior to those generated by the three-year moving average, and the forecasters fail to predict the sign of the average change correctly ($\bar{P}$ is -1.16 and $\bar{A}$ is 3.01). The inequality coefficients for total gross fixed private investment and the non-dwellings components are 0.74 and 0.66

Table 7.9

Underestimation, overestimation and turning-point errors: OECD half-yearly forecasts 1967(I)-1971(II)

	Positive change		
	Under-estimation (1)	Over-estimation (2)	$P_t = A_t$ (3)
Private consumption	7	0	0
Public consumption	5	3	0
Fixed investment	2	3	0
Final domestic demand (excluding stockbuilding)	5	3	0
Exports	6	3	0
Imports	6	2	0
Gross domestic product at market prices	6	2	0
Total	37	16	0

	Underestimation of turning-point errors (10)	Overestimation of turning-point errors (11)
Private consumption	1	0
Public consumption	0	2
Fixed investment	2	3
Final domestic demand (excluding stockbuilding)	1	1
Exports	0	1
Imports	1	0
Gross domestic product at market prices	0	1
Total	5	8

respectively. Total consumers' expenditure has an inequality coefficient of 0.54, the non-durables component's U coefficient being 0.50. Exports are forecast more accurately than imports ($U = 0.43$ and 0.70 respectively); the imports forecasts are outperformed by the one-year and three-year moving averages and the $\bar{A}$ naïve model. The inequality coefficient for gross domestic product is 0.57.

The bias proportion is greater than ten per cent for all variables except total fixed private investment and its non-dwellings component, and is most marked for exports ($U^M = 0.43$), investment in dwellings (0.37) and consumers' durable expenditures (0.23). There is no systematic pattern between $\bar{P}$ and $\bar{A}$. The variance proportion is greater than ten per cent for private non-dwelling investment ($U^S = 0.55$), total private investment

Table 7.9 (continued)

Negative change					
Under-estimation (4)	Over-estimation (5)	$P_t = A_t$ (6)	Turning-point errors (7)	Total no. of observations (8)	E (9)
1	0	1	1	10	0.10
0	0	0	2	10	0.20
0	0	0	5	10	0.50
0	0	0	2	10	0.20
0	0	0	1	10	0.10
1	0	0	1	10	0.10
0	1	0	1	10	0.10
2	1	1	13	70	0.19

A_t no turning-point		A_t turning-point			
P_t no turning-point (12)	P_t turning-point (13)	P_t no turning-point (14)	P_t turning-point (15)	E_1 (16)	E_2 (17)
4	1	0	5	0.00	0.17
7	1	1	1	0.50	0.50
4	2	3	1	0.75	0.67
7	1	1	1	0.50	0.50
8	0	1	1	0.50	0.00
7	1	0	2	0.00	0.33
6	0	1	3	0.25	0.00
43	6	7	14	0.33	0.30

(0.37), GDP (0.36), imports (0.32) and private dwellings investment (0.18). With the exception of non-durable consumption and exports the forecasts underestimate the variance of A_t. Total systematic error is less than thirty per cent only for non-durable consumption and total consumption, both with U^C values of 0.88; systematic error is most marked for private dwelling and non-dwelling investment (U^C = 0.45 in both cases) and gross domestic product (U^C = 0.50).

The cross-section analysis is given in Table 7.11. It is apparent that the performance of the London Business School forecasts against the cross-section naïve models is very variable. The forecasts are superior to all the naïve models in four half-years, 1968(I), 1970(II), 1971(I) and (II); inferior to all the naïve models in two half-years, 1969(I) and (II); inferior to all but the A_{t-1} naïve model in 1970(I) and to the $\bar{A}$, three-year moving average and no-change models in 1968(II). The best forecast half-year is 1970(II) with an inequality coefficient of 0.42; the worst forecast is for 1969(I) with a U of 1.72.

Bias is least noticeable in 1969(II) for which U^M = 0.01 and most marked for 1968(I) with U^M = 0.44; it is also above ten per cent in three further half-years, 1969(I), 1971(I) and (II) for which U^M is equal to 0.19, 0.12 and 0.21 respectively. The variance proportion is highest in

Table 7.10

Accuracy analysis of the London Business School (*The Sunday Times*) half-yearly forecasts: time series 1968(I)-1971(II)

U for naïve models				
A_{t-1}	1-year moving average	3-year moving average	$\bar{A}$	
1.20	1.15	0.90	0.95	Consumers' expenditure: Durables
0.88	0.72	0.59	0.52	Non-durables
1.03	0.94	0.79	0.71	Total
0.76	1.00	1.15	1.00	Gross private fixed investment: Dwellings
1.31	1.10	1.07	0.85	Other
1.39	1.12	1.07	0.86	Total
1.36	1.08	0.81	0.67	Exports of goods and services
1.49	1.28	1.06	0.93	Stockbuilding [a]
1.02	0.58	0.67	0.61	Imports of goods and services
1.27	0.91	0.77	0.68	Gross domestic product at factor cost

a 1968(I)-1970(II)

1971, U^S is 0.48 in the first half of the year and 0.63 in the second; high variance error also occurred in 1968(I), U^S = 0.14, 1968(II), 0.17, and 1969(II), 0.40. Except in the first and second halves of 1970, when unsystematic error is ninety-five and ninety-four per cent respectively, systematic error is quite marked, being highest in 1971 (U^C = 0.39 and 0.16 in the first and second halves respectively) and 1968(I) (U^C = 0.46).

The results of the observation-by-observation analysis for underestimation, overestimation and turning-point errors are presented in Table 7.12. The forecasts that are not turning-point errors are underestimated more often than they are overestimated, while the forecasts that are turning-point errors are overestimated more often than they are underestimated but the differences are not statistically significant at the five per cent level. Underestimation is most marked for non-dwelling investment, exports and imports, and overestimation is most marked for consumption expenditure on non-durables and gross domestic product.

The proportionate forecasting error was correlated with the absolute value of the outcome to see if error and outcome are inversely related as is usually the case. A correlation coefficient that is significant at the five per cent level is obtained only when the errors and outcomes are transformed into logarithms, the correlation coefficient being –0.49.

Table 7.10 (continued)

U	U^M	U^S	U^C	r	α	β	SE (α)	SE (β)	$\bar{P}$	$\bar{A}$	s_P/s_A
0.93	0.23	0.08	0.69	0.53	3.88	0.74	3.10	0.48	–1.16	3.01	0.72
0.50	0.11	0.01	0.88	0.63	0.28	0.58	0.36	0.29	1.08	0.90	1.09
0.54	0.11	0.00	0.88	0.74	0.46	0.77	0.38	0.29	0.80	1.08	0.96
1.35	0.37	0.18	0.45	0.06	–0.63	0.14	5.81	0.94	5.49	0.14	0.43
0.66	0.00	0.55	0.45	0.69	–1.31	1.61	2.21	0.70	2.53	2.75	0.43
0.74	0.06	0.37	0.57	0.56	1.31	1.17	2.43	0.70	2.98	2.18	0.48
0.43	0.43	0.01	0.55	0.88	2.26	0.81	0.91	0.18	2.98	4.68	1.09
0.93	0.00	0.12	0.88	0.41	–6.90	0.61	136.99	0.62	–14.88	–16.04	0.67
0.70	0.13	0.32	0.56	0.01	2.37	0.03	2.01	1.13	1.65	2.41	0.33
0.57	0.15	0.36	0.50	0.65	–0.80	1.30	1.01	0.62	1.52	1.18	0.50

Twenty-two per cent of the forecasts are turning-point errors; misforecast signs are most frequent for stockbuilding (two thirds of the stockbuilding forecasts are turning-point errors) and private investment in dwellings (for which half the forecasts are turning-point errors). Thirty-nine per cent of turning-points are missed in *The Sunday Times* forecasts, most noticeably in inventory investment (two thirds of the time) and gross fixed investment in dwellings and consumers' expenditure on durables and non-durables (both half the time) although the two turning-points in total consumption are correctly predicted. Thirty-six per cent of forecast turning-points prove spurious, including two of the three predicted turning-points in stockbuilding, one of two in consumers' durable expenditure and three out of four in dwellings investment.

6. The Sunday Telegraph forecasts 1967(I)-1971(II)

The accuracy of the forecasts published in *The Sunday Telegraph* is analysed in Table 7.13. The inequality coefficients obtained vary widely, from a low value of 0.15 for consumers' expenditure on non-durables to 1.29 for stockbuilding. On the whole the inequality coefficients tend to be fairly low and the forecasters do not fare too badly in comparison with the naïve models. The forecasts for all but three variables are superior to all the naïve models: the forecasts of stockbuilding are inferior to the

Table 7.11

Accuracy analysis of the London Business School (*The Sunday Times*) half-yearly forecasts: cross-section 1968(I)-1971(II)

	U for naïve models			
A_{t-1}	1-year moving average	3-year moving average	$\bar{A}$	
1.72	1.24	0.93	0.63	1968 (I)
1.27	1.65	0.98	0.97	1968 (II)
0.44	0.94	1.10	1.08	1969 (I)
0.88	0.93	0.86	0.84	1969 (II)
1.44	1.19	0.39	0.78	1970 (I)
0.98	1.38	1.00	0.89	1970 (II)
1.05	1.17	1.39	1.16	1971 (I)
0.97	0.83	0.88	0.89	1971 (II)

one-year, three-year and $\bar{A}$ naïve models and the forecasts for public current and investment spending are both equalled or bettered by the A_{t-1}, one-year moving average and $\bar{A}$ naïve models.

Two aspects of public sector activity are well forecast by *The Sunday Telegraph*; public authorities' current spending has a low inequality coefficient, 0.39, and the statistic is 0.45 for factor cost adjustment, the adjustment to account for indirect taxation and subsidies. Public sector investment is, however, less successfully predicted, its high U value of 0.90 being second only to stockbuilding.

For the other variables we note that exports are forecast more accurately than imports, private fixed investment is forecast better than public fixed investment, and that gross domestic product, in current prices and not seasonally adjusted has the second lowest inequality coefficient, 0.30, and is forecast very much better than gross domestic product seasonally adjusted and in constant prices for which U is 0.70. The first of these GDP coefficients indicates that there have been some offsetting errors.

The bias proportion is ten per cent or greater for eight variables but only for imports, for which U^M is 0.53, is it very marked; U^M is in the range 0.10 to 0.16 for both consumption series, public authorities' current spending, gross private fixed investment, exports and both GDP series. For all the series considered here, excluding real gross domestic product, the mean predicted change is less than the mean actual change.

Seven variables have a variance proportion above ten per cent; the

Table 7.11 (continued)

U	U^M	U^S	U^C	r	α	β	SE (α)	SE (β)	$\bar{P}$	$\bar{A}$	s_P/s_A
0.52	0.40	0.14	0.46	0.88	3.14	0.68	0.22	0.03	2.92	5.12	1.29
1.13	0.07	0.17	0.77	0.66	0.94	0.45	0.01	0.05	−0.49	0.72	1.47
1.72	0.19	0.00	0.81	−0.27	0.49	−0.28	1.64	0.20	2.84	−0.31	0.96
1.09	0.01	0.41	0.58	−0.17	1.16	−0.56	2.35	2.16	1.04	0.57	0.30
1.27	0.05	0.00	0.95	−0.32	2.49	−0.35	1.20	0.21	2.39	1.65	0.91
0.42	0.03	0.03	0.94	0.72	0.87	0.62	0.61	0.07	2.88	2.66	1.16
0.75	0.12	0.48	0.39	0.76	−2.36	1.61	1.51	0.38	1.99	0.84	0.47
0.82	0.21	0.63	0.16	0.43	−0.73	2.90	7.10	2.72	2.34	6.06	0.15

highest values of U^S are for consumers' expenditure on non-durables and gross domestic product in current prices, 0.46 and 0.36 respectively. Public authorities' current spending and exports both have U^S values of 0.26; also above ten per cent are the values for gross fixed public investment, GDP in constant prices and adjustment to factor cost for which U^S

Table 7.12

Underestimation, overestimation and turning-point errors: London Business School (*The Sunday Times*) half-yearly forecasts 1968(I)-1971(II)

	Positive change		
	Under-estimation (1)	Over-estimation (2)	$P_t = A_t$ (3)
Consumers' expenditure:			
Durables	2	2	0
Non-durables	2	5	0
Total	2	4	0
Gross private fixed investment:			
Dwellings	2	2	0
Other	6	0	1
Total	4	2	0
Exports of goods and services	6	1	0
Stockbuilding	0	1	0
Imports of goods and services	6	2	0
Gross domestic product at factor cost	2	5	0
Total	32	24	1

	Underestimation of turning-point errors (10)	Overestimation of turning-point errors (11)
Consumers' expenditure:		
Durables	2	0
Non-durables	0	1
Total	1	0
Gross private fixed investment:		
Dwellings	0	4
Other	0	1
Total	0	2
Exports of goods and services	1	0
Stockbuilding	2	2
Imports of goods and services	0	0
Gross domestic product at factor cost	0	1
Total	6	11

is 0.19, 0.14 and 0.12 respectively. For all the seven variables referred to we observe s_P less than s_A. It is interesting to note that while the variance of A_t is much larger for current-price seasonally unadjusted GDP than for constant-price seasonally adjusted GDP (11.48 compared to 1.46) the variance proportion is lower for the current price series.

Table 7.12 (continued)

Negative change					
Under-estimation (4)	Over-estimation (5)	$P_t = A_t$ (6)	Turning-point errors (7)	Total no. of observations (8)	E (9)
1	1	0	2	8	0.25
0	0	0	1	8	0.12
0	1	0	1	8	0.12
0	0	0	4	8	0.50
0	0	0	1	8	0.12
0	0	0	2	8	0.25
0	0	0	1	8	0.12
1	0	0	4	6	0.67
0	0	0	0	8	0.00
0	0	0	1	8	0.11
2	2	0	17	78	0.22

A_t no turning-point		A_t turning-point			
P_t no turning-point (12)	P_t turning-point (13)	P_t no turning-point (14)	P_t turning-point (15)	E_1 (16)	E_2 (17)
5	1	1	1	0.50	0.50
6	0	1	1	0.50	0.00
5	1	0	2	0.00	0.33
3	3	1	1	0.50	0.75
5	0	1	2	0.33	0.00
3	0	2	3	0.40	0.00
6	1	0	1	0.00	0.50
1	2	2	1	0.67	0.67
8	0	0	0	—	—
5	0	1	2	0.33	0.00
47	8	9	14	0.39	0.36

The cross-section analysis is reported in Table 7.14. The mean value of the inequality coefficients is 0.60 but there is considerable variation about this value. Only three of the individual half-years have inequality coefficients larger than the mean: 1967(II), $U = 0.81$, 1969(I), $U = 1.52$, 1971(II), $U = 0.92$. In 1967(II) the forecasters predicted spurious downturns in consumer durables, private investment and imports. The mean predicted change underestimated the outcome so that bias was twenty-one per cent of the error; accuracy was inferior to that of the $\bar{A}$ model. 1969(I) was a difficult period to forecast; all the naïve models returned their highest U values then. Two substantial turning-point errors, both involving the public sector, contributed to the *Telegraph*'s poor performance: a two per cent fall in public investment was predicted as a seven per cent increase, and a one-and-a-half per cent increase in factor cost adjustment was forecast to fall by two per cent. Bias, overestimation of the average outcome, accounted for fourteen per cent of the mean-square error, eight per cent was due to misforecasting the variance, and the large remainder was random. The forecasters underestimated the growth rate for most of the variables in 1971(II), and bias was nineteen

Table 7.13

Accuracy analysis of *The Sunday Telegraph* half-yearly forecasts: time series 1967(I)-1971(II)

U for naïve models					
A_{t-1}	1-year moving average	3-year moving average	$\bar{A}$		
1.50	0.94	0.87	0.76	Consumers' expediture:	Durables
1.65	0.85	0.85	0.85		Non-durables
0.31	0.36	0.44	0.38	Public authorities' current spending	
0.78	0.90	1.26	0.87	Gross fixed investment:	Public
1.44	0.95	0.90	0.82		Private
1.03	0.89	0.71	0.65	Exports of goods and services	
1.44	1.27	1.09	0.95	Stockbuilding	
0.96	0.80	0.71	0.59	Imports of goods and services	
1.69	1.01	0.95	0.87	Adjustment to factor cost	
				Gross domestic product:	
1.09	0.64	0.62	0.61	Current prices, seasonally unadjusted	
1.28	0.93	0.82	0.74	Constant prices, seasonally adjusted	

per cent; in particular a sixteen per cent increase in consumers' expenditure on durables was forecast as a fall of seven per cent. Accuracy is superior for the one-year and three-year moving averages, and for $\bar{A}$. Moreover 1971(II) yields the lowest U value for the one-year moving average.

The remaining half-years are well forecast. For 1968(I), the inequality coefficient is 0.34, and the correlation between predictions and outcomes is 0.92; for 1968(II), $U = 0.33$ and $r = 0.94$; for 1969(II), the most accurately forecast half year, $U = 0.31$ and $r = 0.86$; for 1970(II), $U = 0.34$ and $r = 0.93$. Total systematic error is only higher than twenty-five per cent for 1970(II) when the mean outcome was markedly underestimated, and marginally for 1971(I), when the forecast spread of changes was somewhat too small. In 1969(II) all the (rounded) error was random.

Our tabulation of the number of forecasts which are overestimates and underestimates and which commit turning-point errors supports our earlier conclusions. From Table 7.15 we see the large number of actual fluctuations in non-durable consumption, all of which are predicted by *The Sunday Telegraph* and most of which are underestimated. For stockbuilding, underestimation of (larger) changes is again the rule but there are

Table 7.13 (continued)

U	U^M	U^S	U^C	r	α	β	SE(α)	SE(β)	$\bar{P}$	$\bar{A}$	s_P/s_A
0.76	0.14	0.04	0.83	0.65	5.16	0.55	2.52	0.23	4.22	7.46	1.18
0.15	0.16	0.46	0.38	0.99	0.01	1.12	0.29	0.04	3.38	3.81	0.88
0.39	0.10	0.23	0.67	0.27	2.45	0.55	2.84	0.69	4.03	4.65	0.49
0.90	0.05	0.19	0.76	−0.13	4.50	−0.27	3.43	0.73	4.36	3.32	0.48
0.49	0.15	0.03	0.81	0.84	1.72	0.94	1.44	0.21	3.08	4.62	0.89
0.39	0.12	0.23	0.65	0.91	2.60	0.71	0.97	0.11	5.10	6.20	1.28
1.29	0.08	0.01	0.91	0.15	−7.88	0.17	253.97	0.18	38.06	−1.57	0.89
0.53	0.53	0.01	0.46	0.82	3.20	0.77	0.94	0.19	2.79	5.35	1.06
0.45	0.00	0.12	0.88	0.86	−0.02	1.04	1.58	0.22	3.90	4.04	0.83
0.30	0.14	0.36	0.49	0.91	−0.50	1.30	0.92	0.21	3.76	4.40	0.70
0.70	0.12	0.14	0.74	0.14	0.00	0.74	0.82	0.48	1.51	1.11	0.65

fewer actual turning-points to trouble the forecasters. However a third of the forecasts now wrongly predict the sign of the outcome. There are four actual turning-points in the constant price GDP series, half of which are downturns which are not forecast. Constant price increases are typically overestimated. The current price GDP series has no downturns and growth from one half-year to the next is usually underestimated if it is not correctly forecast; note that there are three pairs of observations for which (rounded) P_t equals (rounded) A_t. Forecasts of constant price, seasonally adjusted GDP and of consumers' expenditure on durables provide marked exceptions to the preponderance of actual increments and decreases which are under-predicted.

Correlating the absolute value of the percentage error with the absolute value of the outcome for all pairs of observations, excluding stocks, which are not turning-point errors reveals the familiar inverse relationship: r is -0.38 for the linear correlation and -0.49 for the log-linear correlation, and both are significant at the five per cent level.

One sixth of the forecasts predicts an incorrect sign. Of these, approximately two thirds are underestimates. Column 13 and 14 and the associat-

Table 7.14

Accuracy analysis of *The Sunday Telegraph* half-yearly forecasts: cross-section 1967(I)-1971(II)

	U for naïve models			
A_{t-1}	1-year moving avereage	3-year moving average	$\bar{A}$	
2.08	1.16	1.05	0.83	1967 (I)
1.51	0.90	1.08	0.72	1967 (II)
0.97	0.97	0.83	0.62	1968 (I)
1.33	1.04	0.92	0.97	1968 (II)
3.86	2.56	1.60	1.87	1969 (I)
1.00	0.52	0.53	0.71	1969 (II)
1.45	0.99	0.75	0.65	1970 (I)
0.95	0.54	0.55	0.55	1970 (II)
1.50	0.94	1.10	0.83	1971 (I)
1.02	0.62	0.68	0.61	1971 (II)

ed E_1 and E_2 values indicate that spurious turning-points are as common as wrongly forecast actual turning-points. Thus the typical turning-point error entails the forecasters predicting a downturn which does not occur. Turning-point errors are avoided completely in the forecasts of non-durable consumption, public authorities' current spending and exports.

7. A comparison of the forecasts

To facilitate comparison of the forecasters' performance we reproduce, in Table 7.16, the time series inequality coefficients and U^C statistics and, in Table 7.17, the corresponding information for the cross-section analysis.

The time series inequality coefficients range from the very good 0.15 for *The Sunday Telegraph*'s forecasts of consumers' expenditures on non-durables to the remarkable figure of 1.42 for the Treasury's forecasts of public authorities' current spending. The cross-section inequality coefficients vary from the OECD's excellent 0.06 for 1968(I) to the London Business School's 1.72 for 1969(I).

Table 7.14 (continued)

U	U^M	U^S	U^C	r	α	β	SE(α)	SE(β)	$\bar{P}$	$\bar{A}$	s_P/s_A
0.57	0.07	0.00	0.93	0.82	1.54	0.84	1.66	0.23	2.04	3.26	0.98
0.81	0.21	0.03	0.76	0.48	3.41	0.39	1.27	0.27	2.27	4.29	1.23
0.34	0.05	0.17	0.78	0.92	2.34	0.76	1.27	1.13	6.56	7.30	1.21
0.33	0.12	0.02	0.86	0.94	1.07	0.99	1.17	0.14	3.53	4.56	0.95
1.52	0.14	0.08	0.78	0.28	0.53	0.19	0.99	0.25	2.32	0.97	1.47
0.31	0.00	0.00	1.00	0.86	0.63	0.87	1.42	0.20	5.90	5.77	0.99
0.43	0.00	0.11	0.89	0.89	0.95	0.75	0.97	0.15	3.76	3.76	1.19
0.34	0.85	0.02	0.13	0.93	3.75	0.81	0.76	0.12	5.48	8.18	1.15
0.42	0.02	0.24	0.74	0.89	−0.05	1.16	1.18	0.22	2.61	2.99	0.77
0.92	0.19	0.00	0.81	−0.19	8.48	−0.20	2.50	0.40	3.98	7.67	0.95

Table 7.15

Underestimation, overestimation and turning-point errors: *The Sunday Telegraph* half-yearly forecasts 1967(I)-1971(II)

	Positive change		
	Under-estimation (1)	Over-estimation (2)	$P_t = A_t$ (3)
Consumers' expenditure·			
Durables	1	4	0
Non-durables	5	0	0
Public authorities' current spending	6	4	0
Gross fixed investment:			
Public:	4	4	0
Private	3	2	0
Exports of goods and services	6	3	0
Stockbuilding	2	1	0
Imports of goods and services	5	2	0
Adjustment to factor cost	3	2	0
Gross domestic product:			
Current prices, seasonally unadjusted	4	2	3
Constant prices, seasonally adjusted	2	5	1
Total	41	29	4

	Underestimation of turning-point errors (10)	Overestimation of turning-point errors (11)
Consumers' expediture:		
Durables	3	1
Non-durables	0	0
Public authorities' current spending	0	0
Gross fixed investment:		
Public	0	2
Private	2	0
Exports of goods and services	0	0
Stockbuilding	1	2
Imports of goods and services	3	0
Adjustment to factor cost	2	0
Gross domestic product:		
Current prices, seasonally unadjusted	1	0
Constant prices, seasonally adjusted	0	2
Total	12	7

Table 7.15 (continued)

Negative change					
Under-estimation (4)	Over-estimation (5)	$P_t = A_t$ (6)	Turning-point errors (7)	Total no. of observations (8)	E (9)
0	1	0	4	10	0.40
3	2	0	0	10	0.00
0	0	0	0	10	0.00
0	0	0	2	10	0.20
2	1	0	2	10	0.20
0	0	1	0	10	0.00
3	1	0	3	10	0.30
0	0	0	3	10	0.30
3	0	0	2	10	0.20
0	0	0	1	10	0.10
0	0	0	2	10	0.20
11	5	1	19	110	0.17

A_t no turning-point		A_t turning-point			
P_t no turning-point (12)	P_t turning-point (13)	P_t no turning-point (14)	P_t turning-point (15)	E_1 (16)	E_2 (17)
2	3	1	4	0.20	0.43
0	0	0	10	0.00	0.00
10	0	0	0	0.00	0.00
7	1	1	1	0.50	0.50
3	1	1	5	0.17	0.17
8	0	0	2	0.00	0.00
2	2	1	5	0.17	0.29
7	2	1	0	1.00	1.00
2	2	0	6	0.00	0.25
9	1	0	0	0.00	1.00
6	0	2	2	0.50	0.00
56	12	7	35	0.17	0.26

Table 7.16

Inequality coefficients and proportion of error that is non-systematic: half-yearly forecasts, time series

		U				
		Treasury	NIESR	OECD	London Business School	*The Sunday Telegraph*
Consumers' expenditure:	Durables				0.93	<0.76>
	Non-durables				0.50	<0.15>
	Total	0.83	0.72	0.60	0.54	
Public authorities' current spending		1.42	0.88	0.75		<0.39>
Gross fixed investment:	Public	1.10				<0.90>
	Private dwellings				1.35	
	Private non-dwellings				0.66	
	Total private	1.23			0.74	<0.49>
	Total	0.93	1.15	1.33		
Exports of goods and services		0.39	0.54	[0.66]	0.43	<0.39>
Total final expenditure		0.47[a]	0.34[b]	0.48[c]		
Stockbuilding		0.74	0.98		0.93	<1.29>
Imports of goods and services		0.76	0.68	[0.59]	0.70	<0.53>
Adjustment to factor cost		0.67	0.74			<0.45>
Gross domestic product		0.56[d g]	0.32[d g]	0.37[e]	0.57[d i]	{ 0.70 / <0.30> }[d f]

		U^C				
		Treasury	NIESR	OECD	London Business School	*The Sunday Telegraph*
Consumers' expenditure:	Durables				0.69	<0.83>
	Non-durables				0.88	<0.38>
	Total	0.89	0.56	0.57	0.88	

Table 7.16 (continued)

Public authorities' current spending		0.80	0.61	0.38		<0.67>
Gross fixed investment:	Public	0.94				<0.76>
	Private dwellings				0.45	
	Private non-dwellings				0.45	
	Total private	0.66			0.57	<0.81>
	Total	0.61	0.98	0.95		
Exports of goods and services		0.51	0.81	[0.36]	0.55	<0.65>
Total final expenditure		0.86[a]	0.34[b]	0.63[c]		
Stockbuilding		0.76	0.38		0.88	<0.91>
Imports of goods and services		0.80	0.87	[0.78]	0.56	<0.46>
Adjustment to factor cost		0.31	0.47			<0.88>
Gross domestic product		0.93[d g]	0.60[d g]	0.79[e]	0.50[d i]	{0.74 / <0.49>}[d f]

<> Denotes current price seasonally unadjusted data.
[ ] Denotes current price seasonally adjusted data.
a Including stockbuilding.
b Excluding stockbuilding.
c Final domestic demand excluding stockbuilding
d At factor cost
e At market prices, compromise estimate
f Expenditure estimate
g Compromise estimate
i Expenditure estimate 1968(I)-1970(II); compromise estimate, average of expenditure and output measures 1971(I) and 1971(II).

We first look at the forecasts of real gross domestic product, the most widely accepted measure of general economic activity. Having noted that the forecasters define GDP differently and that there are some differences in the time periods covered by the forecasts, it is nevertheless clear that the forecasts by the National Institute and OECD are the most accurate. Inequality coefficients of 0.32 for NIESR and 0.37 for OECD compare favourably with the overall pattern of inequality coefficients that we have seen in earlier chapters. Following NIESR and OECD are, in order, the Treasury ($U = 0.56$), the London Business School (0.57) and *The Sunday Telegraph* (0.70).

The Sunday Telegraph forecasts of current-price seasonally unadjusted gross domestic product are much more accurate than its constant-price seasonally adjusted forecasts, the respective inequality coefficients being 0.30 and 0.70. Three explanations for this readily come to mind. First, the emphasis of *The Sunday Telegraph* team is on forecasting in terms of current prices without seasonal adjustment and one may expect, therefore, that they should show greater expertise at this. Secondly, it may be easier to forecast variables that are not seasonally adjusted than those that are. Thirdly, it may be easier to forecast in terms of current prices than in terms of constant prices. We have no evidence on the validity of explanations one and two; but we do have evidence that provides a test of the third hypothesis. Results obtained from other countries suggest that forecasting in current prices is rather easier than forecasting in constant prices; in Chapter 8 we shall see that inequality coefficients for gross national product in constant prices tend to be larger than inequality coefficients for gross national product in current prices for forecasts made at the same time by the same forecaster as part of the same set of projections; and the differences are quite substantial, the inequality coefficients for the constant price forecasts are up to twice as large as those for the corresponding current price forecasts.[3] Those for *The Sunday Telegraph* forecasts of components of gross domestic product are quite low compared with those obtained for the other forecasters. For exports *The Sunday Telegraph* inequality coefficient is the same as for the Treasury and for imports the same as the OECD; for the other GDP components *The Sunday Telegraph* has the lowest inequality coefficient excepting only stockbuilding where its U coefficient is the highest. How should we interpret these results? Do they really reflect superior forecasting or do they mean that the Morrell team is working with a more predictable set of current price variables? In the light of the two GDP inequality coefficients and the overseas evidence we are confident that *The Sunday Telegraph* inequality coefficients should be raised (or the other inequality coefficients lowered) to allow for *The Sunday Telegraph*'s easier forecasting task. But we do not know how large this adjustment should be. Consequently we limit the discussion in the following paragraph to seasonally adjusted components of gross domestic product in constant prices.

The honours for forecasting the individual components of real GDP must be shared between the Treasury, NIESR, the OECD and the London Business School. The London Business School forecasts total consumers' expenditure the best with an inequality coefficient of 0.54 followed by the OECD ($U = 0.60$), NIESR (0.72) and the Treasury (0.83). The OECD's are the most accurate forecasts of public authorities' current spending ($U = 0.75$) and the Treasury's forecasts are by far the worst ($U = 1.42$). Overall, gross fixed investment is best forecast by the London Business School although it must be remembered that forecasts of public investment are not included. The Treasury, with an inequality coefficient of 0.39, provides the most accurate forecasts of exports, followed by the London Business School ($U = 0.43$) and NIESR (0.54). The OECD forecasts of current-price seasonally adjusted exports are inferior to those by the other forecasters. However, its forecasts of imports on the same basis are superior to the constant price forecasts. The best constant price forecasts of imports are by NIESR with an inequality coefficient, 0.68, marginally lower than the London Business School's 0.70; the Treasury coefficient is 0.76. The OECD forecasts imports better than exports; the other four forecasters predict exports better than imports. The NIESR forecast of total final expenditure excluding stockbuilding is superior to the Treasury's forecast of total final expenditure including stockbuilding and to the OECD forecast of final domestic demand excluding stockbuilding. The Treasury, with an inequality coefficient of 0.74, forecasts stockbuilding with the least error, the U coefficients for the London Business School and NIESR being 0.93 and 0.98 respectively; the OECD does not forecast stockbuilding on a comparable basis. Only the Treasury and NIESR forecast the adjustment to factor cost and the Treasury forecasts ($U = 0.67$) are marginally superior.

We conclude our time series comparisons with a consideration of the extent to which the different forecasters make systematic errors and a brief summary of the principal sources of systematic error in the forecasts. Looking at the nine major categories in Table 7.16 we see that the Treasury has the least systematic error for four variables (consumption, public authorities' current spending, total final expenditure and GDP), NIESR least for three (investment, exports and imports) and *The Sunday Telegraph* least for two (stockbuilding and factor cost adjustment). NIESR has most systematic error for three variables (stockbuilding, consumption and total final expenditure), OECD for two (public authorities' current spending and exports), the London Business School also for two (fixed investment and GDP) and the Treasury and *The Sunday Telegraph* for one each (factor cost adjustment and imports respectively).

Systematic error is low for the Treasury and London Business School forecasts of consumption; for NIESR and *The Sunday Times* the systematic error is mainly underestimation of changes in consumption, for *The Sunday Telegraph* there is underestimation of the average changes also but more important here is the underestimation of the variance of actual changes for non-durables. For public authorities' current spending the largest bias proportion is only thirteen per cent (the Treasury), most systematic error for this variable being underestimation of the magnitude of fluctuations. The errors in the NIESR and OECD forecasts of investment are mainly unsystematic; the systematic errors by the other forecasters primarily consist of underestimating growth rates and underestimating the magnitude of fluctuations although the London Business School and *The Sunday Telegraph* overestimate the rate of growth of private dwelling investment and public investment respectively. Both bias and variance error is to be found in the stockbuilding forecasts; systematic error is most marked for the National Institute, where it stems in the main from the underestimation of fluctuations. Excepting only *The Sunday Telegraph* forecasts, exports are predicted with more systematic error than imports. With the single exception of the exports forecast issued by the OECD, the rate of growth of both exports and imports are underestimated; fluctuations in both balance of payments series are under-predicted except for exports forecast in *The Sunday Telegraph*. The high systematic error for adjustment to factor cost in the Treasury and NIESR forecasts is mainly bias error with growth rates underestimated. Overall when the individual components of GDP are aggregated some of the systematic errors in the components appear to offset each other. For GDP the Treasury error is mainly unsystematic. The OECD underestimates growth of GDP; NIESR is conservative in predicting growth but overestimates fluctuations; the London Business School and *The Sunday Telegraph* do the reverse; however, in its forecasts in nominal terms *The Sunday Telegraph* under-predicts the growth rate so that too modest a rate of inflation is forecast.

It is apparent from the cross-section summary in Table 7.17 that the accuracy with which the five forecasting teams predict half-years tends to move together. There are three major exceptions. 1968(II) saw relatively poor forecasting in real terms, although *The Sunday Telegraph*'s current price forecasts were quite accurate. Against the general trend, the OECD predictions failed to improve from the first to the second half of 1969.

Table 7.17

Inequality coefficients and proportion of error that is non-systematic: half-yearly forecasts, cross-section

U						U^C				
Treasury	NIESR	OECD[a]	London Business School	*The Sunday Telegraph*		Treasury	NIESR	OECD[a]	London Business School	*The Sunday Telegraph*
	0.67	0.83		<0.57>	1967 (I)		0.58	0.70		<0.93>
	1.03	0.95		<0.81>	1967 (II)		0.36	0.37		<0.76>
0.37	0.14	0.06	0.52	<0.34>	1968 (I)	0.37	0.98	0.54	0.46	<0.78>
1.18	1.27	1.13	1.13	<0.33>	1968 (II)	0.85	0.83	0.85	0.77	<0.86>
1.50	1.11	0.86	1.72	<1.52>	1969 (I)	0.94	0.84	0.31	0.81	<0.78>
0.56	0.48	0.87	1.09	<0.31>	1969 (II)	0.49	0.44	0.90	0.58	<1.00>
0.39	0.36	0.50	1.27	<0.43>	1970 (I)	0.36	0.50	0.43	0.95	<0.89>
0.40	0.41	0.48	0.42	<0.34>	1970 (II)	0.67	0.62	0.46	0.94	<0.13>
0.44	0.78	0.57	0.75	<0.42>	1971 (I)	0.85	0.76	0.76	0.39	<0.74>
0.49	0.56	0.41	0.82	<0.92>	1971 (II)	0.67	0.63	0.63	0.16	<0.81>

[a] Exports and imports at current prices, P_t and A_t divided by two for these variables to avoid scale distortion.

<> Data in current prices, seasonally adjusted.

Similarly, there was no improvement in the London Business School forecasts in 1970(I).

The best forecast half-years are 1968(I) when the inequality coefficients for the OECD and the National Institute were 0.06 and 0.14 respectively, and both halves of 1970 (except for the London Business School's bad forecast in the first half of 1970). The low inequality coefficients for 1968(I) indicate that the forecasters correctly estimated the extent of the economy's short-run response to devaluation. The year 1970 seems to have been a fairly easy one to forecast: the naïve models predict quite well, growth rates were about on trend and the lowest annual inequality coefficient obtained for the Treasury in the period 1951-1971, 0.25, was for that year.

The second half of 1968 and the first half of 1969 were badly predicted by the Treasury, NIESR, OECD and the London Business School; *The Sunday Telegraph* forecast 1968(II) well but 1969(I) badly. In both 1968(II) and 1969(I) the forecasters overestimated public authorities' current spending and investment and underestimated exports and imports; typically the forecasters underestimated consumption in 1968(II) and overestimated it in 1969(I), the net result being that gross domestic product was under estimated in 1968(II) and overestimated in 1969(I). The forecasters underestimated the cutback in government spending in both half-years but nevertheless apparently overestimated the impact in 1968(II) of the fiscal measures (cuts in government spending and increases in taxation) in the March 19th 1968 Budget. In 1969(I) they overcompensated for their previous errors and now underestimated the bite of the fiscal measures. Thus they erred in estimating the timing and magnitude of the government's attempts to restrict demand. In 1969(II) and 1970 the forecasts improved though the inequality coefficients for the London Business School were still high in 1969(II) and 1970(I) mainly because of the difficulty in forecasting investment, especially dwelling investment, and expenditure on consumers' durables.

We do not make a direct comparison of the cross-section inequality coefficients of the various forecasters. Such a comparison would probably be unfair to the London Business School forecasting team for their forecasts are more disaggregated, probably harder to make and hence more subject to error than those of the Treasury, NIESR and OECD. This view is supported by our observation that there is little difference between the cross-section inequality coefficients obtained by the Treasury, NIESR, OECD and *The Sunday Telegraph* even though the time series current-price seasonally unadjusted inequality coefficients of *The Sunday Telegraph* were much lower; we put this down to greater disaggregation of the forecasts included in *The Sunday Telegraph*'s cross-sections.

We note that there is considerable variability in the proportion of error that is systematic in different half-years and that, unlike U, there is little tendency for the forecasters' U^C values to move together half-year by half-year. *The Sunday Telegraph* team, whose U^C statistic ranges from unity in 1969(I) to 0.13 in 1970(II), records both the largest and smallest random error proportions.

From Tables 7.3, 7.6, 7.9, 7.12 and 7.15 it is evident that *The Sunday Telegraph* is the most successful predictor of turning-points. However, as its forecasts are not seasonally adjusted, many of the turning-points in its data are likely to be due regular, seasonal fluctuations, which should be easier to predict than genuine economic cycles. Of the other four forecasters, the National Institute clearly performs the best.

Notes

1 From *Economic Trends* (October 1972) we extracted seasonally adjusted constant-price data and seasonally unadjusted current-price data on the aggregate expenditure variables. All outcome data for all variables summing to, and including, the seasonally adjusted constant-price compromise measure of gross domestic product (simple average of the expenditure, output and income measures) were taken from recent issues of the *National Institute Economic Review* except for OECD which were taken from issues of the *OECD Economic Outlook*.

2 J. R. Shepherd, H. P. Evans and C. J. Riley, 'The Treasury short-term forecasting model,' paper presented at the Social Science Research Council Conference on Econometric Model Building in the United Kingdom at the London Business School (July 1972) p. 2.

3 See Tables 8.1, 8.8 and 8.10.

8 International Comparisons

1. Introduction

Previous chapters have examined the accuracy of United Kingdom macroeconomic forecasts and compared the performances of genuine forecasts and naïve models. One further set of comparisons is possible: to compare the accuracy of the U. K. forecasts with similar forecasts made in other countries. This is the object of the present chapter. Successive sections deal with annual, quarterly and half-yearly forecasts.

The methods of analysis used to evaluate the forecasts in other countries vary from study to study. Many studies do not estimate inequality coefficients. However, some studies provide us with raw data from which we can calculate inequality coefficients. Others produce summary statistics of the ratio of the mean-square error of the forecasts to the mean-square error of naïve models from which inequality coefficients may be inferred. Where such inferences cannot be made we may be able to estimate ratios from our data comparable to the ratios available for some other countries. Also when turning-point analyses are not presented by other authors, we have sometimes been able to make use of their data to make our own turning-point calculations.

The nature and coverage of the forecasts being variable, valid comparisons of international accuracy are often difficult to make. We comment on these problems as they arise but list some more obvious ones here.

(1) The frequency and magnitude of fluctuations differ from country to country: it is likely to be easier to forecast developments in a country experiencing fairly steady growth and little cyclical variation than countries subject to large cyclical swings.
(2) The accuracy of statistics and the speed with which they are available varies from country to country.
(3) Some forecasts are made by official agencies, others by private institutions; obviously the information available to the two groups may vary.
(4) Some forecasts are made on a continuing basis by the same organisation; others less regularly by different individuals.

(5) Definitions of variables are not the same in different countries.
(6) Differences in the extent to which countries are subject to direct controls will affect the difficulty of the forecasting task.
(7) Values may be forecast in either real or nominal terms: it seems clear that forecasts in current prices are rather easier to make than forecasts in constant prices.
(8) Many of the inequality coefficients estimated for other countries are for absolute not percentage changes. Fortunately, whenever the analysis involves long time series, percentage change data has been used, so little distortion to our results is likely to have arisen on this account.
(9) Some forecasts may be adjusted for post-forecast policy changes; our U.K. forecasts are not.
(10) Finally, there is the important question of the time-span covered by the forecast. Some forecasts refer to a period some months or quarters in the future; some other forecasts are not made until part of the period being forecast has elapsed. The U.K. forecasts usually fall into this second category.

Most of the forecasts for other countries that we analyse are genuine forecasts in the sense that, though they were initially derived as raw predictions from econometric models, they were subsequently modified by the forecasters to allow for 'judgement', before they were finally published. This is the case also with the U.K. forecasts so in our international comparisons we are comparing like with like. There are some U.S. studies that have compared the predictive powers of different econometric models without adjusting the raw forecasts in any way.[1] We do not consider these in the present study; the comparable U.K. forecasts would be raw econometric forecasts, which are not generally available. The forecasts from the Fair model are not genuine in the sense of being published predictions.[2] However, they are predictions generated by the model for a period outside the sample used to estimate the model and extrapolated values of the exogenous variables are used so that the predictions may be regarded as reconstructions of forecasts that could have been made with the model. Fair compares these predictions with those of the Wharton model and we have accepted them for analysis.

2. Annual forecasts

Table 8.1 presents time series inequality coefficients for some annual forecasts in the Netherlands and the United States for different time periods together with the United Kingdom coefficients from Chapter 3. We present coefficients only for variables comparable to those for which we have U.K. forecasts and we do not list the U.K. coefficients for variables for which we have been unable to locate corresponding forecasts for other countries. Inequality coefficients for the Netherlands were published in a study by de Wolff.[3] A number of other estimates are available for slightly different time periods[4] but we have taken the longest series published. The inequality coefficients for the predictions of various U.S. forecasters analysed by Zarnowitz[5] (and identified by him only by code letters) were inferred from results he presented. Zarnowitz presents indices measuring the ratio of the mean-square error of the forecasts to the root-mean-square error of forecasts by various naïve models. One of these naïve models is constructed on the basis of a no-change assumption. This means that the resulting ratio is the inequality coefficient.[6]

Some of the forecasts are in terms of current prices: these are indicated by being placed within square brackets. Where possible we have included inequality coefficients for both constant and current prices to give some indication of whether it is easier to forecast in terms of current or constant prices; this will help us to interpret comparisons when we only have constant price forecasts for the U.K. and current price forecasts for other countries.

The Dutch forecasts are official forecasts made by the Central Planning Bureau. It is readily apparent that they tend to be superior to the United Kingdom forecasts. The inequality coefficients for the Netherlands forecasts for the most recent period 1958-1963 are lower than all the corresponding U.K. inequality coefficients except for the export series. Some U.K. coefficients for other series are superior to the Netherlands forecasts over the period 1953-1963, most noticeably some of the NIESR May forecasts. It should be noted, however, that the Dutch forecasts are finalised by the December preceding the forecast year and published in February of the forecast year[7] so that they are made earlier than the British forecasts.

We turn now to the forecasts for the United States. Unfortunately all but two of these are in current prices. The two that are in constant prices are the forecasts of gross national product by the Council of Economic Advisers and by the University of Michigan model. All the U.K. forecasts of GDP are superior to those of the Michigan model. The Treasury forecasts for the period 1963-1971 are marginally superior to those by the Council of Economic Advisers, the other U.K. forecasts are slightly worse. Again attention must be drawn to the time at which the forecasts are made: the U.S. forecasts are made before the start of the year to be forecast while the U.K. forecasts are published some way into the year.

Table 8.1

Inequality coefficients for the United Kingdom, the Netherlands and United States: annual forecasts, time series

Country	United Kingdom				Netherlands	
Forecaster	Treasury		NIESR		Central Planning Bureau	
Time period	1951-1971	1963-1971	February 1963-1971	May 1963-1971	1953-1963	1958-1963
Consumers' expenditure	0.47	0.45	0.59	0.34	0.38	0.27
Public authorities' current expenditure	0.72	0.78	0.74	0.73	{0.25[a] 0.67[b]	{0.12[a] 0.49[b]
Gross fixed inverstment	0.53	0.64	0.63	0.56	0.78	0.48
Investment in stocks	0.96	1.04	0.57	0.47	1.01	0.48
Exports	0.56	0.44	0.35	0.45	0.56	0.55
Exports minus imports				[0.81][f]		
Imports	0.51	0.64	0.43	0.30	0.42	0.24
Gross domestic product	0.39	0.29	0.35	0.33		

Country	United States						
Forecaster	Council of Economic Advisers	University of Michigan model	Wharton School model	Various forecasters Forecast Set A	Forecast Set B	Forecast Set C	Forecast Set F
Time period	1962-1972	1953-1967	1963-1967	1953-1963	1953-1963	1953-1963	1953-1963
Consumers' expenditure			[0.10]	[0.22]	[0.32]	[0.31]	[0.35]
Public authorities' current expenditure			[0.23][c]	[0.41][d]	[0.41][d]	[0.32][d]	[0.31][d]
Gross fixed investment			[0.24][e]	[1.12][e]	[0.90][e]	[0.57][e]	[0.51][e]
Investment in stocks			[0.67]				

Table 8.1 (continued)

Exports							
Exports minus imports			[1.35]				
Imports							
Gross domestic product	0.31 [0.18][g]	0.49[g]	[0.06][g]	[0.40][g]	[0.40][g]	[0.37][g]	[0.31][g]

a Government wage bill
b Other public consumption expenditure
c Government purchases of goods and services
d Total government expenditures
e Gross private domestic investment
f 1965-1969 are absolute not percentage changes
g Gross national product
[ ] Forecasts in current prices

Sources for Table 8.1 (continued)

Sources: United Kingdom–Tables 3.1, 3.3 and 6.27.
Netherlands–Pieter de Wolff, 'Macroeconomic forecasting', in *Forecasting on a Scientific Basis*, Proceedings of an International Summer Institute held in Curia, Portugal, September 1966, the NATO Science Committee and the Gulbenkian Foundation, Lisbon (1967).

United States—our calculations. Council of Economics Advisers forecasts for 1962-1967 are given by Geoffrey H. Moore, 'Forecasting short-term economic change', *Journal of the American Statistical Association* (March 1969) p. 11, Table 3; forecasts for 1968-1972 were inferred from statements in the *Economic Report of the President*, 1968-1972 issues. University of Michigan model forecasts as given in Moore, *op cit.* p. 13, Table 5. The actual percentage change series have been calculated from the *Economic Report of the President: 1973*, Table C-2. Wharton School forecasts as given in Michael K. Evans and Lawrence R. Klein, *The Wharton Econometric Forecasting Model* (2nd enlarged edition) University of Pennsylvania, Philadelphia, (1968) Appendix A, p. 175. Forecasts sets A, B, C and F are forecasts gathered from various sources and analysed in Victor Zarnowitz, *An Appraisal of Short-Term Economic Forecasts* Occasional Paper 104 of the National Bureau of Economic Research, Columbia University Press, New York (1967); inequality coefficients are inferred from tabulations presented in Table 17, pp. 94-5.

It is noteworthy that the Council of Economic Advisers' forecasts of gross national product in constant prices are markedly inferior to their forecasts in current prices; this adds support to the hypothesis that forecasting values is easier than forecasting volumes. In view of this the U.K. inequality coefficients for GDP, all of which fall in the range 0.29 to 0.39, compare favourably with the current price forecasts analysed by Zarnowitz which are in the range 0.31 to 0.40. However, the forecast of current price GNP by the Wharton School forecasting team is very good, the inequality coefficient obtained being 0.06 which is markedly lower than any time series inequality coefficient we have obtained; however, it is calculated from only five annual forecasts covering a period of fairly steady growth.

Comparing the U.K. forecasts with the U.S. forecasts for other variables we see that the U.K. consumption forecasts are inferior to all U.S. counterparts except that the inequality coefficient for the NIESR May forecasts is lower than that for Forecast set F. Possible explanations for the relative superiority of the U.S. forecasts are the current price basis on which they are made and the fairly steady continued growth of consumption over the period in question. However, total government expenditures in current prices in the U.S. did not grow steadily over the period (there were declines in 1954 and 1955 and for other years there were some quite marked variations in growth rates) but all the U.S. forecasts are superior to all the U.K. forecasts. The U.K. performance in forecasting investment is better than Forecast Sets A and B and about as accurate as Set C; however they all are inferior to the Forecast Set F and the Wharton forecasts. Superior U.K. forecasting here may arise because, even in current prices, U.S. investment was quite volatile, for instance, declines were registered in 1954, 1957, 1958 and 1961. The Wharton forecasts for investment in stocks are superior to the Treasury forecasts but inferior to those by the National Institute. The Wharton forecasts of exports minus imports are inferior to the U.K. forecasts of exports and imports separately.

A number of studies have used another inequality coefficient developed by Theil, $V = \sqrt{\frac{1}{n}\Sigma(P_t - A_t)^2} \,/\, \sqrt{\frac{1}{n}\Sigma P_t^2 + \frac{1}{n}\Sigma A_t^2}$ which is bounded by zero and one.[8] Table 8.2 gives this inequality coefficient for the Treasury and NIESR forecasts together with coefficients for the Netherlands, Norway, Sweden, Denmark, Australia and Canada. When coefficients have been available for various time periods we have taken the longest run of years.

Except for public expenditures the Norwegian National Budget forecasts are inferior to the U.K. forecasts: the forecasts are, however, made very much earlier than the U.K. forecasts, in the October of the previous year, and it is not clear to what extent they have been vitiated by policy changes. The Australian forecasts of consumers' expenditure are superior to the British forecasts; however the Australian forecasts are in current prices. It is noteworthy that the United Kingdom forecasts of public spending are inferior to those of other countries except for the Netherlands' forecasts of the government wage bill. Apart from the NIESR February forecasts the British investment forecasts are not bettered by those for any other country. Compared with the Australian performance, stocks are forecast better by the NIESR but worse by the Treasury. The forecasts of exports for the United Kingdom are superior to those for other countries: The U.K. total final expenditure forecasts are superior to the Australian gross national expenditure forecasts. The imports forecasts are inferior only to the (current price) Australian forecasts. The United Kingdom gross domestic product is predicted more accurately than gross national product in the other countries. On the whole the United Kingdom comes out well from the comparisons. However, it must be stressed that the forecasts for the other countries are normally made earlier than those for the United Kingdom.

A study evaluating forecasts in the Netherlands and Norway provides the estimates of root-mean-square error for the forecasts and for some naïve models.[9] We may utilise these results to make inter-country comparisons of forecasting accuracy relative to the difficulty of forecasting as measured by the performance of naïve models. The naïve models used in the comparison are the A_{t-1}, A_{t-3} and no-change models. For the United Kingdom the best fitting naïve model is picked for each series and the ratio of the inequality coefficient for the forecasts to the inequality coefficient for the naïve model is calculated. This is comparable to Sims' procedure of taking the ratio of the forecasters' root-mean-square error to

Table 8.2

Inequality coefficients (alternative definition) for the United Kingdom and six other countries: annual forecasts, time series

Country	United Kingdom			Netherlands	Norway
Forecaster	Treasury	NIESR February	NIESR May	Central Planning Bureau	National Budget
Time period	1951-1971	1963-1971	1963-1971	1949-1953	1949-1960
Consumers' expenditure	0.26	0.31	0.18	0.28	0.42
Public authorities' current expenditure	0.33	0.33	0.33	0.58[a] 0.32[b]	0.24
Gross fixed investment	0.29	0.33	0.29	[0.24][e]	0.72
Investment in stocks	0.55	0.30	0.27		
Exports	0.29	0.19	0.24	0.30[g]	0.49
Total final expenditure	0.18	0.18	0.19		
Imports	0.30	0.24	0.15	0.20[i]	0.47
Gross domestic product	0.20	0.16	0.16		0.55[j]

Country	Sweden	Denmark	Australia	Canada
Forecaster	'Official'	'Official'	Various Australian economists	Budget speech
Time period	1949-1952	1949-1952	1956/7-1962/3	1949-1968
Consumers' expenditure			[0.12]	
Public authorities' current expenditure			[0.19][c]	[0.26][d]
Gross fixed investment	0.31	0.29	[0.44][b]	
Investment in stocks			[0.42]	
Exports	0.52[g]	0.35[g]	[0.41]	
Total final expenditure			[0.22][b]	
Imports	0.33[i]	0.34[i]	[0.15]	
Gross domestic product	0.47[j]	0.35[j]	[0.30][j]	

the root-mean-square error of the best fitting naïve model. Table 8.3 gives the ratios. The lower the ratio the better the forecasting compared to the naïve models. All the British forecasts perform worse than the Netherlands' 1958-1963 forecasts for consumers' expenditure, public authorities' current expenditure, gross fixed investment and imports; they do better only for exports. The U.K. performance is somewhat less unsatisfactory when judged against the Netherlands' forecasts for 1953-1963. None of the U.K. forecasts for gross fixed investment or exports are inferior to the Netherlands' forecasts for this period and the NIESR May forecast for imports is superior; however all the other U.K. forecasts are inferior to the corresponding Netherlands' forecasts.

Footnotes to Table 8.2

a Government wage bill
b Other public consumption expenditure
c Public expenditure
d Federal budgêtary expenditures
e Net investment
f Gross private capital formation
g Commodity exports
h Gross national expenditure
i Commodity imports
j Gross national product
[] Forecasts in current prices

Sources: United Kingdom—our calculations.

Netherlands, Sweden and Denmark—Henri Theil, *Economic Forecasts and Policy* North-Holland, Amsterdam, (1961) pp. 88-89.

Norway—T. G. Ridker, 'An evaluation of the forecasting ability of the Norwegian national budgeting system,' *Review of Economics and Statistics* (February 1963) pp. 23-33.

Australia—D. J. Smyth, 'How well do Australian economists forecast?' *Economic Record* (June 1966) pp. 293-311.

Canada—'Fiscal markmanship in Canada,' *Canadian Journal of Economics* (August 1970) pp. 507-11.

Table 8.3

Ratios of inequality coefficients of forecasts to inequality coefficients for the best of three naïve models for the United Kingdom, the Netherlands and Norway: annual forecasts, time-series

Country	United Kingdom				Netherlands		Norway	
Forecaster	Treasury		NIESR February	May	Central Planning Bureau		National Budget	
Time period	1951-1971	1963-1971	1963-1971	1963-1971	1953-1963	1958-1963	1950-1964	1958-1964
Consumers' expenditure	0.69	1.02	1.34	0.77	0.56	0.52	0.95	0.91
Public authorities' current expenditure	0.82	0.96	0.91	0.90	0.79 [a] 0.71 [b]	0.66 [a] 0.48 [b]	1.16	1.51
Gross fixed investment	0.64	0.79	0.78	0.69	0.79	0.58	1.02	1.08
Exports	0.56	0.67	0.57	0.74	0.98	0.93	0.67	0.83
Imports	0.54	0.97	0.65	0.45	0.49	0.31	1.03	1.32
Gross domestic product	0.62	0.63	0.76	0.72			0.72 [c]	0.66 [c]

a Government wage bill

b Other public consumption expenditure

c Gross national product

[ ] Forecasts in current prices

Sources: United Kingdom—our calculations.

Netherlands and Norway—Christopher A. Sims, 'Evaluating short-term macro-economic forecasts: the Dutch performance, '*Review of Economics and Statistics*' May 1967 pp. 225-36.

All the U.K. forecasts of public authorities' current expenditure, gross fixed investment and imports are superior to the corresponding Norwegian forecasts; the forecasts for the other variables are of comparable accuracy to the Norwegian forecasts.

For the U.S.A., Zarnowitz has established the ratio of the root-mean-square error of forecasts to the root-mean-square error generated by naïve models constructed on the assumption that the forecasts are the mean of previously observed observations. We do not have inequality coefficients for such a naïve model; our $\bar{A}$ model is calculated over the sample period and so is based not just on prior values. As an approximation to the Zarnowitz naïve model we use our five-year moving average model; this should be reasonably comparable. The ratio of the inequality coefficients for the forecasts to the inequality coefficient for the five-year moving average is the same as the ratio of the mean-square errors for the two models as the $\sqrt{\frac{1}{n}\Sigma A_t^2}$ term is common to the inequality coefficients and may be cancelled. The ratios for the U.K. and the U.S are presented in Table 8.4. The results are not very clear-cut. For consumers' expenditure the ratio for the Treasury over the period 1951-1971 is better than the U.S. ratios; however, for the period 1963-1971, for which the U.K. naïve models predict better, the Treasury forecasts are inferior to the U.S. forecasts. The NIESR February forecasts are also inferior to all sets of U.S. forecasts; the NIESR May forecasts are better than all but Forecast Set A. For public sector spending the Treasury forecasts over 1951-1971 are the only U.K. forecasts not inferior to all the U.S. forecasts; these Treasury forecasts are superior to Forecast Sets A and C. The Treasury and National Institute investment forecasts are superior to Sets A and B and inferior to Sets C and F. Both the Treasury and NIESR forecasts of GDP are inferior to the predictions of GNP by Forecast Sets B and F; the Treasury forecasts, but not the NIESR forecasts, are better than Forecast Set C; all the U.K. series are superior to Forecast Set A.

Cross-section inequality coefficients have been calculated for the Netherlands and Norwegian forecasts considered earlier.[10] We do not make direct comparisons here because of the different variables included. However, the pattern of the cross-section inequality coefficients over time is of some interest. It will be recalled from Chapter 3 that neither the Treasury nor the National Institute forecasts improved with time. The correlation coefficients obtained were: Treasury, 1951-1971, −0.06; Treasury, 1963-1971, −0.41; NIESR, 1963-1971, February forecasts, 0.20; NIESR May forecasts, 0.15. None of these correlation coefficients are significant at the ten per cent level. The corresponding correlation coefficient for Norway for the period 1949-1960 is −0.38 which is also not significant at the ten per cent level. However, for the Netherlands the correlation coefficient for the period 1953-1963 is –0.91 which is significant at the five per cent level. Once again the United Kingdom forecasts come out unfavourably compared with the Netherlands' forecasts; the Netherlands' forecasts improve with time, the U.K. forecasts do not.

We turn now to a comparison of turning-point errors for the United Kingdom annual forecasts with such errors for the Netherlands, Norway, Australia and the United States. The extent of the comparisons is limited

Table 8.4

Ratios of inequality coefficients to naïve models for the United Kingdom and the United States: annual forecasts, time series

Country	United Kingdom			
Forecaster	Treasury		NIESR	
Time period	1951-1971	1963-1971	February 1963-1971	May 1963-1971
Consumers' expenditure	0.75	1.10	1.44	0.83
Public authorities' current spending	0.59	1.08	1.03	1.01
Gross fixed investment	0.70	0.81	0.80	0.71
Gross domestic product	0.67	0.69	0.83	0.79
Country	**United States**			
Forecaster	Forecast set A	Forecast set B	Forecast set C	Forecast set F
Time period	1958-1963	1953-1963	1958-1963	1953-1963
Consumers' expenditure	[0.77]	[0.91]	[0.96]	[1.02]
Public authorities' current spending	[0.86][a]	[0.46][a]	[0.89][a]	[0.35][a]
Gross fixed investment	[1.26][b]	[1.01][a]	[0.67]	[0.57]
Gross domestic product	[1.03][c]	[0.66][c]	[0.73][c]	[0.52][c]

a Total government expenditures
b Gross private domestic investment
c Gross national product
[] Forecasts in current prices

Sources: United Kingdom–Tables 3.1 and 3.3.
United States–forecasts analysed by Zarnowitz–see Table 8.1. The ratios are from pp. 94-95 of Zarnowitz *op. cit.*

because some studies neither calculate the required statistics nor present the raw data and because some time series are too short to permit meaningful comparisons. Table 8.5 presents the statistics E, the proportion of total forecasts that represented turning-point errors, E_1, the proportion of turning-points that were missed by the forecasters, and E_2, the proportion of turning-point predictions that subsequently proved false. It should be stressed that we expect the predictive performance with respect to turning-points to be better for variables in current prices than for variables in constant prices as far as E is concerned for during a period with rising prices there may be no downturns at all for current price variables.

For consumers' expenditure and fixed investment we can only compare the E coefficients for the U.K. with a combined set of U.S. forecasters. For consumption the NIESR May forecasts are superior to both sets of the U.S. forecasts and the NIESR May forecasts are better than one of the sets; the NIESR February forecasts are worse than both sets. Note that during the NIESR forecast period there were no negative changes for the actual consumption series; there were three such changes during the Treasury forecast period. For the more volatile investment series the three sets of U.K. forecasts are inferior to the two sets of U.S. forecasts. The U.K. forecasts are inferior to the U.S. forecasts of public spending; the NIESR forecasts, but not the Treasury forecasts, are superior for stockbuilding.

The Treasury and NIESR February E statistics for GDP are superior and the NIESR May statistic inferior to all the U.S. E statistics. Only one negative change in actual GDP is included in the Treasury series and none in the NIESR series.

The studies for the Netherlands, Norway and Australia do not undertake a turning-point analysis variable-by-variable; they merely report tabulations combining the variables used in the studies. The U.K. coefficients are those given as totals in Tables 3.12, 3.13 and 3.14. None of the E coefficients for the U.K. are worse than that calculated for the Netherlands; however, only the February NIESR coefficient is better than that obtained for Australia. The proportion of actual turning-points missed by the U.K. forecasters, E_1, is markedly higher than the proportion for the Netherlands and about the same as for Norway. The proportion of predicted turning-points that prove false is about the same in the U.K. and the Netherlands; the statistic for Norway is lower.

3. Quarterly forecasts

We turn now to an international comparison of the accuracy of quarterly forecasts. Here we are limited to comparing the NIESR forecasts with forecasts made for the U.S. We have calculated inequality coefficients for the U.S. forecasts on both a $P1$ and $P2$ basis.

The inequality coefficients for $P1$ forecasts, forecasts made quarter by quarter, are given in Table 8.6. It is apparent from this that the U.K. emerges rather badly from the comparison. For all nine variables the NIESR forecasts for the U.K. are worse than the corresponding U.S. fore-

Table 8.5

Turning-point errors for the United Kingdom and four other countries: annual forecasts

Country		United Kingdom			Netherlands	Norway	Australia
Forecaster		Treasury	NIESR		Central Planning Bureau	National Budget	Various Australian economists
			February	May			
Time period		1951-1971	1963-1971	1963-1971	1953-1963	1949-1960	1956/7-1962/3
Consumers'	E	0.05	0.22	0.00			
expenditure	E_1	0.00	a	a			
	E_2	0.33	1.00	b			
Public auth.	E	0.21	0.11	0.13			
current	E_1	0.75	0.50	1.00			
expenditure	E_2	0.50	0.00	b			
Gross	E	0.21	0.33	0.38			
fixed	E_1	0.67	0.67	0.67			
investment	E_2	0.67	0.33	0.50			
Investment	E	0.26	0.00	0.14			
in stocks	E_1	0.21	0.00	0.00			
	E_2	0.27	0.00	0.25			
Gross	E	0.05	0.00	0.13			
domestic	E_1	0.25	a	a			
product	E_2	0.00	b	b			
Several	E	0.15	0.08	0.10	0.15		[0.09]
variables	E_1	0.28	0.33	0.35	0.16	0.33	
combined	E_2	0.33	0.33	0.35	0.35	0.20	

a Data included no observed turning-points
b Data included no predicted turning-points
c Government expenditures
d Gross private domestic investment
e Gross domestic product
[ ] Forecasts in current prices

casts. The U.S. forecasts were normally made earlier, relative to the date of the outcomes, than U.K. forecasts and, except for the four constant price series for gross national product and the Office of Business Economics forecasts of investment, the U.S. forecasts are in terms of current prices. These two effects probably operate in opposite directions so far as the relative accuracy of the U.K. and U.S. forecasts are concerned.

Looking at the directly comparable real GDP and GNP coefficients we see that the U.S. coefficients range from about two fifths of the NIESR

Table 8.5 (continued)

Country		United States				
Forecaster		Council of Economic Advisers	University of Michigan model	Various forecasters		
Time period		1962-1972	1953-1967	1952-1963	1947-1963	1953-1963
Consumers'	E			[0.08]		[0.03]
expenditure	E_1					
	E_2					
Public auth.	E					[0.03][c]
current	E_1					
expenditure	E_2					
Gross	E			[0.14][d]		[0.18][d]
fixed	E_1					
investment	E_2					
Investment	E					[0.21]
in stocks	E_1					
	E_2					
Gross	E	0.09[e]	0.07[e]	[0.09][e]	[0.11][e]	[0.08][e]
domestic	E_1	0.50[e]	0.25[e]		[0.47][e]	
product	E_2	[b][e]	0.00[e]		[0.20][e]	
Several	E					
variables	E_1					
combined	E_2					

Sources: United Kingdom–Tables 3.12, 3.13 and 3.14.
Netherlands–our calculations; P. de Wolff *op. cit* in Table 8.1, p. 366.
Norway–our calculations; T. G. Ridker *op. cit.* in Table 8.2, p. 29.
United States–our calculations; Council of Economic Advisers and University of Michigan, as in Table 8.1; Various forecasters, V. Zarnowitz *op. cit.* in Table 8.1, p. 49, pp. 54-55 and pp. 118-19.

coefficient (the Wharton model) to about five-eights (Forecast Set G).

Table 8.7 provides a turning-point analysis of *P*1 forecasts. The OBE forecasts are excluded because there are so few observations. It would appear that some of the relatively good U.S. forecasting may be due to the lack of turning-points, for instance all the changes in the actual consump-

Table 8.6

Inequality coefficients for the United Kingdom and the United States: quarterly *P*1 forecasts, time series

Country	United Kingdom	United States		
Forecaster	NIESR	Wharton School model		Fair model
Time period	1965(i)-1970(iv)	1963(ii)-1967(iv)	1966(i)-1968(iv)	1965(iv)-1969(iv)
Consumers' expenditure	0.83	[0.44]	[0.33]	[0.35]
Public authorities' current expenditure	0.95	[0.59]		
Gross fixed investment	1.09		[0.65]	
Gross private dwelling investment	1.10	[0.98]		[0.65]
Gross private non-dwelling investment	1.01	[0.85]		[0.64]
Stockbuilding	0.91	[0.73]		[0.73]
Imports	0.67			[0.54]
Exports minus imports	[1.15][c]	[0.93]		
Gross domestic product	0.86	[0.28][d]	0.34[d] [0.33][d]	0.40[d] [0.18][d]

a Government expenditures

b Gross private domestic investment

c 1969(ii)-1970(iv)

d Gross national product

[] Forecasts in current prices

Sources: United Kingdom–Tables 5.1, 6.10 and 6.19

United States–our calculations; Wharton School model, 1963(ii)-1967(iv), Evans and Klein, *op. cit.* in Table 8.1, pp. 166-69, 1966(i)-1968(iv) in Michael K. Evans, Yoel Haitovsky, and George I. Treyz, 'An analysis of

tion series for the periods covered by the Wharton and Fair forecasts are positive whereas consumption in the U.K. does not rise monotonically. The NIESR forecasts make a higher proportion of turning-point errors than the Fair model and a higher proportion than the Wharton model except for gross fixed investment and exports minus imports. However,

Table 8.6 (continued)

Forecaster	OBE model	Forecast set A	Forecast set C	Forecast set D	Forecast set G
Time period	1967(ii)-1968(iv)	Various quarters 1958-1963	1958-1963	1959-1963	1955-1963
Consumers' expenditure		[0.58]			
Public authorities' current expenditure		[0.64][a]			
Gross fixed investment	0.66[b]	[0.77][b]			
Gross private dwelling investment		[0.90]			
Gross private non-dwelling investment		[0.86]			
Stockbuilding		[0.69]			
Imports					
Exports minus imports		[1.07]			
Gross domestic product	{ 0.37[d] {[0.20][d]		[0.41][d]	[0.40][d]	0.52[d]

the forecasting properties of U.S. econometric models' in Bert G. Hickman, ed., *Econometric Models of Cyclical Behavior, Volume II*, Number 36 of Studies of Income and Wealth by the Conference on Research in Income and Wealth, National Bureau of Economic Research, New York (1972) pp. 1034-73; OBE model, *ibid.* pp. 1084-1106; Fair model, Ray C. Fair, *A Short Run Forecasting Model of the United States Economy*, Heath Lexington Books, Lexington, Massachusetts (1971) pp. 209-12; inequality coefficients for other forecasts inferred from Zarnowitz, *op. cit.* in Table 8.1, pp. 98-99 and pp. 112-13.

Table 8.7

Turning-point errors for the United Kingdom and the United States: quarterly *P*1 forecasts

Country		United Kingdom	United States	
Forecaster		NIESR	Wharton School model	
Time period		1966(i)-1970(iv)	1963(ii)-1967(iv)	1966(i)-1968(iv)
Consumers' expenditure	E	0.29	[0.00]$^{a\,b}$	[0.00]$^{a\,b}$
	E_1	0.40	[a]	[a]
	E_2	0.33	[b]	[b]
Gross fixed investment	E	0.54		[0.20]^{c}
	E_1	0.44		[0.17]^{c}
	E_2	0.40		[0.25]^{c}
Gross private dwelling investment	E	0.50	[0.53]	
	E_1	0.50	[0.25]	
	E_2	0.58	[0.72]	
Gross private non-dwelling investment	E	0.42	[0.18]	
	E_1	0.44	[0.50]	
	E_2	0.25	[0.67]	
Stockbuilding	E	0.46	[0.17]	
	E_1	0.35	[0.33]	
	E_2	0.31	[0.00]	
Imports	E	0.25		
	E_1	0.33		
	E_2	0.20		
Exports minus imports	E	[0.32]^{d}	[0.50]	
	E_1	[0.40]^{d}	[0.33]	
	E_2	[0.31]^{d}	[0.44]	
Gross domestic product	E	0.21	[0.00]^{e}	0.10 [0.00]$^{a\,b\,e}$
	E_1	0.50	[0.00]^{e}	0.50^{e} [a]^{e}
	E_2	0.20	[0.00]^{e}	b e [b]^{e}

a Data included no observed turning-points
b Data included no predicted turning-points
c Gross private domestic investment
d 1969(ii)-1970(iv)
e Gross national product
[ ] Forecasts in current prices

Table 8.7 (continued)

Fair model 1965(iv)-1969(iv)	Various forecasters Forecast Set C Quarters in 1947-1963	Forecast Set D Quarters in 1947-1963	Forecast Set G Quarters in 1947-1963
[0.00][a b]			
[a]			
[b]			
[0.12]			
[0.12]			
[0.12]			
[0.24]			
[0.50]			
[0.50]			
[0.29]			
[0.18]			
[0.18]			
[0.06]			
[0.50]			
[0.00]			
0.00[e] [0.00][a b e]	[0.23][e]	[0.33][e]	0.44[e]
0.00[e] [a][e]	[0.50][e]	[1.00][e]	1.00[e]
0.00[e] [b][e]	[0.50][e]	[1.00][e]	1.00[e]

Sources: United Kingdom–Tables 5.7 and 6.16

United States–Wharton School model and Fair model, our calculations from sources given in Table 8.6; Various forecasters, Zarnowitz, *op. cit.* in Table 8.1, pp. 98-99.

they make a lower proportion of turning-point errors than all three of the forecasts sets analysed by Zarnowitz. The NIESR forecasts miss a smaller proportion of actual turning-points than the Wharton and Fair forecasts of non-dwelling investment, a smaller percentage of imports than the Fair model, and the same proportion or less than the three GNP series analysed by Zarnowitz and the Wharton constant price GNP forecasts. The NIESR forecasts predict a smaller proportion of spurious turning-points than the Wharton model for dwelling investment and exports minus imports, than both the Wharton and Fair models for non-dwelling investment, and a smaller proportion for GDP than all three of the Zarnowitz models for GNP.

Table 8.8

Inequality coefficients for the United Kingdom and the United States: quarterly *P*2 forecasts, time series

Country	United Kingdom	United States	
Forecaster	NIESR	Wharton School model	Fair model
Time period	1965(i)-1970(iv)	1966(i)-1968(iv)	1965(iv)-1969(iv)
Consumers' expenditure	0.90	[0.83][a] [0.56][b]	[0.37]
Gross fixed investment	1.03	[1.08][a c] [1.06][b c]	
Gross private dwelling investment	1.10		[0.98]
Gross private non-dwelling investment	1.01		[0.88]
Stockbuilding	0.99		[0.96]
Imports	0.92		[0.53]
Gross domestic product	0.89	0.78 [a d] 0.49 [b d] [0.78][a d] [0.60][b d]	0.44 [d] [0.23][d]

a Forecasts not adjusted for delay in implementation of 1968 tax surcharge
b Forecasts adjusted for delay in implementation of 1968 tax surcharge
c Gross private domestic investment
d Gross national product
[] Forecasts in current prices

Sources: United Kingdom–Tables 5.1 and 6.10.
United States–our calculations from sources given in Table 8.6.

Table 8.8 gives the inequality coefficients for the chained *P*2 NIESR forecasts together with our estimates of inequality coefficients for the Wharton and Fair forecasts on a *P*2 basis. The *P*2 series for the Wharton School are constructed on the basis of the forecasts made late in a year for the following year so that the forecasts for the first quarter of the year are the same as for the *P*1 series analysed above. This procedure provides us with more data points than any alternative assumption. The forecasts produced by the Fair model on the basis of extrapolation of exogenous variables have been similarly constructed. Two inequality coefficients are estimated for the Wharton School forecasts. The Wharton forecasts are made on the basis of expected government policy changes and they were consistently wrong about the date of implementation of the 1968 tax surcharge. Thus the forecasts made in 1968(i) are too low because they assumed that the surtax would be imposed at an earlier date than it actually was.[11] In addition to inequality coefficients calculated including these forecasts, a second inequality coefficient has been calculated for forecasts reconstructed on the assumption of no tax surcharge imposed for the relevant quarters.[12]

The comparison between the U.K. and U.S. *P*2 forecasts is somewhat less unfavourable to the U.K. than the *P*1 forecasts, as a number of the coefficients obtained for the Wharton School and Fair models are of the same order as are obtained for NIESR. However, the only U.K. coefficient that is lower than the corresponding U.S. coefficient is for gross fixed investment.

The turning-point analysis is presented in Table 8.9. The NIESR coefficients that are lower than the U.S. coefficients are: for E, gross domestic product lower than the unadjusted Wharton coefficient; for E_1, imports lower than the Fair coefficient; for E_2, consumers' expenditure lower than both Wharton coefficients, non-dwelling investment lower than the Fair coefficient, gross domestic product lower than all the Wharton GNP coefficients except that for the adjusted constant price series.

4. Half-yearly forecasts

We have calculated half-yearly forecasts on a *P*2 basis for the Wharton School and Fair models and we compare the accuracy of these forecasts for the U.S. with the U.K. forecasts in Table 8.10. We consider the results variable-by-variable.

The current price consumption forecasts of the Fair model are superior to all the constant price forecasts of consumption for the U.K.; the in-

Table 8.9

Turning-point errors for the United Kingdom and the United States: quarterly *P*2 forecasts

Country		United Kingdom	United States	
Forecaster		NIESR	Wharton School model	Fair model
Time period		1965(i)-1970(iv)	1966(i)-1968(iv)	1965(iv)-1969 (iv)
Consumers' expenditure	E	0.29	[0.17][c] [0.08][d]	[0.00][a,b]
	E_1	0.40	[a][c,d]	[a]
	E_2	0.33	[1.00][c,d]	[b]
Gross fixed investment	E	0.58	[0.25][c,d,e]	
	E_1	0.50	[0.33][c,d,e]	
	E_2	0.43	[0.20][c] [0.25][d,e]	
Gross private dwelling investment	E	0.42		[0.38]
	E_1	0.40		[0.25]
	E_2	0.50		[0.38]
Gross private non-dwelling investment	E	0.46		[0.38]
	E_1	0.56		[0.50]
	E_2	0.22		[0.60]
Stockbuilding	E	0.46		[0.38]
	E_1	0.35		[0.27]
	E_2	0.31		[0.27]
Imports	E	0.25		[0.06]
	E_1	0.33		[0.50]
	E_2	0.20		[b]
Gross domestic product	E	0.21	0.25 [c] 0.08 [d] [0.17][c] [0.08][d]	0.06 [0.00][a,b]
	E_1	0.50	0.50 [c,d] [a][c,d]	0.33 [a]
	E_2	0.20	0.67 [c] 0.00 [d] [1.00][c,d]	0.00 [b]

a Data included no observed turning-points

b Data included no predicted turning-points

c Forecasts not adjusted for delay in implementation of 1968 tax surcharge

d Forecasts adjusted for delay in implementation of 1968 tax surcharge

e Gross private domestic investment

[] Forecasts in current prices

Sources: United Kingdom–Tables 5.8 and 6.17.
United States–our calculations from sources given in Table 8.6.

equality coefficient for the Fair model is bracketed by *The Sunday Telegraph* current price forecasts of consumers' durable and non-durable spending. The U.K. constant price forecasts compare favourably with the Wharton current price forecasts; the London Business School forecasts are better than the policy adjusted Wharton consumption series, the LBS and OECD forecasts are better and the NIESR forecasts are as good as the unadjusted predictions, the Treasury performance is somewhat worse, and again the coefficients are bracketed by *The Sunday Telegraph* results for durables and non-durables.

Turning now to the fixed investment series we see that the London Business School and *The Sunday Telegraph* forecasts of gross fixed private investment are markedly superior to the Wharton forecasts and the Treasury forecasts are about as accurate as Wharton. The London Business School and the Fair model both forecast private investment disaggregated into dwelling and non-dwelling components; the London Business School provides superior forecasts of non-dwelling investment, the Fair model is better at forecasting dwelling investment.

The Treasury is the only U.K. forecaster predicting stockbuilding markedly more accurately than the Fair model; *The Sunday Telegraph* forecasts are much worse.

All the U.K. forecasts of imports are worse than the corresponding predictions for the U.S. from the Fair model.

All the U.K. GDP forecasts are superior to the Wharton School model's forecasts of GNP irrespective of whether or not the delay in the implementation of the surtax in 1968 is taken into account. The NIESR constant price GDP forecasts are better, and the OECD forecasts about as good as the corresponding constant price forecasts by the Fair model; the other U.K. forecasts are inferior. *The Sunday Telegraph* forecasts of current price GDP are superior to the Wharton forecasts of current price GNP but inferior to the Fair predictions.

A comparison of the accuracy with which the U.K. forecasters predict turning-points is made with the performance of the Wharton School and Fair models in Table 8.11.

There were no downturns during the Wharton and Fair forecasting periods for consumers' expenditure, imports and gross national product in current prices and in gross national product in constant prices. For these series the U.S. forecasters predicted no downturns and so made no turning-point errors. As far as turning-points are concerned, then, the task of forecasting the U.S. economy was not very difficult. The same series in the U.K. did experience fluctuations making the British forecasters' task harder so that the zero values for E, E_1 and E_2 obtained by the Treasury

Table 8.10

Inequality coefficients for the United Kingdom and the United States: half-yearly *P2* forecasts

Country		United Kingdom				
Forecaster		Treasury	NIESR	OECD	London Business School	*The Sunday Telegraph*
Time period		1968(I)-1971(II)	1967(I)-1971(II)	1967(I)-1971(II)	1968(I)-1971(II)	1967(I)-1971(II)
Consumers' expenditure		0.83	0.72	0.60	0.54	{<0.76>[a] {<0.15>[b]
Gross fixed investment:	Public	1.10				<0.90>
	Private dwellings				1.35	
	Private non-dwellings				0.66	
	Total private	1.23			0.74	<0.49>
	Total	0.93	1.15	1.33		
Stockbuilding		0.74	0.98		0.93	<1.29>
Imports		0.76	0.68	[0.53]	0.70	<0.53>
Gross domestic product		0.56[f]	0.32[f]	0.37[f]	0.57[f]	{0.70[f] {<0.30>[f]

Country		United States	
Forecaster		Wharton School model	Fair model
Time period		1966(I)-1968(II)	1966(I)-1969(II)
Consumers' expenditure		{[0.72][c] {[0.57][d]	[0.23]
Gross fixed investment:	Public		
	Private dwellings		[0.88]
	Private non-dwellings		[0.96]
	Total private	{[1.25][c e] {[1.20][c e]	

Table 8.10 (continued)

Total		
Stockbuilding		[0.94]
Imports		[0.42]
Gross domestic product	{ 1.37 [c g] { 0.79 [d g]	{ 0.36 [g] { [0.18] [g]
	{ [0.75] [c g] { [0.58] [d g]	

a Consumers' expenditures: durables
b Consumers' expenditures: non-durables
c Forecasts not adjusted for delay in implementation of 1968 tax surcharge
d Forecasts adjusted for delay in implementation of 1968 tax surcharge
e Gross private domestic investment
f Gross domestic product as defined in Table 7.16
g Gross national product
[] Data in current prices, seasonally adjusted
<> Data in current prices, seasonally unadjusted.

Sources: United Kingdom–Table 7.16. United States–our calculations from sources given in Table 8.6.

Table 8.11

Turning-point errors for the United Kingdom and the United States: half-yearly *P2* forecasts

Country		United Kingdom		
Forecaster		Treasury	NIESR	OECD
Time period		1968(I)-1971(II)	1967(I)-1971(II)	1967(I)-1971(II)
Consumers' expenditure	E	0.12	0.10	0.10
	E_1	0.00	0.33	0.00
	E_2	0.33	0.00	0.17
Gross fixed private investment	E	0.50	0.40 [f]	0.50 [f]
	E_1	0.75	0.50 [f]	0.75 [f]
	E_2	0.00	0.50 [f]	0.67 [f]
Gross private dwelling investment	E			
	E_1			
	E_2			
Gross private non-dwelling investment	E			
	E_1			
	E_2			
Stockbuilding	E	0.25	0.40	
	E_1	0.00	0.29	
	E_2	0.29	0.29	
Imports	E	0.25	0.20	[0.10]
	E_1	0.00	0.00	[0.00]
	E_2	1.00	0.40	[0.30]
Gross domestic product constant prices	E	0.00 [h]	0.00 [h]	0.10 [h]
	E_1	0.00 [h]	0.00 [h]	0.25 [h]
	E_2	0.00 [h]	0.00 [h]	0.00 [h]
Gross domestic product current prices	E			
	E_1			
	E_2			

a Data included no observed turning-points

b Data included no predicted turning-points

c Consumers' expenditure: durables

d Consumers' expenditure: non-durables

e Forecasts adjusted or unadjusted for delay in implementation of 1968 tax surcharge

f Gross fixed investment

g Gross private domestic investment

Table 8.11 (continued)

		United States	
London Business School	*The Sunday Telegraph*	Wharton School model	Fair model
1968(I)-1971(II)	1967(I)-1971(II)	1966(I)-1968(II)	1966(I)-1969(II)
0.25	<0.40> [c] <0.00> [d]	[0.00] [a b e]	[0.00] [a b]
0.50	<0.20> [c] <0.00> [d]	[a] [e]	[a]
0.50	<0.43> [c] <0.00> [d]	[b] [e]	[b]
0.50	<0.20>	[0.17] [e g]	
0.33	<0.17>	[0.00] [e g]	
0.40	<0.17>	[0.33] [e g]	
0.50			[0.38]
0.50			[0.00]
0.25			[0.60]
0.12			[0.25]
0.33			[0.50]
0.00			[0.50]
0.67	<0.30>		[0.38]
0.67	<0.17>		[0.75]
0.67	<0.29>		[0.00]
0.00	<0.30>		[0.00] [a b]
	<1.00>		[a]
	<1.00>		[b]
0.12 [h]	0.20	0.00 [abei]	0.00 [abi]
0.67 [h]	0.50	a e i	a i
0.00 [h]	0.00	b e i	b i
	<0.10>	[0.00] [abei]	[0.00] [a i]
	<0.00>	aei	ai
	<1.00>	bei	bi

h Gross domestic product as defined in Table 7.16
i Gross national product
[] Data in current prices, seasonally adjusted
<>Data in current prices, not seasonally adjusted

Sources: United Kingdom–Tables 7.3, 7.6, 7.9, 7.12, 7.15.
United States–our calculations from sources given in Table 8.6.

and the two zero E_1 values and the one zero E_2 value obtained by the OECD are commendable.

There is more comparability in the difficulty of turning-point forecasting between the U.S. and the U.K. for the fixed and inventory investment series as downturns and upturns were experienced during the sample period in both countries. Gross fixed private investment (private and public for NIESR and OECD) is predicted with relatively more turning-point errors by the U.K. forecasters than by the Wharton School and they miss more actual turning-points; however, the Treasury and *The Sunday Telegraph* predict relatively fewer spurious turning-points. The London Business School makes a higher proportion of turning-point errors for gross private dwelling investment than the Fair model, missing proportionately more actual turning-points; however a lower proportion of predicted turning-points prove spurious. For private non-dwelling investment all three turning-point statistics are lower for the London Business School than the Wharton School. For stockbuilding the Treasury and *The Sunday Telegraph* have a lower E statistic than the Fair model, all the U.K. forecasts have lower E_1 statistics but all make some E_2 errors while the Fair model does not.

Notes

[1] Ronald L. Cooper, 'The predictive performance of quarterly econometric models of the United States,' in Bert G. Hickman, ed., *Econometric Models of Cyclical Behavior, Volume II,* Number 36 of Studies in Income and Wealth by the Conference on Research in Income and Wealth, National Bureau of Economic Research, New York (1972) pp. 813-926; J. W. Elliot, 'A direct comparison of short-run GNP forecasting models,' *Journal of Business* (January 1973) pp. 33-60.

[2] Ray C. Fair, *A Short-run Forecasting Model of the United States Economy* Heath Lexington Books, Lexington, Massachusetts (1971).

[3] Pieter de Wolff, 'Macroeconomic forecasting', in *Forecasting on a Scientific Basis* Proceedings of an International Summer Institute held in Curia, Portugal, September 1966, the NATO Science Committee and the Gulbenkian Foundation, Lisbon (1967).

[4] Organisation for Economic Co-operation and Development, *Techniques of Economic Forecasting* O.E.C.D., Paris (1965); C. A. Van Den Beld, 'Short-term planning experience in the Netherlands,' in Bert G. Hickman, ed., *Quantitative Planning of Economic Policy* The Brookings Institution, Washington D.C., (1965)

[5] Victor Zarnowitz, *An Appraisal of Short-Term Economic Forecasts* Occasional Paper 104 of the National Bureau of Economic Research, Columbia University Press, New York (1967).

[6] The index given by Zarnowitz is $R_1 = \sqrt{\frac{1}{n}\Sigma(P_t - A_t)^2} / \sqrt{\frac{1}{n}\Sigma(0 - A_t)^2}$ which is U.

[7] Christopher A. Sims, 'Evaluating short-term macro-economic forecasts: the Dutch performance,' *Review of Economics and Statistics* (May 1967) p. 231.

[8] Henri Theil, *Economic Forecasts and Policy* North-Holland, Amsterdam (1961).

[9] Christopher A. Sims, *op. cit.*

[10] Pieter de Wolff, *op. cit.* and Ridker, *op. cit.*

[11] Michael K. Evans, Yoel Haitovsky and George I. Trepz, 'An analysis of the forecasting properties of U.S. econometric models,' in Bert G. Hickman, ed., *op. cit.* p. 1031.

[12] We do not estimate two sets of coefficients for the quarter-by-quarter $P1$ analyses as for these series the differences are inconsequential.

9 Conclusions

1. Introduction

Summaries have been presented at the end of Chapters 3 to 7 and it would be tedious to repeat detailed conclusions here. However, running through our results are some common themes which deserve emphasis in this final chapter.

2. Forecasting gross domestic product and its components

One encouraging feature that we have found throughout the forecasts is a pervasive tendency for errors in different variables to be offset in aggregation: that is, total final expenditure and gross domestic product are typically forecast more accurately than their components. We do not know why. We should, if anything, expect the tendency to go the other way as an error in one variable is likely to lead to an error in endogenous variables linked to it, so that errors should compound. Perhaps because turning-points in the components are not perfectly synchronised it may be that the aggregated fluctuations are smaller and fewer: hence changes in total expenditure and product are rather easier to predict.

Another persistent finding is that public sector spending (i.e. public authorities' current spending and, where specifically distinguished, public fixed investment) is badly forecast. And the Treasury forecasts of public authorities' current spending are worse than those by other forecasters. In contrast to the pattern typical of other variables, the rate of growth of public authorities' current spending is usually overestimated; it is underestimated only in the quarterly (*P*1 and *P*2) forecasts by the National Institute and in the current-price half-yearly forecasts by *The Sunday Telegraph*. The Treasury does not underestimate the variance of public authorities' current spending, nor is the variance underestimated in the NIESR fourth quarter forecasts, but it is underestimated by all the other forecasters.

Gross fixed investment is uniformly badly forecast and its variance is markedly underestimated. Excessive reliance on investment intentions surveys may account for some of the misforecasting here.

Stockbuilding also is poorly forecast but, rather remarkably, this volatile series is sometimes forecast with a smaller proportion of systematic error and with fewer wrongly forecast turning-points than is fixed investment. Moreover the stockbuilding variable is commonly treated as a residual component; for instance, often the discrepancy between expenditure and compromise estimates of GDP is allocated to stockbuilding.

Consumers' expenditure is usually fairly accurately forecast, with expenditure on non-durables proving markedly easier to forecast than expenditure on durable goods.

The pattern in the relative accuracy of forecasts of exports and imports is difficult to explain. The quarterly and half-yearly forecasts of exports are more accurate than the corresponding imports forecasts (except for the current price forecasts by OECD) but the annual and fourth quarter forecasts of imports have lower inequality coefficients than do those for exports (except for the NIESR February annual forecasts).

3. Exogenous and endogenous forecasts

Variables that are endogenous are forecast, on average, more accurately than variables taken by the forecasters to be exogenous. Table 9.1 presents the average inequality coefficients for the exogenous and endogenous variables. Variables classified as exogenous are public authorities' current spending, gross fixed investment and exports; consumers' expenditure, exports, stockbuilding, total final expenditure, imports, factor cost and gross domestic product comprise the endogenous variables. The only sets of forecasts for which the exogenous variables are better forecast than the endogenous variables are those of the London Business School and *The Sunday Telegraph*. The London Business School does not forecast public authorities' current spending and public investment which other forecasters have found difficult to predict, presumably thus lowering the average of its exogenous coefficients. *The Sunday Telegraph*'s relatively low average inequality coefficient for the exogenous variables is mainly due to its superior forecasting of government current expenditure, and *The Sunday Telegraph* may have an advantage here by forecasting in current prices, for government spending plans may be fulfilled in current prices even if there is an actual shortfall in real terms due to inflation. *The Sunday Telegraph* is also unique in attempting to forecast policy, but it is debatable whether this in itself would result in more accurate predictions of public sector expenditure for the half-year or even year ahead.

Table 9.1

The accuracy of forecasts of exogenous and endogenous variables

	Periods of forecasts	Average inequality coefficients	
		Exogenous variables	Endogenous variables
Annual			
Treasury	1951-1971	0.60	0.54
NIESR (February)	1963-1971	0.57	0.46
NIESR (May)	1963-1971	0.58	0.37
Fourth Quarter			
NIESR (February)	1959-1971	0.77	0.67
NIESR (May)	1959-1971	0.68	0.50
Half-Yearly			
Treasury	1968(I)-1971(II)	0.91	0.67
NIESR	1967(I)-1971(II)	0.86	0.63
OECD	1967(I)-1971(II)	0.91	0.51
London Business School	1968(I)-1971(II)	0.58	0.68
The Sunday Telegraph	1967(I)-1971(II)	0.54	0.58
Quarterly			
NIESR *P*1	1965(i)-1970(iv)	0.86	0.80
NIESR *P*2	1965(i)-1970(iv)	0.96	0.91

4. Economic versus naïve forecasting

The forecasters usually earn their keep in that their predictions tend to be more accurate than those generated by naïve models. To illustrate this we present in Table 9.2, for gross domestic product, the ratios for the inequality coefficients of the forecasters' predictions to those generated by an extrapolative naïve model. The naïve model used in each case is the longest moving average of previous values of A_t calculated for the forecast under consideration (five years for the annual and fourth quarter forecasts, three years for the half-yearly forecasts and one year for the quarterly forecasts). This provides a fair summary test of the forecasts: real gross domestic product is the most widely accepted single measure of United Kingdom economic activity, and the moving average models are usually among the more accurate naïve predictors that might be used as an alternative to genuine forecasting. The annual, half-yearly and fourth quarter NIESR May forecasts come out well from the comparison as all the coefficients are less than one. However, the NIESR fourth quarter forecasts made in February and both its quarterly forecasts do not emerge so favourably.

5. The relative accuracy of annual, half-yearly and quarterly forecasts

Annual forecasts tend to be more accurate than half-yearly forecasts, and in turn half-yearly forecasts tend to be more accurate than quarterly forecasts. This may be seen from Table 9.3 which compares the annual and half-yearly forecasts by the Treasury and the annual, half-yearly and quarterly forecasts by the National Institute. For six of the eight series in Table 9.3 the Treasury half-yearly forecasts have larger inequality coefficients than the annual forecasts, the exception being for the stockbuilding and exports series. Turning to the NIESR results in the same table, we see that the half-yearly coefficients are larger than the annual coefficients except for total final expenditure and gross domestic product, and for the latter the half-yearly coefficient is 0.32 and the annual coefficient is 0.33. All the NIESR annual coefficients are lower than the corresponding quarterly coefficients for both *P*1 and *P*2. The half-yearly coefficients for consumers' expenditure, public authorities' current spending, total final expenditure and gross domestic product are smaller than the correspond-

Table 9.2

Ratio of forecasters' inequality coefficients to inequality coefficients for the longest moving average naïve models: constant-price gross domestic product

	Time period	Ratio of forecasters' inequality coefficient to inequality coefficient for longest moving average naïve model
Annual		
Treasury	1951-1971	0.67
NIESR (February)	1963-1971	0.83
NIESR (May)	1963-1971	0.78
Fourth Quarter		
NIESR (February)	1959-1971	1.14
NIESR (May)	1959-1971	0.75
Half-Yearly		
Treasury	1968(I)-1971(II)	0.82
NIESR	1967(I)-1971(II)	0.47
OECD	1967(I)-1971(II)	0.51
London Business School	1968(I)-1971(II)	0.74
The Sunday Telegraph	1967(I)-1971(II)	0.85
Quarterly		
NIESR *P*1	1965(i)-1970(iv)	0.96
NIESR *P*2	1965(i)-1970(iv)	1.00

Table 9.3

Annual, half-yearly and quarterly inequality coefficients: Treasury and NIESR, time series

	Treasury		NIESR			
	Annual 1963-1971	Half-yearly 1968(I)-1971(II)	Annual (May) 1963-1971	Half-yearly (*P2*) 1967(I)-1971(II)	Quarterly *P1* 1965(i)-1970(iv)	Quarterly *P2* 1965(i)-1970(iv)
Consumers' expenditure	0.45	0.83	0.34	0.72	0.83	0.90
Public authorities' current expenditure	0.78	1.42	0.73	0.88	0.95	0.94
Gross fixed investment	0.64	0.93	0.56	1.15	1.09	1.03
Stockbuilding	1.04	0.74	0.47	0.98	0.91	0.99
Exports	0.44	0.39	0.45	0.54	0.54	0.91
Total final expenditure	0.36 [a]	0.47 [a]	0.42 [b]	0.34 [b]	0.91 [b]	0.99 [b]
Imports	0.64	0.76	0.30	0.68	0.67	0.92
Gross domestic product	0.29	0.56	0.33	0.32	0.86	0.89

a Including stockbuilding.
b Excluding stockbuilding.

ing quarterly *P*1 and *P*2 coefficients; the half-yearly coefficients for exports and imports are approximately the same as the corresponding *P*1 coefficients and lower than the *P*2 coefficients; the half-yearly stockbuilding coefficient is higher than the quarterly *P*1 coefficient and marginally lower than the *P*2 coefficient; and for the badly forecast gross fixed investment series, for which the half-yearly and quarterly coefficients are greater than one, the half-yearly inequality coefficient is higher than both the quarterly coefficients.

The time series inequality coefficients considered in Table 9.3 are calculated over different time periods; this makes the results less conclusive than they otherwise would be. Accordingly, we also present, in Table 9.4, cross-section results: together with the annual results are annual averages of the half-yearly and quarterly cross-section inequality coefficients. For three out of four years the annual inequality coefficient for the Treasury is less than the corresponding average of the half-yearly coefficients, and for 1971 the two statistics are the same. The picture is less clear for the comparison of the NIESR annual and half-yearly cross-section forecasts: the annual forecasts have lower inequality coefficients in 1968, 1970 and 1971, and higher coefficients in 1967 and 1969 than the average of the half-yearly coefficients. The NIESR coefficients for the annual forecasts are all lower than the annual average of the quarterly *P*1 and *P*2 coefficients, the half-yearly averages are lower in 1967, 1969 and 1970, but higher than the average for both *P*1 and *P*2 quarterly forecasts in 1968.

Table 9.4

Annual, half-yearly and quarterly inequality coefficients: Treasury and NIESR, cross-section

	Treasury		NIESR			
	Annual	Half-yearly	Annual (May)	Half-yearly (*P*2)	Quarterly *P*1	Quarterly *P*2
1965			0.53		0.69	0.82
1966			0.30		0.92	1.02
1967			0.86	0.47	0.95	1.06
1968	0.48	0.77	0.21	0.90	0.60	0.76
1969	0.56	1.03	0.74	0.64	0.92	0.86
1970	0.25	0.39	0.31	0.56	1.18	1.06
1971	0.47	0.47	0.64	0.67		

6. Chained forecasts

Our quarterly analysis included an evaluation not only of forecasts revised every quarter ($P1$ forecasts) but also of post-budget chained forecasts made for the current quarter and the next three quarters ahead ($P2$ forecasts). We found that there was surprisingly little difference in the accuracy of the two sets of forecasts, and that accuracy did not deteriorate significantly the further in the future was the period covered by the forecasts. The only way in which $P2$ forecasts were markedly inferior to $P1$ forecasts was in the dating of turning-points. Furthermore, in our assessment of half-yearly forecasts made after the Budget we found that there was no significant difference in the accuracy of the forecasts of the January-June half-year (a considerable proportion of which had elapsed at the time of the forecasts) and in the accuracy of the predictions of the more distant July-December half-year. Our interpretation of these results, that the accuracy of chained forecasts do not deteriorate with the length of the chain, is that the forecasts that form the basis for further (chained) forecasts are no more tenuous than the preliminary data on which current period forecasts are based. We are suggesting, then, that the preliminary estimates of variables in the national accounts are not very reliable, not really more reliable than forecasts. Our general hypothesis is supported by the balance of payments results. Estimates of balance of payments figures are typically available much earlier than national income aggregates and so provide a more up-to-date and sounder basis for forecasting than is permitted for other variables. We thus expect that $P1$ forecasts for the balance of payments should be more accurate, relative to $P2$ forecasts, than other forecasts. And this is the case.

7. Systematic and unsystematic forecasting error

The average proportions of forecasting error that are due to wrongly forecasting mean changes and the variance of changes, U^M and U^S respectively, together with the average unsystematic proportion, U^C, are given in Table 9.5 for various sets of forecasts of gross domestic product and its major components. The proportions tabulated are simple means of the time series coefficients presented in the tables of earlier chapters.[1] Non-systematic factors account for more than fifty per cent of the error, averaged over all the sets of forecasts. There is noticeably less systematic error in the annual forecasts (average U^C in the range 0.81 to 0.88) than in the half-yearly, quarterly and fourth quarter forecasts.

Table 9.5

Types of error: GDP and components

	Period of forecasts	Proportion of series for which		Proportion of observations that are under-predicted	Average value for forecast set		
		$\bar{P} < \bar{A}$	$s_P < s_A$		U^M	U^S	U^C
Annual							
Treasury	1951-1971	0.75	0.75	0.58	0.06	0.06	0.88
NIESR (February)	1963-1971	0.50	0.50	0.48	0.09	0.08	0.83
NIESR (May)	1963-1971	0.50	0.50	0.51	0.07	0.13	0.81
Fourth quarter							
NIESR (February)	1959-1971	0.87	0.87	0.55	0.07	0.30	0.63
NIESR (May)	1959-1971	0.87	0.87	0.58	0.02	0.37	0.61
Half-yearly							
Treasury	1968(I)-1971(II)	0.45	0.64	0.54	0.21	0.07	0.72
NIESR	1967(I)-1971(II)	0.67	0.56	0.65	0.24	0.13	0.62
OECD	1967(I)-1971(II)	0.57	0.71	0.64	0.14	0.23	0.64
London Business School	1968(I)-1971(II)	0.50	0.80	0.52	0.15	0.20	0.66
The Sunday Telegraph	1967(I)-1971(II)	0.73	0.73	0.61	0.13	0.17	0.69
Quarterly							
NIESR *P1*	1965(i)-1970(iv)	0.87	0.87	0.58	0.04	0.29	0.67
NIESR *P2*	1965(i)-1970(iv)	0.87	0.87	0.53	0.02	0.41	0.57

Excepting the Treasury and NIESR (February) annual forecasts and the Treasury and NIESR half-yearly forecasts, the variance proportion tends to be much larger than the bias proportion. This is especially so for the fourth quarter and quarterly forecasts, while for the quarterly *P*2 forecasts the average variance proportion is some twenty times the average bias proportion; for this last set of forecasts the proportion of error that is unsystematic, fifty-seven per cent, is less than for any other set of forecasts reported in the table. In view of these quarterly results it is interesting to examine the average coefficients for the disaggregated NIESR forecasts reported in Table 9.6. Variance error is much more marked than bias for all the quarterly series, the ratio of U^S to U^M varying from 2.4 for the personal income and expenditure *P*1 forecasts to 6.5 for the balance of payments on current account *P*2 forecasts. In every case the ratio of U^S to U^M is higher for the *P*2 than the *P*1 series. The forecasters' inherent conservatism in underestimating the variance of changes is most exposed by our analysis of rolling quarterly forecasts, which demands great accuracy in predicting economic fluctuations. Given that the *P*2 forecasts of any variable are chained to each other, it is likely that, in the absence of countervailing exogenous information, once committed this source of error will be built into forecasts for subsequent quarters. Table 9.6 also gives the corresponding disaggregated balance of payments statistics on a half-yearly basis; we do not observe the same effects with these half-yearly results.

It is not at all clear that any of the forecasts exhibit the expected positive correlation between inaccuracy, measured by U, and the proportions of systematic error, U^M and U^S, whether examined in time series or cross-section. Indeed an inverse relationship appears to hold for some of our results.[2]

8. Conservative forecasting: underestimation of growth and fluctuations

The forecasters, on the whole, are conservative in their predictions. This can be seen from the summary statistics presented in Tables 9.5 and 9.6. For each of the tables giving our time series accuracy analysis we have calculated the proportion of series for which the mean predicted change, $\bar{P}$, is less than the mean actual change, $\bar{A}$. The only series for which this ratio is less than 0.5 are the Treasury half-yearly series in Table 9.5, and the disaggregated quarterly gross fixed investment series in Table 9.6. It is clear that the forecasters tend to underestimate the average rate of growth of the economy. We also calculated the corresponding proportions for the

Table 9.6

Types of error: NIESR disaggregated forecasts

		Average value for forecast set			Proportion of series for which		Proportion of observations that are under-predicted
		U^M	U^S	U^C	$\bar{P} < \bar{A}$	$s_P < s_A$	
Quarterly, 1969(ii)-1970(iv)							
Personal income and expenditure	P1	0.09	0.23	0.68	0.88	0.82	0.67
	P2	0.07	0.32	0.62	0.72	0.89	0.65
Gross fixed investment	P1	0.07	0.27	0.66	0.44	1.00	0.50
	P2	0.08	0.45	0.46	0.44	1.00	0.52
Balance of payments on current account	P1	0.06	0.37	0.57	0.78	0.89	0.68
	P2	0.08	0.52	0.40	0.89	0.89	0.67
Half-yearly, 1965(I)-1970(II)							
Balance of payments on current account	P1	0.08	0.12	0.80	0.78	0.67	0.66
	P2	0.15	0.12	0.73	0.78	0.67	0.65

variances of the predicted and actual series. In none of the sets of forecasts was the variance of the predicted change overestimated more often than it was underestimated. The high proportion of underestimates is very marked in the quarterly forecasts. Underestimation of variances is most evident for the more volatile series, notably investment.

Underestimation of growth rates and of the magnitude of fluctuations has implications for the successful implementation of stabilisation policy On average, deflationary policy will be weaker and expansionary policy will be stronger than if bias was not present in the forecasts; presumably the result of this is to run the economy at a higher rate of utilisation than intended, with resulting pressure on the price level and the balance of payments. Similarly, anti-cyclical policies based on under-predicted fluctuations must surely have been weaker than they otherwise would have been. This may have meant that some cyclical fluctuations that could have been removed were not. However, if stabilisation measures were also typically applied too late so that policy adjustments aimed at stabilising the economy actually proved destabilising (and there is evidence supporting this hypothesis)[3], then misforecasting the variance may have turned out to have been all for the best in that it alleviated the imposed destabilisation. Of course, it is also possible that had the variances been correctly forecast then this would have led to the implementation of policy measures earlier than actually occurred, with the desired stabilising results.

9. Turning-point errors

Table 9.7 summarises the results of the turning-point analysis for forecasts of different length. The coefficients given are for total observations from previous tables. It is apparent that the proportion of observations that are turning-point errors increases as one moves from annual to fourth quarter to half-yearly and to quarterly forecasts.

The decomposition of mean-square error into components measuring the extent of systematic and random sources of inaccuracy suggested very clearly that the forecasters are conservative in their predictions. In view of this it is somewhat surprising that there is no marked difference between the proportion of actual turning-points that are missed by the forecasters, E_1, and the proportion of forecast turning-points that eventually prove spurious, E_2, for conservative forecasting would lead one to expect the reverse. It is only with the quarterly forecasts that a big gap opens between E_1 and E_2; not surprisingly the widest margin between E_1 and E_2 is for the *P*2 series, as again it is in chained quarterly predictions that

Table 9.7

Turning-point errors

	Period of forecasts	E	E_1	E_2
Annual				
Treasury	1951-1971	0.15	0.28	0.33
NIESR (February)	1963-1971	0.08	0.33	0.33
NIESR (May)	1963-1971	0.10	0.35	0.35
Fourth Quarter				
NIESR (February)	1959-1971	0.15	0.50	0.44
NIESR (May)	1959-1971	0.16	0.42	0.39
Half-yearly				
Treasury	1968(I)-1971(II)	0.23	0.30	0.32
NIESR	1967(I)-1971(II)	0.17	0.25	0.28
OECD	1967(I)-1971(II)	0.19	0.33	0.30
London Business School	1968(I)-1971(II)	0.22	0.39	0.36
The Sunday Telegraph	1967(I)-1971(II)	0.17	0.17	0.26
Quarterly				
NIESR *P*1	1965(i)-1970(iv)	0.32	0.38	0.28
NIESR *P*2	1965(i)-1970(iv)	0.33	0.43	0.27

the forecasters' conservative approach to economic fluctuations probably becomes self-generating and thus appears most pronounced. Distant fluctuations are not just under predicted; the relevant turning-points tend to be missed altogether.

10. Cross-section accuracy analysis

The cross-section inequality coefficients show considerable variation in accuracy from period to period. Here it seems that errors are compounded as one might expect, for an error in forecasting one expenditure variable is likely to lead to an error in the same direction in other expenditure variables. There is also marked variability in the accuracy with which the naïve models predict from period to period. Typically the $\bar{A}$ and long moving-average models fit best when the economy is on its trend rate of growth, and these periods are also those most accurately predicted by the forecasters as forecasting is then relatively easy. As with the time series we find that variances are typically underpredicted.

There is evidence from our quarterly analysis that wrongly forecast turning-points are responsible for some of the least accurate cross-sectional forecasting. Systematic error also tends to be larger on these occasions: a relatively high variance proportion often results when turning-point errors are confined to a few of the expenditure variables, with bias reflecting more widespread directional errors.

11. Changes in forecasting accuracy over time

Many of our time series of forecasts are short, so that conclusions concerning improvement or deterioration of forecasts over time must be treated with some caution. However, in general the cross-section results do not indicate that the accuracy of United Kingdom macroeconomic forecasting has improved. Nor is there support for the hypothesis that short-term forecasting has become more difficult. If we measure forecasting difficulty by the performance of the naïve models, the evidence suggests that annual forecasting has become somewhat easier, because the accuracy of naïve forecasts has increased. Judged against the naïve models, then, there may have been some deterioration in the annual forecasts. In addition, some quarterly forecasts have deteriorated absolutely (i.e. not just relative to the naïve models) and there is no sign of any improvement in any of the quarterly forecasts. There is no evidence of either improvement or deterioration in the half-yearly GDP forecasts. Only the accuracy of the half-yearly, disaggregated forecasts of the balance of payments, made by the National Institute of Economic and Social Research, has unambiguously improved during the period covered by our study.

12. Policy changes and the accuracy of forecasts

All the forecasts, except for those published by the NIESR in February, were made after the Budget, so evidence on the extent to which policy changes introduced in the spring falsify prior forecasts is limited. The improvement from February to May in the NIESR annual and fourth quarter forecasts suggests that budgetary measures make a substantial contribution to the errors observed in the earlier series, particularly in view of the similar performance of current period and chained, post-budget forecasts. This improvement is, as expected, greater for fourth quarter forecasts than for annual forecasts, for policy changes are likely to have relatively more impact on the fourth quarter than on the year as a whole, given the delayed response of aggregate demand to many of the measures announced in March or April Budgets. It is interesting that the superior accuracy of May forecasts is more noticeable for the endogenous variables than for the exogenous variables (see Table 9.1); this too supports our view that Budget changes may have marked multiplier effects on economic activity by the end of the year.

In contrast, we have found that the forecasts seem remarkably resilient to post-budget changes: there is no evidence that forecasting is significantly less accurate or errors significantly more systematic in years in which post-budget policy measures are imposed. Such measures are usually introduced in the autumn, and the implication of our results is that the time-lag between announcement and impact of these later policy changes is sufficiently long to have no perceptible effect on outcomes within the current calendar year.

13. International comparisons

Comparison is often difficult because many of the forecasts for other countries are presented in current prices, but it would seem that in general the accuracy of United Kingdom forecasts is much the same as that of short-term macroeconomic forecasts elsewhere; the U.K. forecasts are neither the best nor the worst. However, the failure of the U.K. forecasts to improve over time is especially discouraging in view of the marked improvement in the Netherlands forecasts that has occurred as the result of greater attention to the dynamic structure of the models and of increasing use of econometric techniques.[4]

When forecasts of other economies are presented in both real and money terms, their relative performance supports the evidence from U.K. quarterly income and expenditure forecasts and half-yearly forecasts of gross domestic product, that current-price values are predicted more accurately and with fewer turning-point errors than are variables measured in constant prices.

14. The future of macroeconomic forecasting

Our evaluation of U.K. short-term, macroeconomic forecasts gives no support to the view that economic forecasting is a waste of time. With few exceptions the forecasters' predictions are significantly more accurate than simply extrapolating or averaging past outcomes, or assuming no change, while the performance of U.K. and comparable overseas forecasts is usually very similar. Equally, our conclusions do not provide grounds for complacency. In some areas, for example government current spending and all categories of investment, the quality of the forecasts is consistently poor. Overall there is a tendency to underestimate and often to mistime economic fluctuations. And there is a little evidence that the forecasters' accuracy has improved even though the National Institute and Treasury have been engaged in continuous forecasting exercises for at least ten and twenty years respectively.

However, the prospects for macroeconomic forecasting are encouraging. Only relatively recently have econometric techniques been used to any appreciable extent in the United Kingdom; one advantage of these techniques is that they facilitate detailed post-mortems of where the forecasts went wrong, as a result of which the models may then be more readily revised and subsequent forecasts improved. It is impossible at this stage to know what deficiencies these formal, *ex post* analyses will reveal, but one does not have to be an ardent monetarist to reasonably suppose that better forecasting would result if the monetary sector was explicitly integrated into the models, most of which currently emphasise real relationships. Also, the models might profitably be expanded to include endogenous predictions of some of those variables which have conventionally been treated as being determined exogenously. On the strength of our results it would certainly seem unwise for the forecasters to rely too heavily on external surveys of private sector investment intentions, or on official estimates of future government expenditure. We would further emphasise the importance of improving the reliability and availability of published economic statistics, particularly of preliminary estimates, and of investigating the effect of data revisions on forecasting accuracy.

We assume that the forecasters are continually learning from experience, and hope that the introduction of aggregate econometric analysis in particular will lead to more accurate forecasts. Not that we anticipate that judgement will be ever be entirely replaced by mechanistic predictions (there is no indication that any of the forecasters intend this to happen) nor would we recommend such an extreme course of action. Indeed, inasmuch as it appears that most forecasting error is attributable to non-systematic factors, it may well be that an essential prerequisite for improved economic forecasting is further refinement in the traditional judgement of the forecasters themselves.

Macroeconomic forecasting is costly, especially the construction and testing of large-scale, computerised econometric models. But there are surely increasing returns to be had from improving the accuracy of economic forecasts even though these returns, the social benefits accruing from a higher quality of public and private sector decision-making, are less immediately quantifiable than the costs. The recent development of non-official forecasts and their widespread dissemination are to be welcomed because in model-building and forecasting, as in other aspects of economic life, competition is likely to benefit the ultimate users.

Notes

[1] For the half-yearly forecasts totals have been used rather than subtotals where possible: e.g. for gross fixed investment by the Treasury we have used the coefficient for total investment not the coefficients for public and private gross fixed investment.

[2] The current authors intend to investigate further this apparent peculiarity, and report our findings in due course.

[3] See D. J. Smyth, 'Public finance policy and techniques for economic stability and balanced economic growth,' United Kingdom report in *Public Finance Policy and Techniques for Economic Stability and Balanced Economic Growth, Congres de Budapest, Septembre 1964* Institut International de Finances Publiques, La Haye (1966) pp. 270-97.

[4] C. A. Sims, 'Evaluating short-term macroeconomic forecasts: the Dutch performance,' *Review of Economics and Statistics* (May 1967) pp. 225-36.

Index